GRC Chronicles

NAVIGATING THE CYBER SEAS OF GOVERNANCE, RISK, AND COMPLIANCE

TOLULOPE MICHAEL

Table of Contents

FOREWORD

CHAPTER ONE
The Evolution of GRC: Tracing the Historical Shifts and Milestones......3

CHAPTER TWO
GRC Frameworks Exposed: ISO 27001, NIST, COBIT, and More Decoded 45

CHAPTER 3
The Tug of War: Balancing Business Agility with Risk Management 83

CHAPTER FOUR

CHAPTER FIVE
Third-Party Risks: Managing The Complexities In Vendor Relationships 133

CHAPTER SIX
Cyber Insurance: The New Frontier of Risk Transfer 155

CHAPTER SEVEN
The Rise of AI in GRC: Opportunities, Risks and Ethical Considerations 189

CHAPTER EIGHT
GRC's Role in Mergers And Acquisitions: Due Diligence in the Digital Age 215

Chapter Nine

BOARDROOM CHRONICLES: ENGAGING AND
EDUCATING TOP LEADERSHIP ON CYBER RISKS.........249

CHAPTER 10:

FUTURE FORWARD: PREDICTIONS AND PREPARATIONS
FOR THE NEXT DECADE OF GRC....................................271

BIBLIOGRAPHY

About The Author

FOREWORD

In today's world of business, where every decision sends ripples across the organizational landscape, navigating the cyber seas has emerged as an indispensable skill for enterprises seeking safe harbor in the ever-shifting tides of technology. Welcome to the "GRC Chronicles: Navigating the Cyber Seas of Governance, Risk, and Compliance," a compass for those embarking on a journey through the nuanced waters of Governance, Risk, and Compliance (GRC).

In this compelling chronicle, readers will find more than a mere guide; they will discover a narrative that unfolds against the backdrop of an interconnected world, where the digital currents shape the destiny of organizations. As someone deeply entrenched in the world of GRC, I am thrilled to introduce a volume that transcends conventional boundaries, offering a rich blend of storytelling and profound insights into the realms of governance, risk management, and compliance.

The GRC Chronicles is a roadmap that beckons leaders, practitioners, and enthusiasts to explore uncharted territories. It delves into the intricacies of governance, where policies carve the path; risk, where uncertainty meets strategy; and compliance, where adherence to rules ensures safe passage through the cyber realms.

Far more than a manual, this book serves as a beacon, casting light on the multifaceted challenges and opportunities that define the GRC journey. With each chapter, readers will navigate through tales of triumphs and tribulations, learning from battle-hardened experts and uncovering strategic maneuvers that have steered organizations through the stormiest of cyber weather.

As you embark on this literary voyage through the GRC Chronicles, be prepared to encounter lessons learned, best practices, and the wisdom distilled from the experiences of those who have sailed these seas before. Whether you are a seasoned captain of industry or a novice explorer in the digital expanse, the GRC Chronicles will stand as your trusted companion, offering the knowledge and tools essential for navigating the cyber seas with confidence.

May the stories within these pages inspire and guide you, as you chart your course towards cyber resilience and success. Bon voyage

CHAPTER ONE

THE EVOLUTION OF GRC: TRACING THE HISTORICAL SHIFTS AND MILESTONES

At its core, GRC is a term that embodies a holistic framework, seamlessly weaving together the threads of governance, risk management, and compliance into a cohesive entity that guides enterprises through the complexities of the contemporary business landscape.

Governance, as the foundational pillar, establishes the rules, structures, and processes that define the direction and decision-making within an organization. It is the compass that sets the course, aligning strategies with objectives and ensuring accountability at every level. In the dynamic currents of today's business environment, effective governance becomes the North Star, providing a steady guide through the ebb and flow of market trends, technological disruptions, and global uncertainties.

Risk management, the second pivotal element, acknowledges that every venture, no matter how well-governed, navigates turbulent waters. Risks, both foreseeable and unforeseeable, pose potential challenges to organizational goals. Herein lies the critical role of risk management within the GRC framework. It is the vigilant lookout, scanning the horizon for potential threats, evaluating their potential impact, and steering the organization away from treacherous waters. In an era where digital transformations, geopolitical shifts, and economic fluctuations are the norm, an adept risk management strategy is the compass that ensures a resilient journey.

Compliance, the third cornerstone of GRC, signifies adherence to the intricate web of laws, regulations, and ethical standards that govern business operations. In an era of heightened scrutiny and a globalized marketplace, compliance is not merely a box-ticking exercise; it is the ethical and legal compass that ensures organizations navigate within the bounds of societal expectations and legal requirements. From data protection laws to industry-specific regulations, the compliance facet of GRC is the map that prevents enterprises from straying into forbidden territories, averting legal pitfalls and reputational damage.

The significance of GRC in the contemporary business landscape is profound. It transcends siloed approaches to governance, risk, and compliance, offering a panoramic view of organizational resilience. As a GRC expert, I have witnessed firsthand how a robust GRC framework empowers organizations to not only weather storms but to thrive in the face of uncertainty. It provides leaders with the tools to make informed decisions, mitigates risks that could undermine strategic objectives, and ensures ethical conduct that enhances trust among stakeholders.

In essence, GRC is the guiding philosophy that transforms challenges into opportunities, uncertainties into strategic advantages, and risks into calculated ventures. As we navigate the intricate seas of modern business, the compass of GRC remains steadfast, pointing towards a horizon where governance, risk management, and compliance converge to illuminate the path to sustainable success.

THE PURPOSE OF THIS CHAPTER

Embarking on the historical odyssey of Governance, Risk, and Compliance (GRC) is akin to delving into the annals of a complex narrative that has shaped the very fabric of organizational resilience. The objective of tracing the historical evolution of GRC transcends the confines of mere historical curiosity; it is a deliberate journey into the roots and foundations that have germinated into the contemporary landscape of governance, risk management, and compliance.

Understanding the historical evolution of GRC is tantamount to excavating the layers of organizational development, witnessing the gradual crystallization of principles, frameworks, and strategies that have withstood the tests of time. By unraveling the historical shifts and milestones, we gain profound insights into the catalytic moments that prompted the amalgamation of governance, risk management, and compliance into a unified and indispensable framework.

The historical lens offers clarity into the origins of governance principles, tracing them back to ancient civilizations, where structured systems of rule and order began to take shape. It unravels the narratives of risk in commerce, from the early days of trade routes to the establishment of insurance mechanisms, elucidating the evolutionary journey from acknowledging risk to actively managing it. Simultaneously, the historical exploration unveils the genesis of compliance as a response to societal and legal expectations, unfolding the intricate dance between regulations and the burgeoning needs of businesses.

Significantly, the historical narrative is not a mere exercise in nostalgia; it serves as a compass guiding us through the ebbs and flows of organizational landscapes. The evolution of GRC mirrors the adaptive responses of enterprises to the evolving challenges of their times. It encapsulates the strategic shifts necessitated by industrial revolutions, globalization, and the ever-accelerating pace of technological advancements. Each historical juncture reflects a nuanced adaptation to the prevailing winds of change, offering valuable lessons for navigating the tumultuous waters of contemporary business.

Moreover, this historical exploration is instrumental in comprehending the interconnectedness of governance, risk management, and compliance. The convergence of these three pillars did not occur in isolation; it was a gradual symbiosis, a recognition that effective governance is intertwined with astute risk management, and both are meaningless without a robust framework of compliance. Tracing this evolution provides the context needed to understand the synergies between these components, illustrating how they coalesce into a comprehensive GRC strategy that is indispensable in today's complex business environment.

The historical journey of GRC is a voyage of enlightenment, offering a profound understanding of the forces that have shaped the discipline. It is a testament to the resilience and adaptability of organizations in the face of challenges. By comprehending this historical context, we equip ourselves with the wisdom to navigate the contemporary seas of governance, risk, and compliance with a nuanced understanding of the currents that propel us forward. As we unveil the chapters of the past, we gain the insights necessary to script the narratives of a resilient and strategically fortified future.

EARLY ROOTS OF GOVERNANCE

The exploration of early forms of governance offers a fascinating journey through time, revealing the foundational principles that underpinned the cohesion and functioning of these early communities.

Governance involves, among other things, coordinating identity and action, and the collection, production, and distribution of goods over a given territory (Spanakos, 2022). One of the earliest cradles of civilization, Mesopotamia, witnessed the emergence of city-states such as Sumer, where the need for order and coordination spurred the establishment of rudimentary governance structures. These city-states, nestled between the Tigris and Euphrates rivers, grappled with the challenges of resource allocation, trade, and communal living. Governance in Sumer took the form of city councils and administrators who were tasked with managing irrigation systems, overseeing trade transactions, and resolving disputes. The Code of Ur-Nammu and the more renowned Code of Hammurabi stand as early legal codifications, reflecting the role of governance in providing a framework for justice and social order.

Meanwhile, in ancient Egypt, the Nile River valley fostered a sophisticated civilization that leaned heavily on centralized authority. Pharaohs, regarded as divine rulers, governed with a mix of religious and administrative powers. The elaborate bureaucracy, complete with scribes and administrators, orchestrated the allocation of resources, collection of taxes, and oversight of monumental construction projects. The governance of ancient Egypt exemplifies how a hierarchical structure was vital in maintaining societal equilibrium and facilitating grand endeavors that defined the civilization.

The Greek city-states, birthplaces of democracy, introduced a revolutionary form of governance in the crucible of intellectual ferment. In Athens, the epicenter of democratic experimentation, citizens actively participated in decision-making through assemblies and juries. The governance principles of ancient Greece, encapsulated in the works of philosophers like Plato and Aristotle, laid the groundwork for the idea that the well-being of the state rested on the active engagement and participation of its citizens.

As we traverse the ancient Silk Road, we encounter the governance structures of the Han Dynasty in China. Here, Confucian principles influenced the development of a centralized bureaucracy that emphasized ethical governance, moral conduct, and the Confucian concept of benevolent rule. The Han governance model was instrumental in fostering stability and cultural flourishing over centuries.

In the Indian subcontinent, the Maurya and Gupta Empires showcased governance systems deeply rooted in principles articulated in texts like Arthashastra. These empires established administrative units, taxation systems, and a legal framework, recognizing the integral role of governance in fostering social harmony and economic prosperity.

Across these diverse civilizations, a common thread emerges — the recognition that governance is not merely an administrative function but a fundamental pillar that structures societal relationships, resolves conflicts, and charts the trajectory of collective progress. Whether through divine monarchies, democratic experiments, or bureaucratic hierarchies, early governance principles were indispensable in providing the scaffolding for the flourishing of organized societies. These historical echoes resonate through time, reminding us that the foundations of governance laid in ancient civilizations continue to shape the contours of our modern societal structures.

THE IMPACT OF INDUSTRIAL REVOLUTION

The onset of the Industrial Revolution marked a seismic shift in the background of governance, reshaping the landscape of societal organization and giving birth to large-scale industrial enterprises. This transformative period, spanning the late 18th to the mid-19th century, brought forth not only technological advancements but also profound changes in governance structures and management philosophies.

Prior to the Industrial Revolution, agrarian and craft-based economies predominated, characterized by small-scale production and decentralized decision-making. The emergence of mechanization, powered by innovations like the steam engine, ushered in an era of unprecedented industrialization. With the advent of factories and the concentration of production in urban centers, the traditional models of governance proved inadequate to manage the complexities of these burgeoning industrial enterprises.

One of the key transformations was the rise of a new class of industrialists and capitalists who spearheaded the establishment of large-scale organizations. The governance of these enterprises underwent a paradigm shift, transitioning from familial or small-group management to more structured hierarchies. Entrepreneurs like Josiah Wedgwood and Richard Arkwright not only pioneered technological advancements but also introduced organizational innovations that would define the governance landscape.

The hierarchical organizational structure became a hallmark of this era. The need for efficient coordination of labor, resources, and production processes necessitated a top-down management approach. Clear lines of authority and a division of labor became imperative to manage the intricacies of industrial production. This hierarchical structure, with managers overseeing specific functions, mirrored the mechanistic precision that characterized the industrial machinery of the time.

With the rise of large-scale organizations came the need for standardized processes and procedures. Governance evolved to incorporate bureaucratic principles, borrowing from the organizational theories of thinkers like Max Weber. The emphasis on rules, regulations, and clearly defined roles sought to streamline operations and bring a sense of order to the increasingly complex world of industrial production.

Simultaneously, the challenges of managing a large and diverse workforce prompted the development of early forms of human resource management. From time clocks to labor unions, governance practices were adapted to address the unique demands of industrial labor. The rise of labor movements and the push for workers' rights spurred a reevaluation of governance, leading to the recognition of the social contract between employers and employees.

The Industrial Revolution also catalyzed changes in corporate governance. As enterprises grew in size and complexity, the need for capital infusion led to the emergence of joint-stock companies. Corporate governance structures evolved to accommodate the interests of shareholders, giving rise to boards of directors and governance mechanisms to ensure transparency and accountability.

The transformation of governance during the Industrial Revolution extended beyond organizational structures. It laid the groundwork for the development of regulatory frameworks to address the social and environmental impacts of industrialization. As large-scale organizations became powerful economic entities, governance had to adapt to balance the interests of capital, labor, and the broader society.

The Industrial Revolution not only revolutionized production methods but also precipitated a profound transformation in governance. The rise of large-scale organizations necessitated new management philosophies, hierarchical structures, and standardized processes. This period of industrialization laid the groundwork for the modern governance structures that continue to shape the organizational landscape today.

EMERGENCE OF RISK MANAGEMENT

The interplay between risk and commerce has been a constant throughout human history, shaping the trajectories of civilizations, influencing trade routes, and underpinning economic systems. Examining historical instances where risk played a crucial role in trade and commerce reveals the dynamic nature of economic endeavors and the resilience required to navigate uncertainties.

Silk Road and Transcontinental Trade

Geopolitical Risks: The ancient Silk Road, connecting the East and West, was not merely a conduit for goods but a pathway fraught with geopolitical risks. Merchants and caravans faced the challenges of diverse political landscapes, encountering changing regulations, taxes, and sometimes outright hostility. The risks associated with traversing vast territories were significant, from the threat of banditry to political instability.

Maritime Exploration and Mercantilism

Navigational Risks: The Age of Exploration in the 15th and 16th centuries saw European powers seeking new trade routes to Asia. Venturing into uncharted waters, mariners faced perilous conditions, navigational uncertainties, and the constant threat of storms. The rewards of discovering new trade routes were immense, but the risks were equally daunting.

Tulip Mania and Speculative Bubbles

Market Risks: The Dutch Golden Age witnessed the infamous Tulip Mania in the 17th century, where the prices of tulip bulbs soared to irrational heights before crashing dramatically. This episode exemplifies how speculative bubbles and market risks can influence commerce. Investors faced the risk of sudden market corrections, revealing the delicate balance between opportunity and peril in the world of trade.

Colonial Trade and Mercantile Risks

Colonial Ventures: European colonial powers engaged in extensive trade, but the risks were manifold. Colonists faced challenges such as unfamiliar climates, diseases, and the complexities of establishing trade networks with indigenous populations. The risks inherent in these ventures were not only economic but also had profound social and cultural implications.

GLOBALIZATION AND FINANCIAL RISKS

Financial Innovations: Globalization is the process of interaction and integration among people, companies, and governments worldwide (Wikipedia). The rise of modern commerce and globalization in the 19th and 20th centuries introduced financial instruments and innovations that transformed trade. However, these innovations also brought about new risks, such as currency fluctuations, market volatility, and the interconnectedness of global financial systems. The Great Depression of the 1930s is a stark example of how economic downturns can have far-reaching consequences for international trade.

TECHNOLOGICAL RISKS IN THE DIGITAL AGE

Cybersecurity Concerns: In the contemporary era, the advent of the digital age has revolutionized commerce, but it has also introduced new risks. Cybersecurity threats, data breaches, and the vulnerability of digital infrastructure pose significant challenges to businesses engaged in e-commerce. The risks associated with technological advancements underscore the need for robust risk management strategies.

GLOBAL SUPPLY CHAINS AND PANDEMIC RISKS

Supply Chain Vulnerabilities: Recent history, especially in the wake of the COVID-19 pandemic, highlights the vulnerabilities of global supply chains. Disruptions in transportation, logistics, and production underscore the intricate risks woven into the fabric of modern commerce. Businesses now grapple with the need for resilient supply chain strategies in the face of unforeseen global events.

Examining these historical instances illuminates the interwoven background of risk and commerce. It underscores that, throughout history, successful trade and commerce have not been devoid of risk but rather have thrived on a strategic understanding and management of uncertainties. The lessons from these historical episodes continue to resonate, emphasizing the importance of adaptability, resilience, and foresight in navigating the multifaceted risks inherent in the world of commerce.

The Origins of Risk Management: The Development of Insurance and Risk Mitigation Strategies

The origins of risk management can be traced back to ancient civilizations, where early forms of risk mitigation were developed in response to the uncertainties inherent in various aspects of life. The journey of risk management, from rudimentary risk avoidance strategies to the sophisticated insurance mechanisms of today, is a testament to humanity's ongoing quest to safeguard against the unpredictable.

Ancient Practices and Maritime Insurance

Mesopotamian Codes: In ancient Mesopotamia, as early as the 2nd millennium BCE, there were codes that outlined risk-sharing arrangements. Merchants would pool their resources to spread the risk associated with caravan trade.

Babylonian Maritime Loans: In Babylon, around 1750 BCE, the Code of Hammurabi introduced the concept of maritime loans. If a ship was lost at sea, the lender would not collect repayment, demonstrating an early form of risk transfer.

Roman Guilds and Burial Societies:

Roman Collegia: In ancient Rome, various trade guilds or collegia served as mutual aid societies. Members contributed to a common fund to assist each other in times of need, creating an early form of risk pooling.

Burial Societies: Similar risk-sharing practices were found in burial societies, where members contributed to cover funeral expenses for a deceased member's family.

Chinese Risk Pools and Sea Trade

Risk Pools in China: Chinese merchants engaged in sea trade during the 3rd and 4th centuries developed risk-sharing practices. Merchants pooled their resources to compensate any member who suffered losses during a voyage, showcasing a communal approach to risk management.

Medieval Guilds and the Hanseatic League

Guild Practices: Medieval guilds in Europe adopted risk-sharing practices, particularly in the construction industry. Members contributed to a common fund to assist with rebuilding in case of disasters like fires.

Hanseatic League: The Hanseatic League, a confederation of merchant guilds in Northern Europe during the late Middle Ages, engaged in maritime trade. Members of the league collaborated to protect against piracy and shared the risks associated with sea voyages.

Lloyd's of London and Modern Insurance

Coffeehouse Origins: In 1688, Edward Lloyd's coffeehouse in London became a gathering place for merchants and shipowners. Lloyd began recording shipping information, laying the groundwork for marine insurance.

Over time, Lloyd's evolved into an insurance market where individuals and businesses could underwrite and share risks. It played a pivotal role in the development of modern insurance practices, expanding beyond maritime risks to cover various industries.

Actuarial Science and Statistical Methods

18th-Century Developments: In the 18th century, advances in probability theory and statistics, led by figures like Daniel Bernoulli and Pierre-Simon Laplace, contributed to the mathematical foundation of risk management.

Actuarial Tables: Actuarial tables, introduced in the 19th century, further refined risk assessment by providing statistical models for life expectancy, laying the groundwork for life insurance.

Corporate Risk Management in the 20th Century

Industrialization and Corporate Risks: The industrialization of the 20th century brought about new risks associated with large-scale production. Corporations started to establish risk management departments to identify, assess, and mitigate various risks.

Financial Derivatives: The latter half of the 20th century saw the development of financial derivatives as tools for managing financial risks. Options, futures, and other derivatives allowed businesses to hedge against fluctuations in commodity prices, interest rates, and currency exchange rates.

Enterprise Risk Management (ERM)

Emergence of ERM: In the late 20th century and into the 21st century, the concept of Enterprise Risk Management (ERM) gained prominence. ERM involves a holistic approach to managing risks across an entire organization, integrating risk considerations into strategic decision-making.

Enterprise Risk Management (ERM) is, simply put, risk management practiced at the enterprise level. It puts the core strategic mission of the enterprise at the center of the discussion, driving all possible responses to potential risks in a holistic approach (ILO 2023).

The journey of risk management from ancient practices to modern insurance and sophisticated risk mitigation strategies reflects humanity's evolving understanding of uncertainty. From communal risk-sharing in ancient trade routes to the intricacies of modern financial derivatives, the development of risk management mirrors the dynamic nature of human endeavors and the constant quest to navigate the uncertainties that accompany progress.

COMPLIANCE THROUGH THE AGES: LEGAL AND REGULATORY FRAMEWORKS IN VARIOUS INDUSTRIES

The emergence of legal and regulatory frameworks to ensure compliance in various industries is a multifaceted historical process rooted in the recognition of the need for standardized rules and ethical guidelines. The evolution of these frameworks has been shaped by economic, social, and political dynamics, reflecting the ever-changing landscape of industries and the imperative to protect the interests of stakeholders. Investigating this evolution unveils the intricate interplay between societal demands, corporate practices, and governmental responses.

EARLY REGULATORY MEASURES

Guilds and Craftsmen: In medieval Europe, guilds established rules and regulations to ensure quality standards in craftsmanship. These early forms of regulation aimed at protecting consumers and maintaining the integrity of trade.

Mercantilism: During the mercantilist era, from the 16th to the 18th centuries, governments began intervening in economic activities to enhance national wealth. Regulations were crafted to control trade, protect domestic industries, and ensure adherence to mercantilist principles.

Industrial Revolution and Labor Regulations

FACTORY ACTS

The Industrial Revolution prompted the introduction of labor regulations to address the harsh working conditions in factories. Acts such as the Factory Acts in the 19th century in the United Kingdom aimed at restricting child labor, regulating working hours, and ensuring basic workplace safety.

FOOD AND DRUG REGULATIONS

Pure Food and Drug Act (1906): In the early 20th century, concerns about the safety of food and pharmaceuticals led to the Pure Food and Drug Act in the United States. This landmark legislation laid the foundation for regulatory agencies like the U.S. Food and Drug Administration (FDA) and emphasized consumer protection.

SECURITIES AND EXCHANGE COMMISSION (SEC)

Great Depression and Financial Regulations: The economic fallout of the Great Depression in the 1930s prompted the establishment of the Securities and Exchange Commission (SEC) in the United States. The SEC aimed to regulate the securities industry and protect investors from fraudulent practices, marking a pivotal moment in financial regulation.

ENVIRONMENTAL REGULATIONS

Environmental Protection Agency (EPA): Growing concerns about environmental degradation in the mid-20th century led to the creation of environmental regulatory bodies, such as the Environmental Protection Agency (EPA) in the United States. Environmental regulations began addressing issues like pollution control, waste disposal, and resource conservation.

CONSUMER PROTECTION LAWS

Consumer Product Safety Commission (CPSC): The rise of consumerism in the latter half of the 20th century prompted the establishment of agencies like the Consumer Product Safety Commission (CPSC) in the U.S. to regulate product safety standards and protect consumers from faulty or dangerous products.

ANTI-TRUST AND COMPETITION REGULATIONS

Sherman Antitrust Act (1890): Concerns about monopolistic practices and anti-competitive behavior led to the enactment of the Sherman Antitrust Act in the U.S., marking the beginning of antitrust regulations. Subsequent legislation, including the Clayton Act and the Federal Trade Commission Act, aimed at promoting fair competition and preventing the abuse of market power.

GLOBALIZATION AND INTERNATIONAL STANDARDS

International Organizations: With the globalization of commerce, international organizations like the World Trade Organization (WTO) and the International Organization for Standardization (ISO) have played a role in developing and promoting global standards to ensure fair trade practices and quality control.

TECHNOLOGY AND DATA PRIVACY REGULATIONS

Data Protection Laws: The advent of the digital age has prompted the introduction of data protection and privacy regulations. Legislation such as the General Data Protection Regulation (GDPR) in the European Union reflects the need to safeguard personal information in an era of pervasive digital connectivity.

CORPORATE GOVERNANCE CODES

Sarbanes-Oxley Act (2002): Corporate governance codes and regulations, such as the Sarbanes-Oxley Act in the U.S., have been implemented to enhance transparency, accountability, and ethical behavior within corporations. These measures address issues like financial reporting and corporate responsibility (Laufer 2018).

The development of legal and regulatory frameworks to ensure compliance in various industries is an ongoing process, continually adapting to new challenges and contexts. It reflects a collective effort to strike a balance between fostering economic growth, protecting the rights of consumers and workers, and upholding ethical standards. As industries evolve and globalize, the role of regulations remains crucial in shaping a responsible and sustainable business environment.

LANDMARK REGULATORY MOMENTS: MILESTONES THAT SHAPED COMPLIANCE PRACTICES

The evolution of compliance practices has been significantly influenced by key regulatory milestones that mark pivotal moments in the development of legal and ethical standards across various industries. These milestones, often born out of societal needs, economic shifts, or crises, have played a crucial role in shaping the compliance landscape. Highlighting some key regulatory milestones provides insights into the continuous refinement of compliance practices over time.

PURE FOOD AND DRUG ACT (1906) AND THE FDA

The Pure Food and Drug Act of 1906 in the United States marked a watershed moment in consumer protection. It aimed to eliminate adulteration and misbranding of food and pharmaceuticals. This legislation laid the foundation for the establishment of the Food and Drug Administration (FDA) in 1930, which became a cornerstone in regulating the safety of food, drugs, and medical devices.

SECURITIES ACT OF 1933 AND SECURITIES EXCHANGE ACT OF 1934

In response to the stock market crash of 1929 and the ensuing Great Depression, the U.S. government enacted the Securities Act of 1933 and the Securities Exchange Act of 1934. These regulations established the Securities and Exchange Commission (SEC) and introduced comprehensive disclosure requirements, aiming to protect investors and maintain the integrity of financial markets.

OCCUPATIONAL SAFETY AND HEALTH ACT (OSHA) OF 1970

The OSHA, enacted in the United States, was a response to concerns about workplace safety and health. It established standards for safe and healthy working conditions, created the Occupational Safety and Health Administration, and empowered workers to have a voice in their workplace safety.

FOREIGN CORRUPT PRACTICES ACT (FCPA) OF 1977

The FCPA was one of the first legislations targeting the bribery of foreign officials by U.S. companies. It aimed to promote ethical business practices, transparency, and accountability in international transactions. The FCPA significantly influenced global anti-corruption efforts and paved the way for similar regulations worldwide.

BASEL COMMITTEE ON BANKING SUPERVISION (BCBS) AND BASEL ACCORDS

The Basel Accords, initiated by the BCBS, established international banking standards to ensure the stability of the global financial system. The Basel I, Basel II, and Basel III frameworks introduced risk-based capital requirements, liquidity standards, and regulatory oversight to enhance the resilience of banking institutions.

DATA PROTECTION DIRECTIVE (1995) AND GENERAL DATA PROTECTION REGULATION (GDPR)

The Data Protection Directive in the European Union (EU) and, more recently, the GDPR, represent milestones in data protection regulation. GDPR, implemented in 2018, introduced robust standards for the processing and protection of personal data, empowering individuals and holding organizations accountable for responsible data management.

SARBANES-OXLEY ACT (2002)

Enacted in response to corporate accounting scandals such as Enron and WorldCom, the Sarbanes-Oxley Act introduced stringent regulations for corporate governance, financial reporting, and internal controls. It aimed to restore investor confidence by enhancing transparency and accountability in publicly traded companies.

DODD-FRANK WALL STREET REFORM AND CONSUMER PROTECTION ACT (2010)

Following the 2008 financial crisis, the Dodd-Frank Act was enacted to address systemic risks in the financial industry. It introduced regulatory measures aimed at improving accountability, transparency, and consumer protection, with provisions addressing issues such as derivatives trading and mortgage practices (Laufer 2018).

MIFID II (MARKETS IN FINANCIAL INSTRUMENTS DIRECTIVE II)

Implemented in the European Union in 2018, MiFID II introduced comprehensive reforms to financial markets. It aimed to enhance investor protection, improve market transparency, and increase the accountability of financial institutions in the aftermath of the global financial crisis.

CALIFORNIA CONSUMER PRIVACY ACT (CCPA) AND PRIVACY REGULATIONS

The CCPA, enacted in 2018, marked a significant step in U.S. data privacy regulation. It grants California residents greater control over their personal data, inspiring discussions on the need for federal privacy legislation. Globally, other jurisdictions have also introduced or enhanced data protection laws, reflecting the growing importance of privacy compliance.

These regulatory milestones represent a selection of key moments that have shaped compliance practices across industries. They demonstrate a global trend toward increased scrutiny, transparency, and accountability, highlighting the ongoing efforts to adapt regulatory frameworks to address emerging challenges in an ever-evolving business landscape.

THE CONVERGENCE OF GOVERNANCE, RISK MANAGEMENT AND COMPLIANCE

The late 20th century witnessed a paradigm shift in the business landscape, marked by globalization, technological advancements, and increasing complexity in organizational structures. In response to these challenges, the convergence of governance, risk management, and compliance (GRC) became a strategic imperative for organizations. This convergence was driven by a recognition that these three components, traditionally managed in silos, are interconnected and should be approached holistically to ensure the sustainability and resilience of modern enterprises.

1. **Technological Advancements**

    Information Age: The advent of the Information Age brought about unprecedented technological advancements. The integration of computers, data networks, and software systems into business processes increased the speed and complexity of operations.

    Data Risks: With the digitalization of business processes, the significance of data and information governance became apparent. The potential risks associated with data breaches, cyber-attacks, and technological failures necessitated a comprehensive approach to risk management and compliance.

2. **Globalization and Complex Supply Chains**

    Expanding Global Footprint: The late 20th century saw an acceleration of globalization, with companies expanding their operations across borders. This increased the complexity of business environments, requiring a more nuanced approach to governance and risk management that accounted for diverse regulatory landscapes.

Supply Chain Risks: Global supply chains became intricate, with increased dependencies on external partners. Risks associated with geopolitical events, natural disasters, and disruptions in the supply chain underscored the need for a holistic risk management strategy.

3. Regulatory Landscape and Corporate Scandals

Emergence of Stringent Regulations: High-profile corporate scandals, such as Enron and WorldCom, led to increased regulatory scrutiny. Governments responded by enacting more stringent regulations, emphasizing transparency, ethical conduct, and accountability.

Sarbanes-Oxley Act (2002): The Sarbanes-Oxley Act in the United States, enacted in the wake of accounting scandals, exemplified the convergence of governance and compliance. It mandated stricter financial reporting, internal controls, and governance standards for publicly traded companies.

4. Complexity of Financial Instruments

Financial Innovations: The late 20th century witnessed the proliferation of complex financial instruments and derivatives. The global financial system became more interconnected, introducing new dimensions of risk.

Financial Risk Management: Organizations recognized the need for a comprehensive approach to managing financial risks, incorporating governance structures to ensure effective oversight and compliance with evolving financial regulations.

5. **Rise of Enterprise Risk Management (ERM)**

   Holistic Approach to Risk: ERM emerged as a strategic response to the limitations of siloed risk management functions. It emphasized a holistic approach, integrating risk management practices across all levels of an organization.

   COSO Framework: The Committee of Sponsoring Organizations of the Treadway Commission (COSO) introduced the Integrated Framework in 1992, providing a foundational structure for ERM that integrated risk management with governance and internal controls.

6. **Technology as an Enabler**

   GRC Software Solutions: Advances in technology facilitated the development of Governance, Risk, and Compliance (GRC) software solutions. These tools allowed organizations to streamline processes, automate compliance activities, and gain real-time insights into risk exposure.

   Data Analytics: The use of data analytics in risk management and compliance further enhanced the ability to proactively identify and mitigate risks, aligning governance practices with data-driven decision-making.

7. **Stakeholder Expectations and Corporate Social Responsibility (CSR)**

   Changing Stakeholder Dynamics: Stakeholders, including shareholders, customers, and the public, began placing greater emphasis on corporate responsibility. Organizations were expected to demonstrate ethical behavior, environmental sustainability, and social responsibility.

   Integrated Reporting: Integrated reporting frameworks emerged, emphasizing the integration of financial and non-financial performance metrics. This reflected a convergence of governance and compliance with broader considerations of corporate responsibility.

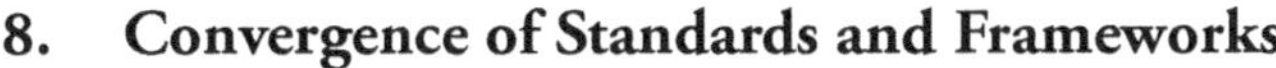

8. **Convergence of Standards and Frameworks**

   Global Standards: The convergence of governance, risk management, and compliance was facilitated by the development of global standards and frameworks. For example, the ISO 31000 standard for risk management and the COSO framework for internal control provided common language and principles.

   Harmonization of Practices: Organizations increasingly sought to harmonize their governance, risk management, and compliance practices to align with globally recognized standards, enabling cross-industry collaboration and benchmarking.

9. **Evolving Role of Chief Risk Officers (CROs) and Chief Compliance Officers (CCOs)**

   CROs and CCOs as Strategic Leaders: The late 20th century saw the emergence of Chief Risk Officers (CROs) and Chief Compliance Officers (CCOs) as strategic leaders within organizations. Their roles expanded beyond traditional risk and compliance functions to encompass broader strategic considerations.

   Board Oversight: Boards of directors recognized the need to establish risk committees and compliance oversight structures, further reinforcing the integration of these functions into overall governance.

10. **Continuous Learning and Adaptability**

    Learning from Crises: Organizations, especially those that experienced crisis, recognized the need for continuous learning and adaptability. Post-crisis assessments led to improvements in governance structures, risk management practices, and compliance protocols.

Agile Governance: The late 20th century set the stage for the adoption of agile governance principles, allowing organizations to respond swiftly to changing business environments, emerging risks, and evolving regulatory landscapes.

Therefore, the convergence of governance, risk management, and compliance in the late 20th century was a response to the dynamic and complex nature of the business environment. It reflected a shift from compartmentalized approaches to a more integrated, strategic, and adaptable framework that acknowledges the interdependencies between these critical elements of organizational success. This evolution continues into the 21st century, where organizations grapple with new challenges and opportunities in an era of rapid technological advancements and global interconnectedness.

TECHNOLOGY AS A CATALYST IN ACCELERATING THE CONVERGENCE OF GRC FUNCTIONS

Technology has played a transformative role in accelerating the convergence of Governance, Risk Management, and Compliance (GRC) functions within organizations. The integration of advanced technologies has not only streamlined processes but has also provided a holistic and real-time view of an organization's risk landscape.

The development and maturation of GRC technology, largely driven by the Sarbanes-Oxley Act, has enabled GRC convergence. It enabled organizations to break down the walls between audit, risk and compliance groups and provided an expanded value as organizations deployed it across their enterprise (Reuters 2009). Here's an exploration of the key ways technology has driven the convergence of GRC functions:

1. **Integrated GRC Platforms:**

   Centralized Solutions: Advanced GRC platforms provide a centralized repository for governance, risk, and compliance data. These platforms integrate diverse functions, enabling organizations to manage policies, assess risks, and monitor compliance from a unified interface.

   Real-Time Reporting: Technology allows for real-time reporting, ensuring that decision-makers have immediate access to critical information. This facilitates agile and informed responses to emerging risks and compliance issues.

2. **Automation of Compliance Processes:**

   Workflow Automation: Technology automates manual and time-consuming compliance processes. Workflow automation ensures that compliance tasks are systematically managed, reducing the likelihood of errors and enhancing efficiency.

   Regulatory Intelligence: Automated tools can continuously monitor and analyze changes in regulatory landscapes. This enables organizations to stay abreast of evolving compliance requirements and adapt their strategies accordingly.

3. **Data Analytics and Predictive Risk Modeling:**

   Big Data Analytics: The use of big data analytics allows organizations to analyze vast amounts of data to identify patterns, trends, and potential risks. This capability is particularly valuable for risk management functions.

   Predictive Risk Modeling: Technology facilitates the development of predictive risk models, enabling organizations to anticipate and proactively address potential risks before they escalate. This forward-looking approach enhances risk management strategies.

4. **Artificial Intelligence (AI) and Machine Learning (ML):**

   Risk Prediction: AI and ML algorithms can analyze historical data to predict potential risks and trends. This capability is invaluable for organizations seeking to enhance their risk management capabilities.

   Automated Monitoring: AI-powered tools can automate the monitoring of internal controls and compliance measures. These systems can detect anomalies, unusual patterns, and potential compliance breaches.

5. **Blockchain Technology for Transparency:**

   Immutable Records: Blockchain technology ensures the immutability of records, enhancing the transparency and traceability of transactions. This is particularly beneficial for compliance functions, offering a tamper-proof audit trail.

   Smart Contracts: Smart contracts on blockchain can automate and enforce compliance with predefined rules, reducing the need for manual intervention and minimizing the risk of contractual breaches.

6. **Cybersecurity Measures:**

   Protection of Sensitive Data: As GRC functions deal with sensitive information, robust cybersecurity measures are essential. Technology provides advanced tools for protecting data integrity, confidentiality, and availability.

   Continuous Monitoring: Automated cybersecurity tools enable continuous monitoring of potential threats, reducing the risk of data breaches and ensuring compliance with data protection regulations.

7. **Mobile and Cloud Solutions:**

   Remote Accessibility: Mobile solutions enable stakeholders to access GRC information from anywhere, facilitating remote governance and risk management. Cloud-based platforms offer scalability and flexibility, accommodating the dynamic needs of modern organizations.

Collaboration and Communication: Cloud-based collaboration tools enhance communication and collaboration among stakeholders involved in GRC functions. This fosters a more integrated and coordinated approach to governance and risk management.

8. User-Friendly Interfaces:

Enhanced User Experience: Modern GRC platforms leverage user-friendly interfaces, making it easier for stakeholders at all levels to engage with GRC processes. This accessibility fosters a culture of compliance and risk awareness throughout the organization.

9. RegTech Solutions:

Regulatory Technology (RegTech): RegTech solutions leverage technology to address regulatory challenges efficiently. These tools assist organizations in navigating complex regulatory landscapes, automating compliance processes, and ensuring adherence to industry-specific standards.

10. Continuous Monitoring and Auditing:

Real-Time Auditing: Technology enables real-time monitoring and auditing of GRC processes. Continuous auditing ensures that compliance measures are consistently applied, and risks are promptly identified and addressed.

Data Visualization: Visualization tools allow stakeholders to comprehend complex GRC data intuitively. Dashboards and reports offer insights into the overall health of governance, risk, and compliance within the organization.

FRAMEWORKS AND STANDARDS THAT SHAPED GRC

In today's world, we know GRC frameworks as "a comprehensive risk management strategy, plan, or foundation that reveals and categorizes all risks an enterprise faces. A GRC framework governs the entire business's approach to risks and legal expectations."(Phipps 2022).

Several Governance, Risk Management, and Compliance (GRC) frameworks and standards have played a pivotal role in shaping the discipline by providing organizations with structured approaches to managing governance, mitigating risks, and ensuring compliance. These frameworks offer guidance and best practices, aiding organizations in developing robust GRC programs tailored to their specific needs. Some major GRC frameworks and standards are:

1. **ISO 31000: Risk Management Standard**

    ISO 31000 is an international standard that provides principles and guidelines for effective risk management. It offers a framework for organizations to develop a risk management strategy, assess risks, and implement risk treatment measures.

    Key Components: The standard emphasizes the importance of risk identification, risk assessment, and risk treatment. It promotes a systematic and iterative approach to managing risks, acknowledging the dynamic nature of the business environment.

2. **COSO Frameworks**

    COSO Internal Control Framework: The Committee of Sponsoring Organizations of the Treadway Commission (COSO) has developed several frameworks. The COSO Internal Control Framework, initially released in 1992 and updated in 2013, provides guidance on designing, implementing, and evaluating internal control.

COSO Enterprise Risk Management (ERM) Framework: COSO's Enterprise Risk Management Framework expands on internal control concepts to provide a comprehensive approach to managing risks across an entire organization. It was first introduced in 2004 and updated in 2017.

3. **COBIT (Control Objectives for Information and Related Technologies)**

    COBIT is a framework developed by ISACA for the governance and management of enterprise information technology. It provides a set of principles, practices, and guidelines to help organizations ensure effective IT governance and risk management.

    Key Components: COBIT focuses on aligning IT with business goals, ensuring the delivery of value, and managing IT-related risks. It is widely used for IT governance, risk management, and compliance initiatives.

4. **ISO 19600: Compliance Management Systems Standard**

    ISO 19600 provides guidelines for establishing, implementing, maintaining, reviewing, and improving compliance management systems within an organization. It is designed to help organizations proactively address and manage compliance with legal and regulatory requirements.

    Key Components: The standard emphasizes the need for a systematic and risk-based approach to compliance management. It covers aspects such as compliance policies, communication, monitoring, and continual improvement.

5. **NIST Cybersecurity Framework:**

   Developed by the National Institute of Standards and Technology (NIST), the Cybersecurity Framework provides a voluntary framework for improving the cybersecurity posture of organizations. It offers a set of guidelines, best practices, and standards to manage and reduce cybersecurity risks.

   Key Components: The framework consists of five core functions – Identify, Protect, Detect, Respond, and Recover. It helps organizations assess and enhance their cybersecurity capabilities and resilience.

6. **ITIL (Information Technology Infrastructure Library):**

   ITIL is a set of practices for IT service management (ITSM) that focuses on aligning IT services with the needs of the business. While not explicitly a GRC framework, ITIL provides guidance on service delivery, service support, and overall IT governance.

   Key Components: ITIL includes a set of best practices for IT service management, covering areas such as incident management, change management, and service level management. It aims to improve the efficiency and effectiveness of IT services.

7. **ISO 22301: Business Continuity Management System Standard:**

   ISO 22301 outlines the requirements for establishing, implementing, maintaining, and continually improving a business continuity management system (BCMS). It provides a framework for organizations to enhance their resilience and ensure the continuity of critical business functions.

Key Components: The standard emphasizes risk assessment, business impact analysis, and the development of a business continuity plan. It helps organizations prepare for and respond to disruptions and disasters.

8. **PCI DSS (Payment Card Industry Data Security Standard):**

PCI DSS is a set of security standards designed to ensure that all companies that accept, process, store, or transmit credit card information maintain a secure environment. While specific to the payment card industry, it is crucial for organizations handling cardholder data.

Key Components: PCI DSS provides requirements for securing payment card transactions, covering areas such as network security, access controls, and regular security testing.

9. **ISO 27001: Information Security Management System Standard:**

ISO 27001 is an international standard for information security management systems (ISMS). It provides a systematic approach to managing sensitive company information, ensuring the confidentiality, integrity, and availability of data.

Key Components: The standard includes a risk management approach to information security, emphasizing the assessment and treatment of information security risks. It covers areas such as information security policies, asset management, and incident response.

10. **GDPR (General Data Protection Regulation):**

    While not a traditional framework, GDPR is a regulation that significantly impacts how organizations handle and process personal data. It sets forth rules for data protection, privacy, and the rights of individuals within the European Union (EU).

    Key Components: GDPR mandates transparency, consent, and accountability in the processing of personal data. Organizations are required to implement measures to protect data and report data breaches promptly.

HOW GLOBALIZATION HAS INFLUENCED GRC ON A GLOBAL SCALE

Globalization has been a transformative force that has significantly influenced the evolution of Governance, Risk Management, and Compliance (GRC) on a global scale. The interconnectedness of economies, the free flow of information, and the increased mobility of goods, services, and capital have presented both opportunities and challenges for organizations.

The complexity of the global corporate environment has made regulatory compliance more crucial than ever. Effective risk control plans give a framework for controlling risks and upholding regulatory requirements, which can help firms navigate the quickly changing business environment (Madhuri 2022). This section focuses on how globalization has shaped the GRC landscape:

1. **Cross-Border Operations and Regulatory Complexity:**

    Globalization has enabled organizations to expand their operations across borders, reaching new markets and diversifying their customer base. Operating in multiple jurisdictions introduces a complex regulatory landscape with varying legal and compliance requirements. Organizations must navigate and comply with a multitude of local, regional, and international regulations.

2. **Increased Supply Chain Complexity:**

Global supply chains have facilitated cost-effective production, access to diverse resources, and increased market competitiveness. The complexity of global supply chains introduces risks related to geopolitical events, natural disasters, and disruptions. Organizations must implement robust risk management strategies to ensure supply chain resilience.

3. **Cybersecurity and Data Protection Challenges:**

Globalization has enabled seamless digital communication and data sharing, fostering collaboration and innovation. The increased reliance on digital technologies exposes organizations to cybersecurity threats and data protection challenges. GRC efforts must address cross-border data privacy regulations and the need for robust cybersecurity measures.

4. **Harmonization of Standards:**

Globalization has spurred efforts to harmonize governance, risk management, and compliance standards. International standards, such as ISO 31000 for risk management, provide a common framework for organizations worldwide. While harmonization simplifies compliance efforts, organizations need to adapt to different cultural, legal, and business environments, requiring a nuanced approach to GRC implementation.

5. **Regulatory Convergence and Global Standards:**

Global regulatory bodies and organizations work towards convergence and the development of common standards. For example, Basel III seeks to establish consistent international banking standards. The challenge here is that, organizations operating in multiple jurisdictions must comply with diverse and evolving regulations. GRC programs need to be agile and capable of adapting to changes in the global regulatory landscape.

6. Ethical and Corporate Social Responsibility (CSR):

Globalization has increased awareness of ethical and CSR practices. Stakeholders, including consumers and investors, expect organizations to operate responsibly on a global scale. Organizations must align GRC efforts with ethical considerations and CSR expectations, taking into account cultural differences and local societal norms.

7. Reputation Management in a Global Context:

Globalization provides organizations with opportunities to enhance their brand and reputation on a global stage. The interconnected nature of the global economy means that reputational risks can quickly escalate, requiring organizations to implement robust reputation management strategies as part of their GRC framework.

8. Third-Party Risk Management:

Globalization has increased collaboration with third-party vendors, partners, and suppliers, fostering innovation and efficiency. Organizations must therefore manage third-party risks, ensuring that partners adhere to the same ethical and compliance standards. This includes understanding and addressing the GRC practices of entities operating in different legal and cultural contexts.

9. Cultural Sensitivity and Diversity:

Globalization brings together diverse talent and perspectives, contributing to innovation and creativity within organizations. Organizations need to foster a GRC culture that respects and integrates diverse perspectives. Understanding and navigating cultural nuances become essential in effective governance and risk management.

10. **Technology and Digital Transformation:**

    Globalization has accelerated digital transformation, enabling organizations to leverage technology for efficiency and competitiveness. The adoption of new technologies introduces risks related to cybersecurity, data privacy, and compliance with evolving digital regulations. GRC efforts need to keep pace with technological advancements.

THE CONTEMPORARY CHALLENGES IN GRC

Contemporary challenges in Governance, Risk Management, and Compliance (GRC) reflect the evolving nature of the discipline in response to the dynamic and complex business environment. As organizations navigate global uncertainties, technological advancements, and changing regulatory landscapes, several challenges emerge that require a strategic and adaptive approach to GRC. Here are key contemporary challenges and their implications:

1. **1. Cybersecurity Threats and Data Privacy:**

    The increasing frequency and sophistication of cybersecurity threats pose significant challenges for organizations. Data breaches not only jeopardize sensitive information but also trigger regulatory scrutiny and legal consequences.

    Implications: GRC programs need to integrate robust cybersecurity measures, continuously monitor threats, and ensure compliance with evolving data protection regulations such as GDPR.

2.   **Digital Transformation:**

The rapid pace of digital transformation introduces new technologies, business models, and risks. Organizations adopting emerging technologies, such as artificial intelligence and the Internet of Things, face challenges in ensuring ethical use, data security, and compliance.

Implications: GRC frameworks must adapt to the evolving technological landscape, incorporating risk assessments and controls for new digital initiatives. Collaboration between IT and GRC functions is crucial for effective governance.

3.   **Globalization and Cross-Border Compliance:**

Operating in multiple jurisdictions requires organizations to navigate diverse and evolving regulatory environments. Harmonizing compliance efforts across borders becomes challenging due to varying legal requirements.

Implications: GRC programs must have the agility to address region-specific regulations while maintaining a cohesive global strategy. Organizations may need to invest in technology solutions that facilitate cross-border compliance.

4.   **Supply Chain Resilience:**

Global supply chains face disruptions due to geopolitical events, natural disasters, and unforeseen crisis. The interdependence of suppliers makes it challenging to ensure the resilience of the entire supply network.

Implications: GRC strategies should include comprehensive risk assessments of the supply chain, focusing on identifying vulnerabilities and implementing measures to enhance resilience.

5. **Regulatory Complexity and Change:**

The regulatory landscape is constantly evolving, with new regulations emerging and existing ones undergoing revisions. Keeping up with regulatory changes and ensuring compliance becomes a demanding task.

Implications: GRC programs need to adopt agile frameworks that can quickly adapt to regulatory changes. Continuous monitoring, regulatory intelligence, and effective communication are vital components.

6. **Environmental, Social, and Governance (ESG) Concerns:**

There is an increasing focus on ESG considerations, including environmental sustainability, social responsibility, and ethical governance. Organizations face challenges in aligning their practices with evolving ESG expectations.

Implications: GRC programs should expand their scope to incorporate ESG factors. Organizations need to transparently communicate their ESG efforts to stakeholders and integrate ESG considerations into risk assessments.

7. **Third-Party and Vendor Risks:**

Challenge: Organizations often rely on third-party vendors and partners, introducing risks related to data security, compliance, and ethical practices. Managing and monitoring these risks can be complex.

Implications: GRC frameworks must include robust third-party risk management protocols, including due diligence, ongoing monitoring, and contractual provisions that align with the organization's risk tolerance.

8. **Crisis Management and Resilience:**

   Organizations face an increasing number of potential crises, ranging from public relations issues to natural disasters. The ability to respond effectively and recover quickly is critical.

   Implications: GRC programs should include crisis management plans, scenario testing, and regular drills to ensure the organization is well-prepared to handle unforeseen challenges. Resilience becomes a key aspect of risk management.

9. **Ethical Considerations and Corporate Culture:**

   Ethical lapses can lead to reputational damage and regulatory scrutiny. Maintaining a strong ethical culture throughout the organization poses ongoing challenges.

   Implications: GRC efforts should focus on promoting a culture of integrity and ethical behavior. Training programs, ethical leadership, and transparent communication are essential components.

10. **Data Governance and Privacy Concerns:**

    With the increasing reliance on data for decision-making, organizations face challenges in ensuring the responsible and compliant use of data. Privacy concerns and the potential misuse of data are critical issues.

    Implications: GRC programs should include robust data governance frameworks, ensuring data quality, security, and compliance with privacy regulations. Transparency in data practices is crucial for maintaining trust.

Emerging Technologies of Today Affecting The GRC of Tomorrow

Emerging technologies, including Artificial Intelligence (AI), blockchain, and data analytics, are reshaping the future of Governance, Risk Management, and Compliance (GRC). These technologies are offering innovative solutions to enhance the efficiency, transparency, and effectiveness of GRC processes. The convergence of innovative solutions, data analytics, and interconnected systems is ushering in a new era, where organizations must adapt to stay ahead in the ever-changing business environment.

This intersection of technology and GRC is not only influencing how businesses operate but is also fundamentally transforming the risk management and compliance strategies of tomorrow. In this dynamic scenario, understanding and harnessing these emerging technologies become paramount for organizations seeking to enhance their GRC frameworks and navigate the complexities of the modern business landscape. Here's an exploration of how each of these technologies is influencing the future of GRC:

1. **Artificial Intelligence (AI):**
   a. Risk Prediction and Mitigation: AI algorithms analyze vast datasets to identify patterns and trends, enabling organizations to predict and proactively mitigate risks. This is particularly valuable in identifying emerging risks and vulnerabilities.

   b. Automated Compliance Monitoring: AI-powered tools automate the monitoring of regulatory changes, helping organizations stay up-to-date with evolving compliance requirements. Machine learning algorithms can adapt to changes and predict potential compliance issues.

   c. Natural Language Processing (NLP) for Policy Management: NLP enables machines to understand and process human language. In GRC, NLP is utilized for policy management, contract analysis, and regulatory document interpretation, streamlining compliance processes.

d. Fraud Detection and Investigation: AI-powered fraud detection systems analyze transactional data in real-time, flagging suspicious activities and potential fraud. This is crucial for financial institutions and organizations dealing with sensitive information.

e. Cognitive Automation in Audit Processes: Cognitive automation, a combination of AI and robotic process automation (RPA), is transforming audit processes. It automates routine audit tasks, allowing auditors to focus on complex analyses and strategic insights.

2. **Blockchain Technology:**

a. Immutable Recordkeeping: Blockchain provides a tamper-proof and transparent ledger, ensuring the integrity of records. This is valuable for maintaining an immutable record of compliance activities, audits, and contractual agreements.

b. Smart Contracts for Automated Compliance: Smart contracts on blockchain enable the automatic execution and enforcement of compliance rules. This ensures that predefined compliance measures are executed without the need for manual intervention.

c. Supply Chain Transparency: Blockchain enhances transparency in the supply chain by providing a decentralized and secure ledger. Organizations can trace the origins of products, ensuring compliance with ethical and regulatory standards.

d. Data Privacy and Consent Management: Blockchain can be employed for secure and decentralized management of data privacy and consent. Individuals can have more control over their data, and organizations can demonstrate compliance with data protection regulations.

3. Data Analytics:

    a. Predictive Analytics for Risk Management: Predictive analytics uses historical data and statistical algorithms to forecast future events. In GRC, this is instrumental for identifying potential risks and making data-driven decisions to mitigate them.

    b. Continuous Monitoring of Compliance Metrics: Data analytics tools provide continuous monitoring of key compliance metrics. Organizations can track adherence to policies, identify deviations, and take corrective actions in real-time.

    c. Visualization for Enhanced Reporting: Data visualization tools convert complex GRC data into intuitive charts and dashboards. This facilitates better understanding and communication of risk and compliance information to stakeholders.

    d. Behavioral Analytics for Fraud Prevention: Behavioral analytics assess patterns of user behavior to detect anomalies and potential fraud. This is particularly effective in financial services and cybersecurity for identifying abnormal activities.

    e. Scenario Analysis for Crisis Management: Data analytics enables scenario analysis for crisis management. Organizations can simulate various scenarios to assess potential impacts, allowing them to develop proactive crisis response strategies.

IMPACT AND CONSIDERATIONS

Improved Decision-Making: These technologies empower organizations to make more informed and data-driven decisions in real-time, enhancing overall governance.

Efficiency and Automation: Automation of routine tasks and processes improves efficiency, allowing GRC professionals to focus on strategic initiatives and high-value activities.

Enhanced Transparency: Blockchain ensures transparent and traceable transactions, fostering trust among stakeholders and regulators. This is particularly relevant in compliance and audit activities.

Adaptive Compliance: AI and blockchain enable adaptive compliance, where systems can evolve and adapt to changing regulatory environments more effectively.

Advanced Risk Management: The use of AI and data analytics allows organizations to adopt a proactive approach to risk management, identifying and mitigating risks before they escalate.

CHALLENGES AND ETHICAL CONSIDERATIONS

Despite the benefits, the adoption of these technologies raises challenges such as data privacy concerns, ethical considerations in AI, and the need for regulatory frameworks to keep pace with technological advancements. Among the many downsides are; risks of security breaches and data privacy violations, workforce displacement and job loss, ethical dilemmas and bias.

A very important challenge is also digital divide and inequality. "While technology has the potential to bridge gaps and provide equal opportunities, there is a risk of exacerbating existing inequalities. Access to technology, reliable internet connectivity, and digital literacy may not be evenly distributed, leading to a digital divide that leaves certain communities or individuals marginalized. Bridging this divide and ensuring equitable access to technology and its benefits remains a challenge" (Ahmed 2023).

CHAPTER TWO

GRC FRAMEWORKS EXPOSED: ISO 27001, NIST, COBIT, AND MORE DECODED

Frameworks have a pivotal impact in establishing effective Governance, Risk Management, and Compliance (GRC) practices within organizations. These frameworks provide structured methodologies, best practices, and guidelines that help organizations develop and implement robust strategies for governance, risk mitigation, and compliance adherence. A nuanced understanding of these frameworks contributes significantly to organizational resilience by fostering a systematic and adaptive approach to managing the complexities of the business environment.

1. **Establishing A Structured Approach**

    A structured approach towards GRC is essential to not only mitigate risks but also to enhance governance practices and ensure compliance with an ever-growing array of regulations.

By aligning governance, risk management, and compliance within a cohesive structure, businesses can not only respond more effectively to emerging challenges but also proactively shape their destinies in an era where adaptability and resilience are paramount. In this context, understanding the elements of a structured GRC framework and their symbiotic relationships is essential for organizations aspiring to thrive amidst the complexities of the modern business environment. Let's take a closer look at them:

Governance Frameworks: Governance frameworks, such as COSO (Committee of Sponsoring Organizations of the Treadway Commission), provide guidelines for establishing and maintaining internal control. These frameworks help organizations define the roles, responsibilities, and decision-making processes within the governance structure.

Risk Management Frameworks: Frameworks like ISO 31000 offer a structured approach to risk management. They guide organizations in identifying, assessing, and mitigating risks systematically. This structured process enhances the organization's ability to anticipate and respond to potential threats.

Compliance Frameworks: Standards like ISO 19600 for compliance management systems provide a systematic approach to ensuring that organizations adhere to legal and regulatory requirements. Compliance frameworks help establish processes for monitoring, reporting, and mitigating compliance risks.

2.   **Enhancing Communication and Coordination**

Governance Frameworks: By clearly defining governance structures and decision-making processes, governance frameworks facilitate effective communication among stakeholders. This clarity ensures that responsibilities are well-understood and enables coordinated efforts across the organization.

Risk Management Frameworks: A shared risk management framework enhances communication about risk appetite, tolerance, and mitigation strategies. It promotes a common understanding of risk factors and encourages collaboration in managing risks.

Compliance Frameworks: Compliance frameworks establish a common language for discussing and addressing regulatory requirements. This shared understanding fosters communication between legal, compliance, and operational teams, ensuring a cohesive approach to compliance.

3. Improving Efficiency and Resource Allocation

Governance Frameworks: Effective governance frameworks streamline decision-making processes, reducing delays and inefficiencies. This efficiency is crucial for organizations to respond promptly to challenges and opportunities.

Risk Management Frameworks: By providing a systematic approach to risk assessment and prioritization, risk management frameworks help organizations allocate resources effectively. This ensures that mitigation efforts are focused on the most significant risks.

Compliance Frameworks: Compliance frameworks assist organizations in prioritizing regulatory requirements based on their impact and significance. This prioritization allows for the efficient allocation of resources to address the most critical compliance challenges.

4. Adapting to Change and Uncertainty:

Governance Frameworks: Governance frameworks often emphasize the need for adaptability and responsiveness. This adaptability is crucial for organizations facing dynamic business environments and evolving stakeholder expectations.

Risk Management Frameworks: A nuanced understanding of risk management frameworks helps organizations anticipate and navigate uncertainties. It encourages a proactive approach to identifying emerging risks and adjusting strategies accordingly.

Compliance Frameworks: Compliance frameworks guide organizations in building flexibility into their compliance programs. This flexibility is essential for adapting to changes in regulations and ensuring ongoing adherence to evolving compliance requirements.

5. **Strengthening Organizational Resilience:**

Governance Frameworks: Well-defined governance structures contribute to organizational resilience by ensuring that decision-makers have a clear understanding of their roles and responsibilities. This clarity is foundational to effective crisis management and strategic adaptation.

Risk Management Frameworks: Organizations with mature risk management practices are better equipped to anticipate and respond to disruptions. A nuanced understanding of risk frameworks enables proactive risk mitigation and enhances overall organizational resilience.

Compliance Frameworks: Compliance frameworks support organizational resilience by providing a systematic approach to addressing regulatory challenges. A proactive and adaptable compliance program ensures that the organization can navigate changes in the regulatory landscape without significant disruptions.

UNDERSTANDING ISO 27001

AN INTRODUCTION

ISO 27001, the International Organization for Standardization's Information Security Management System (ISMS) standard, stands as a cornerstone in the realm of information security. It provides a systematic and comprehensive approach to managing and protecting an organization's valuable information assets.

UNDERSTANDING ISO 27001:

SCOPE AND OBJECTIVES

ISO 27001 is designed to help organizations establish, implement, maintain, and continually improve an Information Security Management System. The standard outlines a risk-based approach to identify, assess, and manage information security risks, ensuring the confidentiality, integrity, and availability of sensitive information.

KEY COMPONENTS

Risk Assessment: ISO 27001 emphasizes a risk-based approach to information security. Organizations are required to assess and prioritize risks, implement controls to mitigate them, and continually monitor and review their effectiveness.

Continuous Improvement: The standard promotes a cycle of continual improvement through regular assessments, audits, and updates to adapt to evolving threats and vulnerabilities.

APPLICABILITY

ISO 27001 is applicable to organizations of all sizes, types, and industries, recognizing the universal importance of information security. Whether in finance, healthcare, or any other sector, organizations can tailor the standard to suit their specific needs.

EVOLUTION OF ISO 27001

INITIAL ITERATIONS

The first version of ISO 27001 was introduced in 2005, building on the earlier British Standard (BS) 7799-2. This initial iteration laid the groundwork for a systematic approach to information security management. Subsequent revisions, particularly the 2013 version, incorporated a risk-based approach and strengthened alignment with other management system standards like ISO 9001 and ISO 14001. This update aimed to enhance compatibility and integration with broader organizational processes. As of 2023, ISO 27001 continues to evolve to address the dynamic nature of cybersecurity threats. Ongoing updates reflect advancements in technology, changes in the threat landscape, and feedback from organizations implementing the standard.

GLOBAL RECOGNITION AND ADOPTION

UNIVERSAL APPLICABILITY

ISO 27001 has gained global recognition for its universal applicability. Organizations worldwide, irrespective of size or industry, have adopted the standard to fortify their information security posture.

REGULATORY COMPLIANCE

Many countries and industries recognize ISO 27001 as a benchmark for information security. Compliance with ISO 27001 often aligns with regulatory requirements, facilitating legal adherence in various jurisdictions.

INDUSTRY RECOGNITION

ISO 27001 has gained widespread acceptance in industries where information security is critical, such as finance, healthcare, and technology. Organizations seeking to demonstrate their commitment to protecting sensitive data often pursue ISO 27001 certification.

SUPPLIER AND CLIENT ASSURANCE

ISO 27001 certification serves as a powerful assurance mechanism for both suppliers and clients. Organizations that handle sensitive information are increasingly requiring their partners to implement ISO 27001 to ensure robust security practices throughout the supply chain.

INTERNATIONAL REPUTATION

The international reputation of ISO 27001 as a comprehensive and adaptable standard for information security contributes to its continued global recognition. It is seen not just as a compliance requirement but as a strategic investment in securing critical assets.

THE STRUCTURE OF THE ISO 27001 FRAMEWORK

ISO 27001 is structured around several key components, each playing a vital role in creating a robust framework for information security. These components are interconnected, forming a systematic and dynamic approach to safeguarding sensitive information. Let's break down the essential components of ISO 27001:

1. **Information Security Management System (ISMS):**

   The ISMS is the overarching framework that encompasses all the components of ISO 27001. It is a systematic approach to managing sensitive information, integrating policies, procedures, and controls to protect the confidentiality, integrity, and availability of data.

2. **Context Establishment and Leadership:**

   Organizations define the scope of their ISMS, identifying the internal and external factors that can affect the security of information. Leadership and Commitment: Top management demonstrates leadership and commitment to information security by establishing a policy, assigning roles and responsibilities, and ensuring resources are allocated for ISMS implementation.

3. **Risk Assessment and Treatment:**

Risk Assessment: Organizations systematically identify and assess risks to the confidentiality, integrity, and availability of information. This involves evaluating the likelihood and impact of potential risks.

Risk Treatment: Based on the risk assessment, organizations develop and implement risk treatment plans. This may involve implementing security controls, avoiding certain risks, or accepting them based on the organization's risk appetite.

4. **Information Security Controls:**

Control Objectives and Controls: ISO 27001 outlines a set of control objectives and controls across various domains such as information security policies, human resources, physical security, communication security, and access control.

Selection of Controls: Organizations select and implement controls based on their risk assessment and treatment decisions. Controls address specific risks and vulnerabilities identified in the organization's context.

5. **Performance Evaluation:**

Monitoring and Measurement: Organizations establish processes for monitoring and measuring the performance of information security controls and the ISMS. This includes regular assessments, audits, and reviews.

Internal Audits: Internal audits are conducted to ensure that the ISMS is implemented effectively, and information security controls are operating as intended.

6. **Continual Improvement:**

Nonconformities and Corrective Actions: If nonconformities or deficiencies are identified through audits or monitoring, organizations take corrective actions to address these issues and prevent their recurrence.

Continual Improvement Process: ISO 27001 emphasizes the importance of continually improving the effectiveness of the ISMS. This involves learning from experiences, adapting to changes in the organization's context, and enhancing information security practices.

7. **Communication and Documentation:**

Communication: ISO 27001 requires effective communication about information security within the organization. This includes communication of the ISMS policy, objectives, roles, and responsibilities.

Documentation: Organizations maintain documented information to support the operation of the ISMS, including the information security policy, risk assessment results, and evidence of compliance with controls.

8. **Annex A: Information Security Control Objectives and Controls:**

Domains and Categories: Annex A of ISO 27001 provides a comprehensive set of information security control objectives and controls organized into domains and categories. It serves as a reference for organizations in selecting controls based on their risk assessment.

INTERACTIONS AND DYNAMICS

Risk-Driven Approach: The risk assessment and treatment process guides the selection and implementation of controls. This ensures that controls are tailored to the organization's specific risks and vulnerabilities.

Continuous Feedback Loop: Monitoring, measurement, and internal audits create a continuous feedback loop. Findings from these activities inform corrective actions and improvements, contributing to the ongoing effectiveness of the ISMS.

Leadership and Culture: The leadership's commitment to information security, as demonstrated in the context establishment, sets the tone for a security-conscious organizational culture. This culture permeates through the selection of controls, their implementation, and the continual improvement process.

ADAPTABILITY OF ISO 27001 ACROSS INDUSTRIES AND ORGANIZATIONAL SIZES

Finance Sector :ISO 27001 is widely adopted in the financial sector to protect sensitive customer information, ensure compliance with financial regulations, and maintain the integrity of financial systems.

Healthcare Industry: Healthcare organizations leverage ISO 27001 to secure patient data, comply with healthcare regulations such as HIPAA, and ensure the availability and integrity of critical healthcare systems.

Technology Companies: Technology companies, including startups and established enterprises, implement ISO 27001 to secure intellectual property, customer data, and proprietary information. It is particularly crucial for companies offering cloud services and software solutions.

Manufacturing and Industrial Sectors: ISO 27001 is adaptable to the manufacturing and industrial sectors, where organizations need to protect sensitive designs, production data, and control systems. It helps ensure the integrity of manufacturing processes and protects against cyber threats.

Small and Medium Enterprises (SMEs): ISO 27001 is scalable and adaptable for SMEs. It allows smaller organizations to implement a robust information security management system proportionate to their size and complexity, enhancing their overall security posture.

Global Corporations: Large multinational corporations often implement ISO 27001 across their global operations. The standard provides a common framework for information security management, ensuring consistent practices across diverse business units and locations.

Key Factors Contributing to Adaptability

Scalability: ISO 27001 is scalable, allowing organizations to tailor the implementation to their specific needs and scale of operations. This makes it suitable for both large enterprises and smaller organizations.

Risk-Based Approach: The risk-based approach of ISO 27001 ensures that organizations can prioritize and address risks based on their unique business context. This adaptability makes it relevant across different industries facing varying threats.

Universal Applicability: ISO 27001's universal applicability, irrespective of industry or sector, makes it adaptable to organizations of diverse sizes and functions. Its principles can be applied across different business processes and activities.

Alignment with Business Objectives: ISO 27001 aligns with the business objectives of organizations, ensuring that information security measures support and enhance overall business goals. This alignment contributes to its broad adaptability.

Compliance with Regulations: ISO 27001 facilitates compliance with various industry-specific regulations and standards. Its adaptability allows organizations to integrate additional requirements based on their industry-specific regulatory landscape.

NIST Framework For Cybersecurity

The National Institute of Standards and Technology (NIST) Cybersecurity Framework is a comprehensive set of guidelines, best practices, and standards designed to enhance cybersecurity in critical infrastructure sectors. Its origins can be traced to the Executive Order 13636, "Improving Critical Infrastructure Cybersecurity," issued by President Barack Obama in February 2013.

Some NIST cybersecurity assignments are defined by federal statutes, executive orders and policies. For example, the Office of Management and Budget (OMB) mandates that all federal agencies implement NIST's cybersecurity standards and guidance for non-national security systems, Priority areas to which NIST contributes – and plans to focus more on – include cryptography, education and workforce, emerging technologies, risk management, identity and access management, measurements, privacy, trustworthy networks and trustworthy platforms (NIST 2021).

Origins of the NIST Cybersecurity Framework

EXECUTIVE ORDER 13636 (2013)

The Executive Order acknowledged the increasing cybersecurity threats facing the United States and highlighted the need to improve the cybersecurity of critical infrastructure. It directed NIST to develop a framework that would provide a set of standards, guidelines, and practices to help organizations manage and mitigate cybersecurity risks. In response to the Executive Order, NIST engaged in an extensive collaborative effort with industry, academia, and government agencies to develop the Cybersecurity Framework. This collaboration aimed to gather insights, expertise, and perspectives from a wide range of stakeholders to ensure the framework's effectiveness and relevance.

They released a preliminary version of the framework in August 2013, seeking public input through workshops, webinars, and public comments. The feedback received during this public consultation process was instrumental in refining and shaping the final version of the framework.

RELEASE OF THE NIST CYBERSECURITY FRAMEWORK (2014)

The NIST Cybersecurity Framework, officially titled "Framework for Improving Critical Infrastructure Cybersecurity," was released in February 2014. This document outlined a voluntary, risk-based approach to cybersecurity, providing a flexible and adaptable framework that organizations could use to assess and improve their cybersecurity posture.

KEY COMPONENTS OF THE NIST CYBERSECURITY FRAMEWORK

The NIST Cybersecurity Framework consists of three main components:

Framework Core: The Core includes five functions: Identify, Protect, Detect, Respond, and Recover. These functions provide a high-level, strategic view of the lifecycle of cybersecurity risk management.

Framework Implementation Tiers: The Tiers help organizations assess the maturity of their cybersecurity practices and provide a roadmap for moving from a basic level of cybersecurity awareness to a more adaptive and risk-informed approach.

Framework Profiles: Profiles allow organizations to align the framework's components with their specific business requirements, risk tolerance, and resources. A profile serves as a customized roadmap for implementing the framework.

Roots in Enhancing Cybersecurity

RISK-BASED APPROACH

The NIST Cybersecurity Framework is rooted in a risk-based approach, emphasizing that organizations should understand and manage cybersecurity risks in the context of their business objectives. This approach enables organizations to prioritize actions based on the potential impact of cybersecurity threats to their operations.

FLEXIBILITY AND ADAPTABILITY:

The framework is designed to be flexible and adaptable to various sectors, sizes of organizations, and types of critical infrastructure. It recognizes that a one-size-fits-all approach is not practical in the diverse landscape of critical infrastructure sectors.

VOLUNTARY NATURE:

The voluntary nature of the framework allows organizations to use it as a tool for self-assessment and improvement without imposing regulatory requirements. This approach encourages widespread adoption and collaboration across industries.

ALIGNMENT WITH EXISTING STANDARDS:

The framework aligns with existing cybersecurity standards, guidelines, and best practices. It does not reinvent the wheel but rather consolidates and integrates well-established cybersecurity principles into a cohesive and accessible framework.

CONTINUOUS IMPROVEMENT:

The framework emphasizes the importance of continuous improvement by encouraging organizations to regularly assess their cybersecurity posture, learn from incidents, and update their strategies accordingly. This dynamic and iterative approach reflects the evolving nature of cybersecurity threats.

GLOBAL RECOGNITION:

While initially developed for U.S. critical infrastructure, the NIST Cybersecurity Framework has gained global recognition. Organizations worldwide leverage its principles, and its concepts have influenced the development of cybersecurity standards and frameworks globally.

The NIST Cybersecurity Framework, born out of a presidential directive and shaped by collaboration with stakeholders, stands as a foundational tool for organizations seeking to enhance their cybersecurity resilience. Its risk-based, flexible, and voluntary nature has contributed to its widespread adoption across various industries, solidifying its role as a key resource in the ongoing effort to address the dynamic and evolving challenges of cybersecurity.

CORE COMPONENTS OF THE NIST FRAMEWORK

The NIST Cybersecurity Framework's core functions—Identify, Protect, Detect, Respond, and Recover—form the foundation of a comprehensive and strategic approach to managing cybersecurity risk. These functions guide organizations in developing, implementing, and improving their cybersecurity programs. Let's delve into each of these core functions:

1. **Identify:**

    The "Identify" function focuses on understanding and managing cybersecurity risks to systems, assets, data, and capabilities.

    Key Activities:

    a. Asset Management: Identify and document all assets, including hardware, software, data, and personnel, that are critical to business operations.

b. Risk Assessment: Conduct a risk assessment to identify and prioritize cybersecurity risks, considering potential threats, vulnerabilities, and impacts.

c. Business Environment: Understand the organization's business context, including its mission, priorities, and stakeholders.

Benefits:

a. Establishes a foundation for effective risk management.

b. Enhances understanding of the organization's cybersecurity posture.

c. Informs the development of risk mitigation strategies.

2. **Protect**

The "Protect" function focuses on implementing safeguards to ensure the delivery of critical services and the protection of assets.

Key Activities:

a. Access Control: Limit access to systems and data based on user roles and responsibilities.

b. Data Security: Implement measures to protect data, including encryption and data integrity checks.

c. Security Training and Awareness: Provide ongoing training and awareness programs to educate personnel about cybersecurity risks and best practices.

Benefits:

a. Strengthens defenses against cyber threats.

b. Safeguards critical assets and data.

c. Enhances the organization's ability to resist and recover from cyber incidents.

3. **Detect**

The "Detect" function focuses on identifying and detecting cybersecurity events promptly.

Key Activities:

a. Anomaly and Event Detection: Implement monitoring systems to detect unusual or suspicious activities.

b. Continuous Monitoring: Establish continuous monitoring capabilities to promptly identify and respond to cybersecurity incidents.

c. Incident Detection Processes: Develop processes to detect and respond to incidents, including the use of intrusion detection systems.

Benefits:

a. Enables early detection of cybersecurity incidents.

b. Minimizes the impact of incidents through timely response.

c. Improves the organization's situational awareness of potential threats.

4. **Respond:**

The "Respond" function focuses on developing and implementing response plans to effectively manage and mitigate the impact of a detected cybersecurity incident.

Key Activities:

a. Incident Response Planning: Develop and maintain incident response plans that outline roles, responsibilities, and actions to be taken in the event of a cybersecurity incident.

b. Communication and Coordination: Establish communication channels and coordination mechanisms for effective incident response.

c. Containment and Eradication: Take immediate actions to contain and eradicate the threat, preventing further damage.

Benefits:

a. Reduces the impact of cybersecurity incidents.

b. Speeds up the recovery process.

c. Enhances the organization's ability to learn from incidents and improve response capabilities.

5. **Recover:**

The "Recover" function focuses on restoring services and capabilities affected by a cybersecurity incident and implementing improvements based on lessons learned.

Key Activities:

a. Recovery Planning: Develop and maintain recovery plans that address the restoration of critical services and functions.

b. Improvement Planning: Identify areas for improvement based on lessons learned from incidents.

c. Communication with Stakeholders: Communicate with stakeholders to keep them informed about the recovery process.

Benefits:

a. Expedites the recovery of critical services and functions.

b. Facilitates organizational learning and continuous improvement.

c. Strengthens the organization's resilience to future incidents.

Integration and Iterative Process

The NIST Cybersecurity Framework emphasizes the importance of an iterative and continuous improvement process. Organizations are encouraged to regularly assess their cybersecurity posture, update their risk management strategies, and refine their cybersecurity programs based on evolving threats and lessons learned from incidents.

The core functions work together in a holistic manner, providing organizations with a structured and adaptable framework for managing cybersecurity risks across the entire lifecycle of their systems and data. By integrating these functions into their cybersecurity programs, organizations can enhance their resilience, responsiveness, and overall ability to safeguard against cyber threats. (NIST 2023)

How Various Organizations Can Implement The NIST Framework

Implementing the NIST Cybersecurity Framework requires a tailored approach that considers the unique characteristics and needs of each organization. The framework's flexibility allows organizations to adapt its principles to varying contexts, sizes, and industries. Here are practical insights into how organizations can implement the NIST framework, considering different organizational contexts:

1. **Customizing the Framework:**

    Understand Organizational Context: Conduct a thorough assessment of the organization's mission, objectives, and business processes. Identify critical assets, systems, and data that are essential to business operations then consider the organization's risk tolerance and industry-specific requirements.

Tailor the Functions, Categories, and Subcategories: Customize the five core functions (Identify, Protect, Detect, Respond, Recover) based on the organization's priorities and risk profile. Select and prioritize categories and subcategories within each function that align with the organization's specific context.

2. **Building a Risk Management Foundation:**

Conduct a Risk Assessment: Identify and assess cybersecurity risks, considering potential threats, vulnerabilities, and impacts. Prioritize risks based on their potential impact on critical business functions.

Develop a Risk Management Plan: Establish a risk management plan that outlines how the organization will manage and mitigate identified risks then Integrate risk management into decision-making processes across the organization.

3. **Implementing the Core Functions:**

Identify: Develop an asset inventory and document critical business processes. Also establish a risk governance structure and assign responsibilities for risk management.

Protect: Implement access controls, encryption, and other safeguards based on the organization's risk assessment. Also endeavor to provide cybersecurity training and awareness programs for employees.

Detect: Deploy monitoring systems for anomalous activities and incidents then establish incident detection processes and procedures.

Respond: Develop incident response plans that include roles, responsibilities, and communication protocols. Work towards conducting regular incident response exercises to test and improve response capabilities.

Recover: Develop recovery plans for restoring critical services and functions. Analyze incidents and implement improvements to enhance recovery processes.

4. Integration with Existing Processes:

Align with Existing Standards and Regulations: Integrate the NIST framework with existing cybersecurity standards, regulations, and industry best practices applicable to the organization. Additionally, leverage synergies with other frameworks, such as ISO 27001 or COBIT, to streamline implementation.

Incorporate into the SDLC and Business Processes: Integrate cybersecurity considerations into the software development life cycle (SDLC) and other business processes. Ensure that cybersecurity is a fundamental aspect of organizational decision-making and strategic planning.

5. Continuous Improvement:

Establish a Continuous Improvement Culture: Foster a culture of continuous improvement by regularly assessing the effectiveness of cybersecurity measures. Also encourage employees to report incidents and contribute to lessons learned.

Regularly Review and Update the Framework: Conduct periodic reviews of the NIST framework implementation to ensure its continued relevance. Update the framework based on changes in the organization's business environment, technology landscape, and threat landscape.

6. Resource Allocation and Budgeting:

Allocate Resources Appropriately: Allocate resources based on the organization's risk assessment and risk management plan ensuring that the budget for cybersecurity aligns with the organization's risk profile and priorities.

Prioritize High-Impact Areas: Identify and prioritize high-impact areas for cybersecurity improvements based on the organization's critical functions and assets. Allocate resources to address vulnerabilities that pose the greatest risk.

7. **Communication and Collaboration:**

Establish Communication Channels: Develop clear communication channels for reporting cybersecurity incidents and disseminating information. Foster a collaborative environment that encourages information sharing among different departments and stakeholders.

Collaborate with External Partners: Collaborate with external partners, suppliers, and stakeholders to enhance overall cybersecurity resilience. Establish cybersecurity requirements for third-party vendors and partners.

8. **Monitoring and Metrics:**

Implement Monitoring and Metrics: Establish key performance indicators (KPIs) and metrics to measure the effectiveness of cybersecurity controls. Regularly monitor and assess cybersecurity performance against established metrics.

Incident Analysis and Lessons Learned: Analyze cybersecurity incidents to understand their root causes and identify areas for improvement. Use lessons learned to enhance incident response plans and recovery processes.

COBIT: Control Objectives for Information and Related Technologies

Control Objectives for Information and Related Technologies (COBIT) is a globally recognized framework that provides a comprehensive set of guidelines and best practices for effective IT governance. Developed by the Information Systems Audit and Control Association (ISACA) and the IT Governance Institute (ITGI), COBIT is designed to align IT activities with business objectives, ensure the delivery of value, and manage risks associated with the use of information and technology. COBIT is widely used by organizations to enhance the governance and management of their IT processes. (ISACA 2016)

KEY PRINCIPLES OF COBIT:

Business Alignment: COBIT emphasizes the alignment of IT with business goals and objectives. It ensures that IT initiatives and activities contribute directly to the achievement of organizational objectives.

Governance and Management: The framework provides a clear distinction between IT governance and management. Governance focuses on strategic alignment, value delivery, risk management, resource optimization, and performance measurement. Management focuses on planning, building, running, and monitoring IT processes.

Holistic Approach: COBIT takes a holistic approach to IT governance, covering all aspects of IT processes and their interrelationships. It considers people, processes, technology, and information as integral components of a comprehensive governance system.

Process Orientation: COBIT is process-oriented, defining a set of processes that organizations can tailor to meet their specific needs. The framework organizes processes into four domains: Plan and

Organize, Acquire and Implement, Deliver and Support, and Monitor and Evaluate.

Maturity Models: COBIT includes maturity models that help organizations assess and improve their capability to manage and govern IT processes. Maturity models provide a roadmap for organizations to evolve from basic, ad-hoc processes to optimized, well-managed processes.

COBIT Framework Components

FRAMEWORK

The COBIT framework provides a high-level structure for organizing its principles, processes, and guidelines. It serves as the overarching guide for implementing effective IT governance.

COBIT defines the components to build and sustain a governance system: processes, organizational structures, policies and procedures, information flows, culture and behaviors, skills, and infrastructure. It addresses governance issues by grouping relevant governance components into governance and management objectives that can be managed to the required capability levels.

PROCESS DESCRIPTIONS

COBIT defines a set of IT-related processes, categorized into the four domains mentioned earlier. Each process is described in detail, outlining its purpose, objectives, inputs, activities, outputs, and metrics.

CONTROL OBJECTIVES

Control objectives are specific goals that organizations aim to achieve through the implementation of COBIT. These objectives ensure that IT processes are effective, efficient, and aligned with business objectives.

MANAGEMENT GUIDELINES

COBIT provides management guidelines that help organizations implement and tailor the framework to their specific context. These guidelines offer practical advice for optimizing IT governance and management.

MATURITY MODELS

Maturity models in COBIT assess the maturity of IT processes on a scale from 0 to 5. This allows organizations to gauge the level of control and effectiveness in each process and prioritize improvement efforts.

IT ASSURANCE FRAMEWORK

COBIT integrates an IT assurance framework that supports the establishment of trust and confidence in IT processes. It assists organizations in ensuring the reliability and integrity of information.

COBIT's Contribution to Aligning IT with Business Objectives

COBIT helps organizations align IT strategy with overall business strategy. By identifying and prioritizing IT-related goals that directly contribute to business objectives, COBIT ensures that IT resources are allocated strategically. COBIT emphasizes the delivery of value through IT processes. It ensures that IT investments and activities contribute positively to the organization's objectives, resulting in tangible benefits. COBIT provides a robust framework for managing IT-related risks. It helps organizations identify, assess, and mitigate risks associated with IT processes, ensuring that risks are managed in alignment with business goals.

RESOURCE OPTIMIZATION AND PERFORMANCE MEASUREMENT

COBIT assists in optimizing IT resources by providing guidelines for efficient and effective use. It helps organizations allocate resources based on priorities, ensuring that IT investments align with business needs. COBIT establishes metrics and key performance indicators (KPIs) for IT processes. This allows organizations to measure and monitor the performance of IT activities and continuously improve their effectiveness.

HISTORICAL CONTEXT AND EVOLUTION OF COBIT

The historical context of COBIT (Control Objectives for Information and Related Technologies) is rooted in the need for effective IT governance and control. The framework has undergone several iterations, each building upon the previous version to address emerging challenges and adapt to evolving industry practices. Here's an exploration of the historical context and evolution of COBIT:

HISTORICAL CONTEXT:

EARLY 1990S: EMERGENCE OF IT GOVERNANCE CONCERNS:

In the early 1990s, as organizations increasingly relied on information technology for their business processes, concerns about IT governance, control, and security began to surface. There was a growing recognition that IT needed to be managed strategically and aligned with business objectives.

1996: COBIT 1.0 - FIRST ITERATION:

* ISACA (Information Systems Audit and Control Association) introduced the first version of COBIT in 1996.

* COBIT 1.0 aimed to provide a framework for IT governance and control, offering a set of control objectives and maturity models.

Evolution of COBIT Versions

1998: COBIT 2.0 - EXPANSION AND REFINEMENT:

* COBIT 2.0 was released in 1998, expanding the framework to cover more areas of IT governance.

* It included a focus on aligning IT with business goals and introduced the concept of IT processes.

2000: COBIT 3.0 - INTEGRATION WITH IT PROCESSES:

* COBIT 3.0, released in 2000, marked a significant evolution by integrating IT processes into the framework.

* It introduced the Plan, Acquire, Implement, Deliver, and Monitor (PAIDM) framework structure.

2005: COBIT 4.0 - FURTHER ENHANCEMENT:

* COBIT 4.0, released in 2005, continued to refine and enhance the framework.

* It provided a more structured approach to IT governance and control, emphasizing the need for a systematic understanding of IT processes.

2012: COBIT 5.0 - COMPREHENSIVE FRAMEWORK:

* COBIT 5.0, released in 2012, represented a significant leap forward by becoming a comprehensive business framework for the governance and management of enterprise IT.

* It incorporated and integrated other relevant standards and frameworks, such as Val IT and Risk IT, into a unified framework.

* COBIT 5 introduced the concept of governance and management enablers and focused on creating business value through IT.

2019: COBIT 2019 - BUILDING ON COBIT 5:

* In 2019, ISACA released an update called COBIT 2019, building upon COBIT 5.

* COBIT 2019 continued to emphasize the importance of governance and management enablers, providing practical guidance for implementation.

* It retained COBIT 5's focus on aligning IT with business objectives and managing IT-related risks.

KEY THEMES IN THE EVOLUTION OF COBIT

Integration of IT Processes: COBIT's evolution has consistently emphasized the integration of IT processes into a cohesive framework. This integration allows organizations to manage and govern IT comprehensively.

Alignment with Business Objectives: With each version, COBIT has placed a strong emphasis on aligning IT activities with business goals. This alignment ensures that IT contributes directly to the achievement of broader organizational objectives.

Enablers for Governance and Management: COBIT has introduced the concept of governance and management enablers, emphasizing the factors that influence successful governance and management practices.

Adaptation to Industry Changes: COBIT has evolved to adapt to changes in the IT and business landscape, incorporating new technologies, emerging risks, and industry best practices.

Practical Implementation Guidance: COBIT versions, particularly COBIT 5 and COBIT 2019, have provided practical guidance for the implementation of the framework. This has made it more accessible and actionable for organizations.

Use Cases for COBIT In Governance, Risk Management and Compliance

Control Objectives for Information and Related Technologies (COBIT) addresses specific Governance, Risk, and Compliance (GRC) challenges by providing a comprehensive framework that integrates governance and management practices for IT processes. There are a variety of ways in which COBIT addresses key GRC challenges:

1. **Alignment with Business Objectives:**

   Many organizations struggle to align IT initiatives with broader business objectives, leading to inefficiencies and a lack of strategic value from IT investments.

   COBIT Solution: COBIT emphasizes the alignment of IT with business goals. By providing a structured approach to link IT processes to organizational objectives, COBIT ensures that IT activities contribute directly to business success.

2. **Risk Management:**

   Effectively managing IT-related risks is a common challenge. Organizations face difficulties in identifying, assessing, and mitigating risks associated with IT processes.

   COBIT Solution: COBIT integrates risk management into its framework. It provides guidelines for assessing and managing risks throughout the IT processes, ensuring that risk management is an integral part of IT governance and decision-making.

3. **Regulatory Compliance:**

   Adhering to a complex and evolving regulatory landscape poses challenges for organizations. Keeping up with compliance requirements and demonstrating adherence is a constant struggle.

COBIT Solution: COBIT incorporates compliance requirements into its framework, making it easier for organizations to map their IT processes to regulatory obligations. This helps in establishing and maintaining compliance with various standards and regulations.

4. Process Integration and Standardization:

Lack of standardized and integrated processes often leads to inefficiencies, duplication of efforts, and difficulty in managing complex IT environments.

COBIT Solution: COBIT provides a set of integrated and standardized IT processes organized into domains. This structure allows organizations to establish consistent and repeatable processes, leading to operational efficiency and improved control.

5. Governance and Management Enablers:

Organizations may struggle with identifying the key factors that enable effective governance and management of IT.

COBIT Solution: COBIT introduces the concept of governance and management enablers, which include principles, policies, processes, organizational structures, culture, and information. This holistic approach ensures that various elements work together to support effective governance and management practices.

6. Maturity Models for Continuous Improvement:

Achieving and sustaining a mature level of IT governance and control is an ongoing challenge for organizations.

COBIT Solution: COBIT incorporates maturity models that allow organizations to assess the maturity of their IT processes. This provides a roadmap for continuous improvement, allowing organizations to evolve their IT governance capabilities over time.

7. **Holistic Approach to IT Governance:**

    Organizations may struggle with fragmented approaches to IT governance, lacking a holistic view of the entire IT landscape.

    COBIT Solution: COBIT takes a holistic approach by considering people, processes, technology, and information as integral components. This ensures that IT governance is comprehensive, addressing all aspects that contribute to effective and efficient IT management.

8. **Practical Implementation Guidance:**

    Organizations often face difficulties in translating governance frameworks into practical implementation.

    COBIT Solution: COBIT provides practical implementation guidance, including management guidelines, to help organizations tailor the framework to their specific context. This makes it more actionable and facilitates successful implementation.

9. **Communication and Collaboration:**

    Communication gaps between IT and other business units can hinder effective collaboration, leading to misunderstandings and conflicts.

    COBIT Solution: COBIT emphasizes the need for clear communication channels and collaboration between IT and other business functions. This ensures that IT activities are aligned with organizational goals and contribute to overall business success.

    Invariably COBIT addresses specific GRC challenges by providing a structured and integrated framework that aligns IT with business objectives, incorporates risk management and compliance requirements, and fosters a culture of continuous improvement. Its holistic approach and practical implementation guidance make it a valuable resource for organizations seeking to enhance their IT governance and control capabilities.

THE COMPLEMENTARY NATURE OF GRC FRAMEWORKS

The strategic integration of different Governance, Risk, and Compliance (GRC) frameworks is a pragmatic approach that leverages the strengths of each framework to create a more comprehensive and effective risk management strategy. Rather than viewing GRC frameworks as mutually exclusive, organizations can gain strategic advantages by recognizing their complementary nature. Here are key considerations and benefits of integrating different GRC frameworks:

1. **Specialized Focus:**

    Different GRC frameworks often have specialized focuses. For instance, ISO 27001 might be more focused on information security, while COSO ERM may emphasize enterprise risk management. Integrating these frameworks allows organizations to benefit from the depth of expertise in specific areas.

2. **Industry-Specific Requirements:**

    Industries often have unique regulatory and compliance requirements. Integrating industry-specific GRC frameworks enables organizations to address sector-specific challenges. For example, financial institutions might benefit from integrating Basel III for financial risk management alongside broader frameworks like COBIT.

3. **Maturity Models and Continuous Improvement:**

    GRC frameworks often provide maturity models to assess an organization's maturity in governance and risk management. By strategically integrating these models, organizations can create a more nuanced understanding of their overall maturity, facilitating continuous improvement initiatives.

4. **Global and Local Compliance:**

Different GRC frameworks may address global and local compliance requirements. For a multinational organization, integrating frameworks like ISO 27001 (global) and NIST Cybersecurity Framework (U.S. focus) can help in aligning with both international and local cybersecurity standards.

5. **Flexibility and Adaptability:**

The business environment is dynamic, and risks evolve. Integrating flexible frameworks allows organizations to adapt to changing circumstances. This flexibility is especially crucial when industries face rapid technological advancements or shifts in regulatory landscapes.

6. **Holistic Risk Management:**

GRC frameworks often provide different perspectives on risk management. By integrating these frameworks, organizations can create a more holistic view of risks, considering financial, operational, reputational, and cybersecurity risks collectively.

7. **Resource Optimization:**

Integrating GRC frameworks enables organizations to optimize resources by avoiding duplication of efforts. Instead of managing separate compliance initiatives, organizations can streamline processes and allocate resources more efficiently.

8. **Enhanced Reporting and Communication:**

Different frameworks may have varying reporting structures and key performance indicators (KPIs). Integrating these frameworks allows organizations to tailor reporting to different stakeholders effectively. For instance, using COBIT for IT governance reporting and COSO ERM for board-level risk reporting.

9. Technology Alignment:

Technology plays a crucial role in GRC. Integrating technology-specific frameworks (e.g., ISO 27001 for information security and NIST Cybersecurity Framework for cybersecurity) allows organizations to align their technology risk management strategies more effectively.

10. Adherence to Best Practices:

GRC frameworks often incorporate best practices from various sources. By integrating these frameworks, organizations can ensure a more comprehensive adoption of industry best practices, leading to a stronger risk management posture.

COMMON CHALLENGES FACED WHEN IMPLEMENTING GRC

Implementing Governance, Risk, and Compliance (GRC) frameworks in organizations is often a complex process that comes with various challenges. These challenges can span from resistance to change, resource constraints, to the need for cultural shifts. Some common challenges are:

1. Resistance to Change:

Employees and leadership may resist changes associated with implementing GRC frameworks. This resistance can be due to a fear of the unknown, perceived disruptions to existing workflows, or concerns about additional workloads.

Solution:

Communication and Training: Clear communication about the benefits of GRC and providing training sessions can alleviate concerns and increase buy-in.

Engagement: Involving employees in the planning and decision-making processes can foster a sense of ownership and reduce resistance.

2. Resource Constraints:

Many organizations face resource limitations, including financial, human, and technological resources. Implementing GRC frameworks may require investments in technology, hiring of skilled personnel, and dedicating time and effort.

Solution:

Prioritization: Prioritize GRC initiatives based on risk assessments and organizational priorities.

Phased Implementation: Implement GRC frameworks in phases to spread resource requirements over time.

3. Cultural Shifts:

GRC implementation often necessitates a cultural shift, especially in organizations where risk management and compliance were not previously prioritized. Changing ingrained habits and attitudes can be challenging.

Solution:

Leadership Support: Leadership should champion the cultural shift, demonstrating commitment and setting an example.

Communication: Regularly communicate the reasons behind the cultural shift, emphasizing the benefits to the organization.

4. **Lack of Clear Communication:**

Poor communication about the objectives, benefits, and expected changes related to GRC implementation can lead to confusion and misunderstanding among employees.

Solution:

Communication Plan: Develop a comprehensive communication plan that includes regular updates, FAQs, and opportunities for feedback.

Transparency: Be transparent about the goals and expected outcomes of GRC initiatives.

5. **Complexity of GRC Frameworks:**

Some GRC frameworks can be intricate and comprehensive. The complexity may overwhelm organizations, especially smaller ones, making it difficult to understand and implement all aspects.

Solution:

Tailoring: Tailor the GRC framework to fit the organization's size, industry, and specific needs.

Incremental Implementation: Start with a phased and incremental approach to gradually introduce and acclimate the organization to the framework.

6. **Integration with Existing Processes:**

Integrating GRC frameworks with existing processes can be challenging, especially if these processes are deeply ingrained or if there is a lack of compatibility.

Solution:

Process Mapping: Conduct a thorough assessment of existing processes and map them to the requirements of the GRC framework.

Collaboration: Involve relevant stakeholders in the integration process to ensure a smooth transition.

7. **Lack of Skilled Personnel:**

GRC implementation may require specialized skills in risk management, compliance, and technology. The organization might lack personnel with these skills.

Solution:

Training Programs: Invest in training programs to upskill existing employees.

Consultation: Consider seeking external expertise or consultants to guide the organization through the implementation process.

8. **Measuring Effectiveness:**

Organizations may struggle with defining and measuring the effectiveness of GRC initiatives. This can lead to uncertainty about the return on investment.

Solution:

Key Performance Indicators (KPIs): Establish clear KPIs aligned with organizational goals to measure the impact of GRC initiatives.

Regular Assessments: Conduct regular assessments and audits to evaluate the effectiveness of implemented GRC measures.

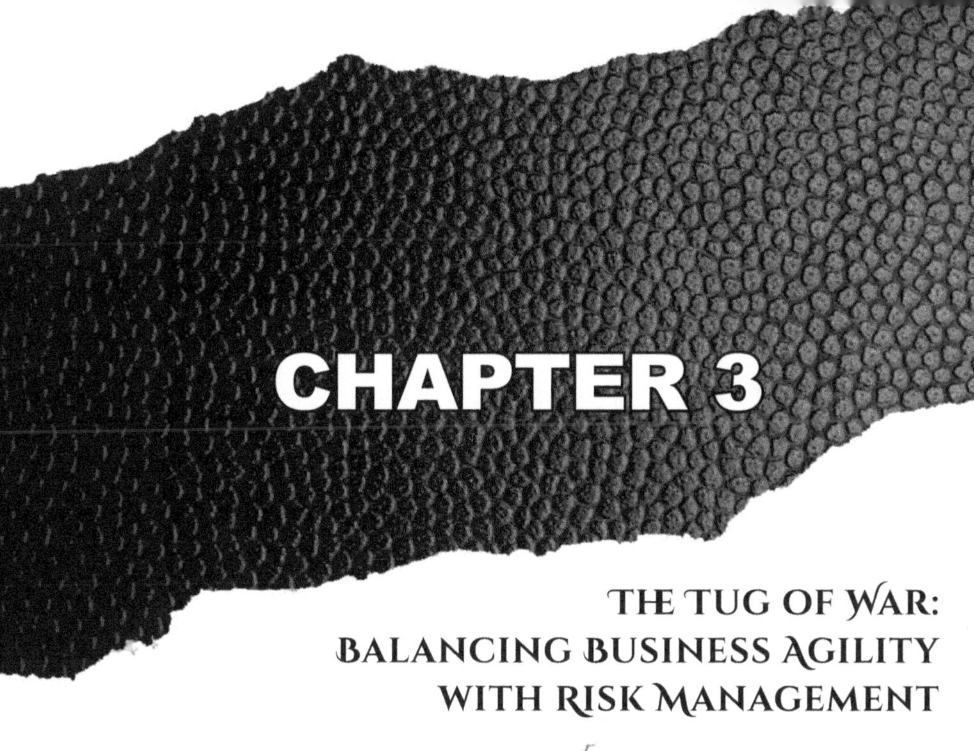

THE TUG OF WAR: BALANCING BUSINESS AGILITY WITH RISK MANAGEMENT

Organizations often find themselves entangled in a metaphorical tug of war, pulled between the compelling need for business agility and the imperative of robust risk management. This dual demand creates a dynamic equilibrium where the pursuit of adaptability collides with the necessity of mitigating risks. In this chapter, we embark on a journey through the intricacies of this tension, exploring the challenges, opportunities, and strategies that define the delicate balance between business agility and risk management.

THE AGILE IMPERATIVE

Our world today is marked by unprecedented technological advancements, global interconnectedness, and rapid market shifts, hence the call for business agility echoes louder than ever. Agility is not merely a competitive advantage; it is a prerequisite for survival. Organizations must navigate through uncertainty, respond swiftly to market dynamics, and capitalize on emerging opportunities. The Agile methodology, born out of the software development realm, has evolved into a guiding philosophy shaping entire enterprises. The ability to pivot, innovate, and deliver value rapidly is the heartbeat of modern business.

Yet, in the pursuit of agility, organizations traverse a landscape fraught with risks. The shadows of uncertainty loom large, encompassing cyber threats, regulatory complexities, market volatility, and more. The faster an organization moves, the more exposed it becomes to unforeseen pitfalls. The imperative to balance speed with resilience is where the metaphorical tug of war comes to life. This tension between the drive for agility and the necessity for risk management defines the contemporary business narrative.

TENSIONS EXPLORED:

1. Speed vs. Stability: Organizations grapple with the challenge of achieving speed in decision-making and operations without compromising the stability required to weather unforeseen disruptions.

2. Innovation vs. Compliance: The pursuit of innovation may clash with the need for regulatory compliance, requiring organizations to tread carefully to avoid legal ramifications.

3. Flexibility vs. Control: Maintaining flexibility in business processes can conflict with the imperative of control necessary for risk mitigation and governance.

STRATEGIES FOR EQUILIBRIUM

Achieving equilibrium in this tug of war necessitates strategic navigation. Organizations must deploy nuanced approaches that allow them to be agile without sacrificing robust risk management. Key strategies include:

Integrated Risk-Aware Culture: Cultivating a culture where every member of the organization is attuned to risk, fostering a proactive approach to risk management without impeding agility.

Agile Risk Frameworks: Developing risk management frameworks that are as nimble and adaptable as the business processes they aim to safeguard.

Collaboration and Transparency: Breaking down organizational silos and fostering collaboration between traditionally isolated functions, such as IT, compliance, and risk management.

Continuous Monitoring and Adaptation: Implementing systems that provide real-time insights into emerging risks, enabling organizations to adapt their strategies swiftly in response to changing circumstances.

REAL-WORLD NARRATIVES

Through real-world narratives and case studies, this chapter delves into the experiences of organizations that have successfully negotiated the delicate balance between business agility and risk management. From startups navigating uncharted territory to established corporations reinventing their strategies, these stories illuminate the challenges, tensions, and triumphs encountered in the pursuit of equilibrium.

CHARTING THE FUTURE:

As organizations navigate the intricacies between agility and risk management, this chapter serves as a guide to charting a course forward. It offers insights, practical strategies, and inspiration for leaders, decision-makers, and practitioners seeking to harness the dual forces of adaptability and resilience. In the contemporary business landscape, where change is the only constant, finding the balance in the tug of war is not just a strategic imperative; it is the essence of sustainable success.

EMBRACING BUSINESS AGILITY: A STRATEGIC IMPERATIVE IN A DYNAMIC WORLD

Business agility is more than a buzzword; it is a dynamic capability that defines an organization's ability to swiftly and effectively respond to changes in its environment. It encompasses the capacity to adapt, innovate, and make strategic decisions in the face of evolving markets, technological advancements, and shifting consumer expectations. At its core, business agility is a mindset, a set of practices, and a cultural orientation that positions an organization to thrive amidst uncertainty.

THE SIGNIFICANCE OF BUSINESS AGILITY

1. **Responding to Rapid Changes:**

   Markets: In an era of rapid globalization and digitalization, markets evolve swiftly. Business agility enables organizations to read market signals, adapt their strategies, and seize emerging opportunities before competitors.

   Technology: Technological advancements are relentless. Agile organizations harness technology as an enabler, staying ahead of the curve and leveraging innovations to enhance their products, services, and operations.

   Consumer Expectations: Consumer preferences are dynamic. Agile businesses are attuned to changing consumer expectations, allowing them to tailor their offerings in real-time and deliver a superior customer experience.

2. **Fostering Innovation:**

   Business agility and innovation are intertwined. Agile organizations create an environment that encourages experimentation, welcomes diverse perspectives, and tolerates calculated risks. This fosters a culture where innovation thrives, propelling the organization ahead in a competitive landscape.

3. Gaining Competitive Advantage:

The ability to pivot swiftly in response to market shifts provides a distinct competitive advantage. Agile organizations can seize new opportunities, outmaneuver competitors, and rapidly adapt their strategies to changing circumstances, positioning themselves as market leaders.

4. Enhancing Organizational Resilience:

Resilience is a hallmark of agile organizations. Instead of being disrupted by unforeseen challenges, they absorb shocks, adapt their strategies, and recover swiftly. This resilience is grounded in a proactive approach to risk management and a readiness to navigate uncertainties.

HOW AGILITY FOSTERS KEY ORGANIZATIONAL OUTCOMES

Agility, as a core organizational attribute, acts as a catalyst for driving key outcomes that are pivotal for sustained success and adaptability in today's dynamic business landscape. From increased responsiveness, to improved operational efficiency and overall customer satisfaction, let's dig a little deeper into them.

1. Innovation: Agile organizations empower teams to experiment and iterate quickly. This results in a continuous flow of innovations, from product enhancements to process improvements. By fostering a culture of creativity and adaptability, business agility becomes a catalyst for sustained innovation.

2. Competitive Advantage: In a fast-paced business landscape, the ability to respond faster than competitors is a strategic differentiator. Agile organizations excel in sensing market shifts, making timely decisions, and executing with precision, giving them a competitive edge.

3. Resilience: Resilience is not about avoiding challenges but navigating through them effectively. Agile organizations build resilience by embracing change, anticipating risks, and maintaining a proactive stance. This resilience enables them to weather disruptions and emerge stronger on the other side.

Real-world Illustrations

Netflix: The entertainment giant's transition from a DVD-by-mail service to a global streaming powerhouse exemplifies business agility. By recognizing the shift in consumer behavior and swiftly adapting its business model, Netflix became a market leader.

Amazon: Amazon's success is rooted in its ability to pivot and diversify rapidly. From an online bookstore to a multifaceted e-commerce giant, cloud computing provider, and beyond, Amazon's agility fuels its constant evolution.

Unveiling The Imperatives: Factors Driving The Need for Business Agility

The concept of business agility has been around for a few decades and been a main topic of research in both industry and academia due to the need for organizations to cope with unpredictable, dynamic and constantly changing environments (Sherehiy et al. 2007).

The demand for business agility arises from a confluence of transformative forces. These forces, propelled by digital transformation, customer-centricity, and the breakneck pace of technological advancements, have reshaped the very fabric of how organizations operate. Understanding these imperatives unveils why agility is not just a strategic choice but an essential survival skill in the dynamic world of business.

1. Digital Transformation:

The Digital Imperative:

The digitization of business processes, operations, and customer interactions is no longer a trend; it's a fundamental shift. Organizations are compelled to embrace digital transformation to stay relevant, gain operational efficiency, and unlock new avenues for growth.

Digital transformation necessitates a fundamental shift in how organizations approach technology. The traditional, rigid IT structures are replaced by agile methodologies that emphasize iterative development, rapid deployment, and continuous adaptation. Business agility becomes the linchpin for navigating the complexities of digital evolution.

2. Customer-Centricity:

Empowered Consumers:

The voice of the customer has never been louder. Empowered by information, choice, and social connectivity, consumers demand personalized experiences, seamless interactions, and products tailored to their preferences.

Meeting these heightened expectations requires organizations to be agile in responding to changing customer needs. Agile methodologies, such as design thinking and customer journey mapping, become essential tools for organizations aiming to pivot swiftly in response to evolving customer preferences.

3. **Pace of Technological Advancements:**

Technological Turbulence:

Technological advancements occur at an unprecedented pace. From artificial intelligence and machine learning to blockchain and the Internet of Things, organizations must grapple with a continually evolving technological landscape.

Agility is the key to successfully navigating the technological turbulence. Organizations must swiftly adopt, adapt, and integrate emerging technologies into their operations. The ability to experiment, iterate, and deploy new technologies is a defining feature of agile organizations.

4. **Globalization and Market Dynamics:**

Shifting Market Dynamics:

Globalization has blurred geographical boundaries, expanding market reach and intensifying competition. Organizations must contend with an environment where market dynamics can shift rapidly due to geopolitical events, economic fluctuations, or industry disruptions.

Agile organizations possess the ability to pivot their strategies, supply chains, and market approaches in response to global shifts. The capacity to sense changes in the global landscape and adapt swiftly is a hallmark of business agility.

5. **Data-Driven Decision-Making:**

Data as a Strategic Asset:

The era of big data has transformed data into a strategic asset. Organizations harness data to derive insights, inform decision-making, and gain a competitive edge.

Agile organizations leverage data not just for retrospective analysis but as a real-time guide for decision-making. The ability to extract actionable insights from data and adapt

strategies based on this information is central to business agility.

6. **Competitive Pressures:**

Rapid Innovation Cycles:

Industries are characterized by rapid innovation cycles, with competitors introducing new products, services, and business models at an accelerated pace.

Agility becomes a potent weapon in this competitive landscape. Organizations that can innovate swiftly, respond to market shifts, and outmaneuver competitors gain a distinct competitive advantage.

Navigating The Unknown: The Essence of Risk Management

Risk management is the systematic process of identifying, assessing, prioritizing, and mitigating potential threats and uncertainties that may impact an organization's objectives. It is a strategic discipline that enables organizations to understand, anticipate, and respond to risks, minimizing potential negative impacts and optimizing opportunities. Risk management extends its reach to encompass crisis and business continuity planning. Beyond day-to-day risk considerations, organizations must formulate robust plans to ensure the resilience of essential functions during disruptions, safeguarding their ability to weather storms and emerge stronger.

Risk management begins with the comprehensive identification of potential risks. This involves scrutinizing internal and external factors that could disrupt operations, hinder growth, or jeopardize the achievement of organizational goals. Risk management, defined correctly, has to look at both the downside of risk and the upside. It cannot just be about hedging risk (Damodaran 2014).

Once identified, risks are assessed for their likelihood and potential impact. This step involves categorizing risks based on severity and prioritizing them to focus efforts on the most critical threats. Effective risk management involves developing and implementing mitigation strategies. This may include preventive measures, contingency plans, and proactive responses to minimize the impact of identified risks.

Risk management is not a one-time effort but a continuous process. Organizations must monitor the business landscape, adapt to changes, and refine their risk management strategies to address emerging threats and capitalize on new opportunities.

IMPACT ON LONG-TERM SUSTAINABILITY:

FINANCIAL STABILITY:

Proactive risk management safeguards financial stability by identifying potential financial threats and ensuring that the organization has the necessary measures in place to weather economic downturns, market fluctuations, or unforeseen financial challenges.

OPERATIONAL RESILIENCE:

A well-executed risk management strategy enhances operational resilience. By identifying and mitigating operational risks, organizations can maintain smooth operations, prevent disruptions, and ensure continuity even in the face of unexpected events.

REPUTATION MANAGEMENT:

Reputation is a valuable asset. Effective risk management protects an organization's reputation by addressing risks related to compliance, ethical practices, and potential crises. Safeguarding reputation is crucial for long-term sustainability in today's interconnected and scrutinizing world.

STRATEGIC DECISION-MAKING:

Informed by risk assessments, organizations can make strategic decisions with a clear understanding of potential consequences. This enhances the likelihood of successful strategic initiatives and minimizes the chances of unexpected setbacks.

REGULATORY COMPLIANCE:

Risk management is closely tied to regulatory compliance. Organizations that effectively manage risks are better positioned to comply with industry regulations and legal requirements, avoiding penalties and legal challenges that could jeopardize sustainability.

INNOVATION AND ADAPTATION:

Risk management is not solely about avoiding threats but also about embracing opportunities. By understanding and managing risks, organizations can innovate, adapt to changing market conditions, and capitalize on new avenues for growth, fostering long-term sustainability.

Risk Management As A Driver for Industry Compliance

Picture the realm of business as a complex, ever-shifting landscape. In this intricate terrain, compliance with industry regulations and legal requirements stands as a sentinel, guarding the gates against potential chaos. Now, imagine risk management as the silent architect, intricately designing and fortifying the structures that uphold this bastion of compliance.

At its core, the role of risk management in ensuring compliance is akin to a masterful dance, where anticipation, agility, and precision take center stage. Let's unravel this performance in a way that unveils the unique nuances, like the unveiling of a hidden masterpiece.

1. **The Grand Blueprint:**

   Imagine the regulatory landscape as a grand tapestry, woven with intricate threads of legal nuances and industry standards. Risk management assumes the role of the master architect, meticulously drafting the blueprint that aligns every organizational contour with these regulatory patterns.

2. **The Sentinel's Vigilance:**

   Compliance is the vigilant sentinel, standing guard at the entrance of legal adherence. Risk management becomes the silent watcher, identifying potential threats and vulnerabilities that could breach the compliance walls. It's the meticulous eye that spots the chinks in the armor before they become chasms.

3. **The Dance of Anticipation:**

   In this dynamic performance, risk management anticipates regulatory changes like a seasoned dancer predicting the next move. It's a dance of foresight, where understanding the evolving legal landscape allows the organization not just to react but to proactively adjust its steps, ensuring compliance remains in harmony with the shifting rhythm of regulations.

4. **Harmonizing the Choreography:**

   Compliance is the structured choreography, each step dictated by legal frameworks. Risk management steps in as the choreographer, ensuring that every move is not only in compliance but also optimized for organizational agility. It crafts processes that are both compliant and flexible, allowing the organization to adapt without missing a beat.

5. **The Tapestry of Documentation:**

   Legal requirements often demand a meticulous tapestry of documentation. Risk management is the scribe, ensuring that every detail, every process, and every decision is documented with precision. It's not just about satisfying the regulatory gaze; it's about creating a comprehensive narrative of compliance that stands scrutiny.

6. **The Orchestra of Controls:**

Imagine controls as the musical notes that ensure regulatory harmony. Risk management orchestrates these controls, fine-tuning them to create a symphony of compliance. It's the conductor, ensuring that every control is not just a standalone note but part of a seamless composition.

7. **Navigating the Legal Maze:**

Legal requirements often resemble a labyrinth, intricate and potentially confounding. Risk management takes on the role of the navigator, guiding the organization through this maze with a keen understanding of the legal terrain. It's the compass that ensures every decision aligns with the legal cardinal points.

8. **Resilience in the Spotlight:**

Compliance isn't a static performance; it's an ongoing play with evolving acts. Risk management shines in the spotlight of resilience, ensuring that the organization not only achieves compliance but sustains it through the twists and turns of regulatory evolution. It's the art of being compliant today and resiliently adapting for compliance tomorrow.

CONSEQUENCES OF NON-COMPLIANCE AND IMPACT ON BUSINESSES

The consequences of non-compliance in the realm of business operations are akin to a series of dominoes, each one triggering a cascading effect that can have severe repercussions. Imagine a delicate ecosystem, where adherence to rules and regulations acts as the equilibrium; disrupt this balance, and the consequences unfold with a domino effect. As EHS software company Nimonik accurately puts it, the cost and risk of non-compliance can very easily outweigh the cost of investing in compliance efforts.

1. **Legal Ramifications:**

    Dominos Begin: The first domino to fall is often legal consequences. Non-compliance exposes the organization to lawsuits, fines, and legal actions. Whether it's violating industry regulations or breaching contractual obligations, legal ramifications are swift and unforgiving.

2. **Reputational Damage:**

    Cascading Effect: Legal consequences trigger a chain reaction, knocking down the domino of reputational damage. News of non-compliance spreads like wildfire in the age of social media, tarnishing the organization's image. The public perception of integrity and trustworthiness takes a hit.

3. **Loss of Stakeholder Trust:**

    Collateral Damage: Reputational damage, the second domino, leads to a loss of stakeholder trust. Customers, partners, investors, and employees may distance themselves from the organization, eroding the foundation of relationships that sustain business operations.

4. **Financial Impact:**

Ripple Effect: The financial repercussions follow swiftly. Fines and legal fees deplete financial resources, impacting liquidity. The loss of stakeholder trust affects revenue streams as customers, and partners may seek alternatives. The financial domino effect compromises the organization's ability to operate and invest in growth.

5. **Operational Disruption:**

Core Operations Impacted: With finances under strain, the next domino to fall is operational disruption. Reduced funds lead to a strain on resources, affecting day-to-day operations. Staffing, supply chains, and production may suffer, disrupting the core functions of the organization.

6. **Loss of Market Position:**

Market Turmoil: Operational disruption, the fifth domino, results in a loss of market position. Competitors seize the opportunity, and the organization may find it challenging to regain its foothold. This loss of market position can have long-term consequences for future growth and competitiveness.

7. **Regulatory Scrutiny:**

Compounding Challenges: Non-compliance attracts regulatory scrutiny, initiating another domino effect. Increased regulatory oversight adds an additional layer of challenges. The organization may face heightened scrutiny in various aspects, including audits, reporting, and compliance checks.

8. **Supply Chain Complications:**

Extended Ripples: The supply chain, often intricately connected, is the next victim. Non-compliance within the organization can extend its ripples to suppliers and partners. They may face similar scrutiny, operational disruptions, and reputational damage, creating a domino effect across the entire ecosystem.

9. **Employee Morale and Productivity:**

   Internal Consequences: The internal repercussions of non-compliance include a decline in employee morale and productivity. As the domino effect unfolds, employees may face uncertainties about the organization's stability, affecting their engagement and commitment.

10. **Long-Term Viability at Stake:**

    Final Domino: The ultimate consequence of non-compliance is the jeopardy of the organization's long-term viability. The compounding impact of legal, financial, operational, and reputational challenges can create a situation where recovery becomes increasingly difficult, putting the very existence of the organization at stake.

ORGANIZATIONAL CHALLENGES OF BALANCING AGILITY AND RISK MANAGEMENT

Striking the right balance between agility and risk management is akin to walking a tightrope suspended between innovation and stability. While both agility and risk management are essential for organizational success, finding the equilibrium between the two presents a set of intricate challenges. Let's delve into these challenges, each representing a hurdle on the path to achieving a harmonious coexistence:

1. **Cultural Clash:**

   Agility's Urge vs. Risk Aversion: The clash of organizational cultures can be pronounced. Agile methodologies often thrive in a culture that encourages experimentation and quick iterations, while risk management is rooted in a culture that seeks to minimize uncertainties. Bridging this cultural gap requires a nuanced approach that values both innovation and stability.

2. Silos and Communication Barriers:

Isolated Departments: In many organizations, agility and risk management operate in silos, isolated from each other. Communication barriers between these departments can hinder the flow of information, leading to a lack of coordination. Bridging these silos requires fostering cross-functional collaboration and breaking down communication barriers.

3. Speed vs. Thoroughness Dilemma:

Agility's Need for Speed vs. Risk Management's Thorough Assessments: Agility demands quick decision-making and rapid implementation, while risk management necessitates thorough assessments and careful consideration. Striking a balance between these conflicting requirements is a delicate act, often leading to a dilemma of speed versus thoroughness.

4. Unclear Roles and Responsibilities:

Blurred Lines: Ambiguity in defining roles and responsibilities in the context of agility and risk management can create confusion. Team members may be unsure about their contributions to either aspect, leading to inefficiencies. Clarifying roles and establishing clear responsibilities is crucial for a harmonious balance.

5. Resistance to Change:

Comfort Zones vs. Innovation: Organizations often resist change, especially when it comes to established processes. The comfort of familiar routines can clash with the disruptive nature of agile transformations. Encountering resistance to change hampers the integration of agility and risk management practices.

6. **Resource Allocation Challenges:**

   Competing Demands for Resources: Both agility initiatives and robust risk management require dedicated resources. Competing demands for time, talent, and budget can strain organizational resources. Balancing the allocation of resources between agility and risk management initiatives becomes a significant challenge.

7. **Lack of Integrated Tools and Technologies:**

   Technological Misalignment: Often, organizations use disparate tools and technologies for agility and risk management. Integrating these systems seamlessly is a technological challenge. A lack of cohesive tools can hinder real-time visibility and coordination between agile and risk management processes.

8. **Short-Term vs. Long-Term Orientation:**

   Balancing Immediate Wins with Future Resilience: Agility may prioritize short-term wins, while risk management often has a long-term focus. Striking a balance between immediate gains and long-term resilience requires a strategic alignment that harmonizes short-term agility with the enduring stability provided by effective risk management.

9. **Lack of Agile Governance Structures:**

   Governance Gaps: Implementing agile governance structures that align with risk management principles can be challenging. Traditional governance structures may not accommodate the fluidity of agile practices, creating gaps that need careful consideration and adjustment.

10. **Measurement and Metrics Misalignment:**

    Aligning Success Metrics: Determining how success is measured in both agility and risk management can be challenging. Metrics that emphasize speed and innovation may not align with those focused on risk reduction and compliance. Finding a common ground for measuring success is a persistent challenge.

INTEGRATED GRC APPROACHES

Enter Integrated Governance, Risk, and Compliance (GRC) approaches – a strategic framework designed to harmonize diverse elements and guide organizations through the intricate dance of governance, risk management, and compliance. Imagine it as a master conductor orchestrating a symphony where governance, risk, and compliance instruments seamlessly blend to create organizational harmony.

THE SYMPHONY OF INTEGRATED GRC:

1. Harmonizing Governance: Governance, the first movement in this symphony, is the set of processes, structures, and policies that guide organizational decision-making. Integrated GRC ensures governance aligns with strategic objectives, fostering transparency and accountability across all levels.

2. Balancing Risk Management: The second movement introduces risk management – the art of identifying, assessing, and mitigating risks. Integrated GRC acknowledges that risk is not the enemy but an inherent part of innovation. It integrates risk management seamlessly into decision-making, enabling the organization to take calculated risks in pursuit of strategic goals.

3. Compliance as a Melody: Compliance, the third movement, is the adherence to laws, regulations, and internal policies. Integrated GRC transforms compliance from a box-ticking exercise to a harmonious melody woven into the organizational fabric. It ensures that compliance is not a standalone effort but an integral part of every business process.

KEY ELEMENTS OF INTEGRATED GRC:

1. Holistic Visibility: Integrated GRC provides a panoramic view of an organization's governance, risk, and compliance landscape. It breaks down silos, offering a unified perspective that enables leaders to make informed decisions with a comprehensive understanding of potential impacts.

2. Strategic Alignment: The framework ensures that governance, risk management, and compliance efforts are aligned with the organization's strategic objectives. It transforms these functions from individual pursuits into synchronized efforts working towards a common goal.

3. Continuous Monitoring and Adaptation: Integrated GRC is not a static composition; it's a dynamic symphony that requires continuous monitoring and adaptation. It introduces real-time insights, allowing organizations to adjust their strategies swiftly in response to changing risk landscapes and compliance requirements.

4. Efficiency and Resource Optimization: By integrating GRC functions, redundant efforts are minimized, and resources are optimized. The symphony of governance, risk management, and compliance becomes more efficient, freeing up resources for innovation and strategic initiatives.

5. Cultural Integration: Integrated GRC fosters a culture where every member of the organization is a steward of governance, a guardian against risks, and a custodian of compliance. It promotes a collective responsibility that permeates through all levels and functions.

BENEFITS OF INTEGRATED GRC:

Asides solving for complex organizational structures and communication breakdown across an organization, having a GRC program has numerous benefits which include;

1. Risk-Informed Decision-Making: Leaders armed with a holistic GRC perspective make risk-informed decisions. This ensures that risks are not merely avoided but strategically embraced when aligned with the organization's objectives.

2. Enhanced Resilience: The integrated symphony of GRC creates a resilient organization that can navigate uncertainties with agility. It transforms challenges into opportunities and setbacks into stepping stones for growth.

3. Adaptive Compliance: Compliance is not a rigid obligation but an adaptive response to evolving regulations. Integrated GRC allows organizations to stay compliant while remaining flexible to changing compliance landscapes.

4. Improved Stakeholder Trust: As the GRC symphony plays in harmony, stakeholders trust that the organization is not only governed, secure, and compliant but also strategically adept and resilient in the face of challenges.

ALIGNING RISK MANAGEMENT WITH AGILITY INITIATIVES

Aligning agility initiatives with risk management frameworks requires a delicate dance that harmonizes the need for speed and innovation with the imperative of identifying, assessing, and mitigating risks. This alignment is crucial for organizations aiming to navigate the complexities of the modern business landscape. Let's explore how organizations can seamlessly integrate agility initiatives with risk management frameworks:

1. **Establish a Common Language:**

    Bridging Terminological Gaps: Ensure that both agility and risk management teams speak a common language. Often, these teams use different terminology and metrics. Establishing a shared lexicon creates a foundation for effective communication and collaboration.

2. **Integrate Risk Management into Agile Processes:**

Sprint-Embedded Risk Assessments: Embed risk management practices directly into agile processes. Integrate risk assessments as a part of sprint planning, ensuring that teams consider potential risks and mitigation strategies during each iteration.

3. **Collaborative Decision-Making:**

Cross-Functional Collaboration: Facilitate collaboration between agile teams and risk management professionals. Foster an environment where decisions are made collaboratively, drawing on the expertise of both agile practitioners and risk management specialists.

4. **4. Real-Time Risk Visibility:**

Agile Boards for Risk Tracking: Leverage agile project management tools to incorporate risk tracking into agile boards. This provides real-time visibility into identified risks, their status, and the effectiveness of mitigation strategies, enabling swift responses.

5. **Risk-Informed Backlog Prioritization:**

Prioritizing Features with Risks in Mind: When building product backlogs, prioritize features with an awareness of potential risks. This ensures that risk mitigation is considered early in the development process, preventing the accumulation of unforeseen challenges.

6. **Iterative Risk Assessments:**

Regularly Revisit Risk Assessments: Embrace the iterative nature of both agile and risk management. Regularly revisit risk assessments, particularly during sprint reviews and planning sessions, to adapt strategies based on evolving project dynamics.

7. **Agile Governance Structures:**

Flexible Governance Models: Introduce agile governance structures that accommodate the fluidity of agile methodologies. Traditional governance may not align with the rapid pace of agile initiatives. Tailor governance structures to ensure they complement rather than hinder agility.

8. **Continuous Learning and Improvement:**

Retrospectives for Risk Reflection: Incorporate risk reflection into agile retrospectives. Encourage teams to reflect on how risks were handled during a sprint, fostering a culture of continuous learning and improvement in both agility and risk management practices.

9. **9. Cross-Training and Skill Development:**

Skill Enhancement Initiatives: Cross-train team members in both agile and risk management practices. This not only enhances their skill sets but also promotes a holistic understanding of how agility and risk management can work together synergistically.

10. **Agile Mindset in Risk Management:**

Embrace the Agile Mindset in Risk Management: Instill an agile mindset within the risk management team. Encourage adaptability, flexibility, and responsiveness to change, aligning risk management practices with the dynamic nature of agile initiatives.

11. **Technology Integration:**

Unified Tools for Agile and Risk Management: Explore integrated tools that unify agile project management and risk management functionalities. Having a centralized platform promotes visibility, collaboration, and efficiency in managing both agile initiatives and risk mitigation strategies.

AGILE RISK MANAGEMENT: NAVIGATING UNCERTAINTIES IN THE DYNAMIC BUSINESS LANDSCAPE

Agile Risk Management – a dynamic and adaptive methodology designed to navigate uncertainties in a way that fosters agility without compromising control. Picture it as a compass guiding organizations through the turbulent seas of innovation, where the traditional anchors of risk management are replaced by flexible strategies that embrace change.

FOUNDATIONS OF AGILE RISK MANAGEMENT:

Iterative and Incremental: Agile Risk Management is rooted in iterative and incremental processes. Instead of attempting to predict all risks upfront, it acknowledges that uncertainties evolve. It embraces an incremental approach, continually reassessing and adapting risk responses as the project or business landscape unfolds.

Dynamic Risk Assessments: Traditional risk assessments are often static, conducted at the project's onset. Agile Risk Management integrates dynamic risk assessments, allowing organizations to identify and respond to emerging risks throughout the project lifecycle. This continuous evaluation ensures that risks are addressed in real-time.

Adaptive Risk Responses: Rather than relying solely on risk mitigation, Agile Risk Management emphasizes adaptive responses. This involves leveraging the organization's ability to pivot, adjust strategies, and capitalize on opportunities that may arise from identified risks. It's about turning challenges into catalysts for innovation.

KEY COMPONENTS OF AGILE RISK MANAGEMENT:

1. Risk Identification Workshops: Agile teams engage in collaborative workshops to identify risks collectively. These sessions foster open communication, bringing together

diverse perspectives to uncover potential risks that may not be apparent in a traditional risk assessment.

2. Risk Backlogs: Similar to product backlogs in agile methodologies, Agile Risk Management introduces risk backlogs. This prioritized list of risks allows teams to focus on addressing the most critical risks first, ensuring that risk responses align with the organization's strategic priorities.

3. Frequent Retrospectives: Agile Risk Management incorporates frequent retrospectives, not just for project performance but specifically for assessing how risks were handled. This reflective process promotes a culture of continuous improvement, where lessons learned are integrated into future risk responses.

4. Real-Time Risk Boards: Visualizing risks in real-time is a core aspect of Agile Risk Management. Teams use visual boards to track and communicate the status of identified risks, making it easier for stakeholders to understand the risk landscape and participate in risk response planning.

ROLE OF AGILE RISK MANAGEMENT IN FOSTERING A DYNAMIC YET CONTROLLED BUSINESS ENVIRONMENT

1. Balancing Agility with Control: Agile Risk Management strikes the delicate balance between fostering agility and maintaining control. It enables organizations to respond rapidly to changing circumstances while ensuring that these responses are well-considered and aligned with the organization's risk appetite.

2. Proactive Risk Response: Rather than being reactive, Agile Risk Management encourages proactive risk response. Teams anticipate potential risks and are empowered to take

pre-emptive actions, minimizing the impact of uncertainties before they escalate.

3.   Enhanced Organizational Resilience: By weaving risk management into the fabric of agility, organizations become more resilient. They not only navigate uncertainties with speed but also possess the capability to absorb shocks, adapt swiftly, and emerge stronger from challenges.

4.   Cultivating a Risk-Aware Culture: Agile Risk Management fosters a culture where risk awareness is ingrained in the organization's DNA. Team members at all levels actively contribute to risk identification and response, promoting a shared responsibility for managing uncertainties.

5.   Facilitating Informed Decision-Making: Through real-time risk visibility and dynamic assessments, Agile Risk Management equips decision-makers with the information needed to make informed choices. It ensures that risk considerations are integrated into strategic decision-making processes.

CHAPTER FOUR

REGULATORY LANDSCAPES: A GLOBAL OVERVIEW OF COMPLIANCE MANDATES

It has been said that where there is no law, there is no offense but for businesses in today's world, the opposite is very true. The ethical and legal integrity of organizational practices are ensured by a stringent set of rules to ensure fairness to all concerned.

As businesses navigate this complex landscape woven with intricate threads of laws and regulations, adherence to compliance mandates becomes not only a legal imperative but a strategic necessity. Organizations implementing effective global compliance programs face particular challenges in navigating disparate regulatory regimes in the numerous jurisdictions in which they may operate. Maintaining and updating regional or country-specific policies and program oversight procedures requires substantial resources and continuous updates(Ropes and Gray 2018).

The repercussions of non-compliance reverberate across industries, impacting reputation, operational continuity, and financial stability. It is within this context that this chapter seeks to cast a spotlight on the sprawling realm of regulatory landscapes, offering a comprehensive global overview that mirrors the complexity and diversity of modern governance requirements.

Against this backdrop, this chapter seeks to cast a spotlight on the sprawling realm of regulatory landscapes, offering a comprehensive global overview that mirrors the complexity and diversity of modern governance requirements. The regulatory environment has evolved into a multifaceted tapestry, woven by the legislative frameworks of major regions and the nuances of industry-specific compliance mandates. It is within this context that we embark on a journey to unravel the intricacies of compliance, examining its contours on a global scale.

Our focus is to illuminate the regulatory landscapes governing businesses across major regions – from the stringent data protection mandates of Europe, such as the General Data Protection Regulation (GDPR), to the dynamic and evolving frameworks of Asia-Pacific, and the ever-changing post-Brexit compliance landscape in the United Kingdom. We delve into the regulatory intricacies shaping industries, exploring how financial services, healthcare, and the technology sector navigate the labyrinth of compliance requirements.

Yet, this exploration is not confined to the static understanding of current regulations. We peer into the future, anticipating shifts in the global regulatory fabric influenced by geopolitical dynamics and technological advancements. The chapter endeavors to equip businesses with the insights and foresight needed to navigate this intricate landscape successfully.

As we unravel the threads of compliance that weave through the global business fabric, we recognize its dual nature – presenting both challenges and opportunities. Challenges in interpretation, harmonization, and resource allocation coexist with the opportunities for strategic alignment and streamlined governance. In the digital era, technology emerges as both a disruptor and a facilitator, providing tools like Governance, Risk, and Compliance (GRC) platforms that aid organizations in managing compliance obligations on a global scale.

Through the lens of this chapter, we invite readers to gain a nuanced understanding of the critical role that compliance plays in sustaining the integrity and longevity of organizations. We aspire to empower businesses with the knowledge required to not only meet current compliance mandates but also to anticipate and adapt to the ever-evolving regulatory landscapes that define the modern business milieu.

REGULATORY FRAMEWORKS IN MAJOR REGIONS OF THE WORLD

NORTH AMERICA: UNITED STATES AND CANADA

In the United States, the regulatory landscape is marked by the formidable Health Insurance Portability and Accountability Act (HIPAA), enacted in 1996. HIPAA is a linchpin for safeguarding healthcare data, setting rigorous standards for the privacy and security of protected health information (PHI). Covering entities in the healthcare and health insurance sectors, HIPAA exemplifies a commitment to preserving the confidentiality of sensitive medical information.

Across the northern border in Canada, the Personal Information Protection and Electronic Documents Act (PIPEDA) governs the collection, use, and disclosure of personal information by private-sector organizations. PIPEDA, a cornerstone of Canadian privacy legislation, reflects the nation's dedication to balancing innovation with the protection of individuals' personal data.

EUROPE: GDPR AND POST-BREXIT LANDSCAPE

In the European Union, the General Data Protection Regulation (GDPR) stands as a revolutionary force in data protection. Enacted in 2018, GDPR establishes stringent requirements for the processing of personal data and grants individuals unprecedented control over their information. The post-Brexit landscape introduces a distinctive regulatory framework in the United Kingdom, separate from the EU. This divergence necessitates a nuanced approach for businesses trading with the UK, navigating evolving compliance dynamics.

ASIA-PACIFIC: CHINA AND INDIA

In the Asia-Pacific region, China's cybersecurity laws wield substantial influence over data protection and secure technology operations. Governed by the Cyberspace Administration of China (CAC), these laws impact businesses operating within or engaging with China, emphasizing the nation's commitment to a secure digital environment. Meanwhile, India's data protection laws, currently being fortified by the forthcoming Personal Data Protection Bill, further exemplify the region's focus on robust privacy measures.

LATIN AMERICA AND MIDDLE EAST

In Latin America, a patchwork of data protection laws is emerging, with countries like Brazil implementing the Lei Geral de Proteção de Dados (LGPD) to bolster data privacy. This trend signifies a growing emphasis on robust privacy frameworks in the region. In the Middle East, the regulatory landscape is witnessing a transformation with evolving data protection and cybersecurity regulations. Navigating these regulations requires a nuanced understanding of the cultural, legal, and technological factors shaping the compliance terrain.

GLOBAL TRENDS AND TECHNOLOGICAL INFLUENCES

Beyond region-specific regulations, overarching global trends are reshaping the regulatory landscape. The rise of technology introduces new dimensions to compliance, with Governance, Risk, and Compliance (GRC) platforms becoming indispensable for managing obligations on a global scale. These platforms facilitate a holistic approach to governance, enabling organizations to align with diverse regulatory frameworks seamlessly.

Moreover, emerging technologies such as artificial intelligence and blockchain are influencing the way organizations approach compliance. These technologies offer innovative solutions to complex regulatory challenges, providing tools for enhanced security, transparency, and accountability. As businesses traverse this dynamic global landscape, the intersection of technology and regulation becomes a focal point for organizations aiming not only to meet current mandates but also to future-proof their compliance strategies.

In navigating this global regulatory mosaic, businesses are confronted with both challenges and opportunities. The challenges lie in interpreting, harmonizing, and allocating resources to comply with diverse frameworks. Yet, opportunities abound for strategic alignment and the development of unified approaches to governance. As organizations adapt to this ever-evolving regulatory terrain, the importance of proactive and adaptable compliance strategies becomes paramount, ensuring resilience and ethical conduct in an interconnected world.

Insight into Overarching Trends Impacting Global Regulatory Landscapes

There are several overarching trends significantly influencing regulatory frameworks today. The increasing globalization of operations has led to a complex interplay of regulatory requirements across borders. Simultaneously, rapid technological advancements, including artificial intelligence and blockchain, are shaping the way organizations operate and are challenging regulators to keep pace with innovation. This intersection of globalization and technology introduces both opportunities and challenges for businesses navigating the regulatory terrain.

One notable trend is the heightened focus on data privacy and protection. Regulatory bodies worldwide are increasingly emphasizing the safeguarding of individuals' privacy rights, leading to the implementation of stringent data protection regulations such as the General Data Protection Regulation (GDPR). This shift has profound implications for businesses that handle personal data, necessitating comprehensive measures to ensure compliance with evolving global standards.

The escalating frequency and sophistication of cyber threats represent another significant trend. Regulators are responding by incorporating cybersecurity requirements into compliance frameworks, reflecting the need for organizations to adopt robust measures to protect sensitive information. The digital era has brought about a rapid transformation in business processes, with regulators adapting to govern aspects such as electronic transactions, digital identity, and online operations.

Environmental, Social, and Governance (ESG) standards have emerged as a critical trend, with increasing attention on sustainability and corporate responsibility. Regulatory bodies are incorporating ESG factors into compliance frameworks, requiring businesses to demonstrate a commitment to environmental and social responsibility in addition to ensuring good governance practices.

Amidst these trends, technology serves both as a compliance enabler and a disruptor. Advanced software, including Governance, Risk, and Compliance (GRC) platforms, streamlines compliance management, offering real-time monitoring, risk assessment, and reporting capabilities. Artificial intelligence and predictive analytics enhance risk assessment, aiding organizations in proactively identifying compliance risks. Blockchain ensures transparency in transactions, reducing the risk of fraudulent activities and enhancing regulatory compliance.

Cross-border data flows and the related challenges of data localization are integral to the evolving regulatory landscape. The global nature of data flows prompts regulators to address cross-border data transfer challenges, while some jurisdictions mandate data localization, requiring companies to store data within specific geographic boundaries.

Cloud computing services, despite enhancing business agility, pose challenges related to data sovereignty and compliance. Regulators are adapting guidelines to address these concerns, and compliance automation tools are becoming increasingly essential. Automation streamlines compliance processes, ensuring timely and accurate adherence to regulatory requirements.

The evolving field of Regulatory Technology (RegTech) leverages AI and data analytics to assist organizations in navigating complex regulatory landscapes. RegTech solutions provide real-time insights, automated reporting, and compliance monitoring, contributing to the overall efficiency of compliance processes.

It goes without saying that the dynamic interplay between globalization, technological advancements, and regulatory evolution is redefining the expectations and challenges for businesses. Organizations that strategically embrace technology and proactively adapt to the evolving regulatory landscape position themselves to thrive in this complex and interconnected global environment.

INDUSTRY-SPECIFIC COMPLIANCE

EXPLORING REGULATIONS IMPACTING THE FINANCIAL SECTOR GLOBALLY

The financial sector operates in a highly regulated environment globally, with regulations designed to ensure stability, protect consumers, and maintain the integrity of financial markets. Here's an exploration of key regulations impacting the financial sector on a global scale:

1. **Basel III Framework:**

   Basel III is an international regulatory framework established by the Basel Committee on Banking Supervision. It aims to strengthen regulation, supervision, and risk management within the banking sector.

   Impact: Requires banks to maintain higher capital reserves, introduces liquidity and leverage ratios, and emphasizes risk-based supervision.

2. **Dodd-Frank Wall Street Reform and Consumer Protection Act (USA):**

   Enacted in response to the 2008 financial crisis, Dodd-Frank is a comprehensive financial reform legislation in the United States.

   Impact: Introduces measures to enhance financial stability, regulate derivatives markets, and establish the Consumer Financial Protection Bureau (CFPB) to protect consumers.

3. **MiFID II (Markets in Financial Instruments Directive II - EU):**

   MiFID II is a European Union directive designed to improve the functioning of financial markets and enhance investor protection.

   Impact: Introduces transparency requirements, expands regulation to non-equity instruments, and imposes stricter rules on high-frequency trading.

4. **Financial Stability Oversight Council (FSOC - USA):**

   The FSOC was established under the Dodd-Frank Act to identify and address risks to the financial stability of the United States.

   Impact: Monitors systemic risks, designates systemically important financial institutions (SIFIs), and recommends regulatory actions to mitigate systemic threats.

5. **Anti-Money Laundering (AML) and Know Your Customer (KYC) Regulations:**

   AML and KYC regulations are global initiatives aimed at preventing money laundering and terrorist financing.

   Impact: Requires financial institutions to implement robust AML and KYC procedures, conduct customer due diligence, and report suspicious transactions to regulatory authorities.

6. **Solvency II (EU):**

   Solvency II is an EU directive regulating insurance and reinsurance companies across the European Economic Area.

   Impact: Sets out capital requirements, risk management standards, and reporting obligations for insurance companies to ensure financial stability and protect policyholders.

7. **Securities and Exchange Board of India (SEBI) Regulations:**

   SEBI is the regulatory authority overseeing the securities market in India.

   Impact: Regulates securities exchanges, securities offerings, and market intermediaries, promoting fair and transparent practices within the Indian financial markets.

8. **Prudential Regulation Authority (PRA - UK):**

   The PRA is a regulatory body in the UK responsible for prudential supervision of banks, insurers, and major investment firms.

   Impact: Sets prudential standards, conducts stress tests, and ensures the stability and resilience of financial institutions in the UK.

9. **Bank of International Settlements (BIS) Standards:**

   The BIS establishes global standards and guidelines for central banks and financial institutions.

   Impact: Develops regulatory frameworks such as Basel III, provides a forum for central bank cooperation, and contributes to global financial stability.

10. **Financial Action Task Force (FATF) Recommendations:**

    The FATF is an intergovernmental organization that sets global standards for combating money laundering, terrorist financing, and other threats to the integrity of the international financial system.

    Impact: Countries adhering to FATF recommendations implement measures to combat financial crimes, strengthen regulatory frameworks, and enhance international cooperation.

    Regulations in the financial sector are diverse and span multiple jurisdictions, reflecting the interconnected nature of global financial markets. Financial institutions must be able to ensure compliance, manage risks, and contribute to the overall stability and integrity of the global financial system.

REGULATORY BODIES : THE FINANCIAL STABILITY BOARD

The Financial Stability Board (FSB) plays a crucial role in the global financial landscape, acting as a coordinating body for international financial regulation and fostering stability in the international financial system. Here's an in-depth exploration of the FSB's functions, objectives, and significance:

1. **Establishment and Mandate:**

    The FSB was established in April 2009 in response to the global financial crisis that began in 2007-2008. The primary mandate of the FSB is to promote international financial stability by coordinating the development of effective regulatory, supervisory, and other financial sector policies.

2. **Membership and Structure:**

   The FSB consists of representatives from central banks, regulatory authorities, and finance ministries of major economies, along with international financial institutions. It operates as a collaboration among its member jurisdictions, international financial institutions, and standard-setting bodies.

3. **Key Functions:**

   Policy Development: The FSB facilitates the development of international financial regulatory policies by providing a forum for collaboration among regulatory authorities and standard-setting bodies.

   Coordination: It coordinates the work of various national authorities and international standard-setting bodies to ensure consistent and effective implementation of regulatory reforms across jurisdictions.

   Monitoring and Assessment: The FSB conducts assessments of vulnerabilities affecting the global financial system, identifying and addressing risks that could potentially lead to systemic disruptions.

   Setting Standards: The FSB collaborates with standard-setting bodies such as the Basel Committee on Banking Supervision, the International Organization of Securities Commissions (IOSCO), and the International Association of Insurance Supervisors (IAIS) to develop and promote international standards for financial regulation.

4. **Key Objectives:**

   Systemic Risk Identification: The FSB aims to identify and mitigate systemic risks that could threaten the stability of the global financial system.

Policy Implementation: It works towards the effective implementation of agreed-upon international financial regulatory standards and policies by member jurisdictions.

Enhancing Transparency: The FSB seeks to enhance transparency and accountability in the financial sector by promoting the disclosure of relevant information and the adoption of sound governance practices.

Cross-Border Cooperation: Facilitating cooperation and information-sharing among member jurisdictions to address cross-border financial issues and challenges is a core objective.

5.   5. Crisis Management and Resolution:

Resolution Frameworks: The FSB develops and promotes effective resolution frameworks for financial institutions, ensuring that mechanisms are in place to handle the failure of systemically important institutions without destabilizing the broader financial system.

Crisis Response: In times of financial crises, the FSB plays a coordinating role in facilitating international cooperation and response to stabilize and restore confidence in the financial markets.

6.   Evaluation and Review:

Peer Reviews: The FSB conducts peer reviews of its member jurisdictions, assessing their adherence to agreed-upon international financial standards and policies.

Effectiveness Assessment: Regularly evaluates the effectiveness of its own processes, functions, and policies to ensure continuous improvement and responsiveness to emerging challenges.

7. **Global Reach:**

    Inclusivity: The FSB's broad membership ensures that it encompasses major economies and financial centers, providing a platform for inclusive discussions and coordinated actions that have a global impact.

    By addressing systemic risks, promoting regulatory consistency, and facilitating crisis response and resolution, the FSB plays a critical role in enhancing the stability and resilience of the global financial system. Its ongoing efforts contribute to a more transparent, accountable, and secure international financial landscape.

EXAMINING HEALTHCARE COMPLIANCE REQUIREMENTS WORLDWIDE

Healthcare compliance requirements vary across jurisdictions, reflecting the unique regulatory landscapes of different countries. These requirements are designed to ensure patient safety, protect sensitive health information, and maintain the overall integrity of healthcare systems. Here's an examination of healthcare compliance requirements worldwide, highlighting key aspects and trends:

1. **United States:**

    HIPAA (Health Insurance Portability and Accountability Act): HIPAA is a comprehensive U.S. federal law that governs the protection of patients' health information. HIPAA establishes standards for the privacy and security of protected health information (PHI), mandates the use of electronic transactions, and outlines the rights of patients regarding their health information. Enforced by the Office for Civil Rights (OCR), non-compliance can result in substantial penalties.

    HITECH Act (Health Information Technology for Economic and Clinical Health): An extension of HIPAA, the HITECH Act promotes the adoption of electronic health records (EHRs) and strengthens HIPAA's privacy and security provisions. It encourages the use of EHRs, imposes notification requirements in the event of a data breach, and enhances penalties for HIPAA violations.

2. European Union:

GDPR (General Data Protection Regulation):GDPR is a comprehensive data protection regulation applicable to all industries, including healthcare, within the European Union. It requires healthcare providers to obtain explicit consent for processing patient data, ensures the right to erasure, and mandates the appointment of data protection officers. Supervised by national data protection authorities, non-compliance can result in significant fines.

Medical Device Regulation (MDR) and In Vitro Diagnostic Regulation (IVDR): These regulations focus on ensuring the safety and reliability of medical devices and in vitro diagnostics. It mandates rigorous testing and documentation for medical devices, along with increased transparency and traceability.

3. Canada:

PIPEDA (Personal Information Protection and Electronic Documents Act): PIPEDA is Canada's federal privacy law regulating the collection, use, and disclosure of personal information. It requires healthcare providers to obtain consent for the collection and use of patient information, and to safeguard this information through appropriate security measures.

4. Australia:

My Health Records: Australia's My Health Record system is a centralized electronic health record system for individuals. Patients have control over who accesses their records, and healthcare providers must adhere to strict privacy and security standards.

5. **Japan:**

    Act on the Protection of Personal Information (APPI): APPI governs the handling of personal information in Japan, including healthcare data. Mandates the proper handling and protection of personal information, with specific requirements for obtaining consent.

6. **Global Trends and Challenges:**

    Interoperability: Achieving interoperability between different healthcare systems and EHRs is a global challenge, impacting the seamless exchange of patient information.

    Telehealth and Remote Patient Monitoring: The increasing adoption of telehealth services and remote patient monitoring introduces new compliance challenges, requiring regulations to adapt to technological advancements.

    Cybersecurity: The healthcare sector faces growing cybersecurity threats, emphasizing the need for robust measures to protect patient data from unauthorized access and data breaches.

COMMON CHALLENGES: NAVIGATING A DIVERSE REGULATORY LANDSCAPE

Navigating diverse regulatory landscapes presents a myriad of challenges for organizations, particularly in industries such as finance, healthcare, and technology. Three major challenges often encountered are related to interpretation, harmonization, and resource constraints.

1. Interpretation Challenges

Divergent Definitions and Terminologies:

Issue: Regulatory frameworks may use different definitions and terminologies for similar concepts, leading to confusion and inconsistent interpretation.

Challenge: Organizations must invest time and resources in clarifying these nuances to ensure accurate compliance.

Ambiguity in Regulatory Text:

Issue: Regulatory texts may be inherently ambiguous or open to interpretation, leaving room for different understandings of compliance requirements.

Challenge: Organizations face the challenge of interpreting regulations consistently and making decisions that align with the intended spirit of the law.

Rapidly Evolving Regulations:

Issue: Regulations are subject to frequent updates and amendments, making it challenging for organizations to stay current.

Challenge: Continuous monitoring and adaptation are necessary to interpret and implement evolving compliance requirements effectively.

2. Harmonization Challenges

Cross-Border Disparities:

Issue: Regulatory requirements often differ significantly across borders, especially in global industries.

Challenge: Achieving consistency and uniformity in compliance measures becomes difficult when faced with conflicting or incongruent regulations.

Industry-Specific Standards:

Issue: Different industries may have their own specific regulatory standards, adding complexity for organizations operating in multiple sectors.

Challenge: Developing a cohesive compliance strategy requires harmonizing industry-specific standards with broader regulatory frameworks.

Varied Enforcement Practices:

Issue: Enforcement practices can vary widely, even within the same regulatory framework, leading to uncertainty for organizations.

Challenge: Organizations must navigate this variability to understand the practical implications of compliance and non-compliance.

3. Resource Constraint Challenges

Financial Constraints:

Issue: Complying with diverse regulations often demands significant financial investments in technology, personnel, and training.

Challenge: Smaller organizations may find it challenging to allocate the necessary resources, potentially compromising their ability to achieve comprehensive compliance.

Human Resource Expertise:

Issue: Ensuring that personnel possess the necessary expertise to interpret and implement diverse regulations is a significant challenge.

Challenge: Recruiting, training, and retaining skilled professionals capable of navigating complex regulatory landscapes can strain organizational resources.

Technology Costs:

Issue: Implementing and maintaining technologies for compliance, such as data security systems, can be expensive.

Challenge: Organizations must balance the costs of technology investments against the benefits of achieving and maintaining compliance.

MITIGATION STRATEGIES:

1. Regulatory Intelligence and Monitoring: Regularly monitor regulatory changes through automated systems and dedicate resources to staying informed.

2. Invest in Compliance Technology: Leverage technology solutions, such as Governance, Risk, and Compliance (GRC) platforms, to streamline compliance management and reporting.

3. Cross-Functional Collaboration: Foster collaboration between legal, compliance, and operational teams to ensure a holistic understanding of regulatory requirements.

4. Engage with Regulatory Authorities: Actively participate in industry forums and engage with regulatory authorities to seek clarification on ambiguous regulations.

5. Prioritize Risk Assessments: Conduct regular risk assessments to identify the most critical compliance issues and allocate resources accordingly.

6. Professional Development: Invest in continuous professional development for personnel to enhance their understanding of evolving regulatory landscapes.

7. Legal Counsel Engagement: Collaborate with legal counsel to obtain expert guidance on complex regulatory interpretations and potential implications.

    Successfully navigating diverse regulatory landscapes demands a proactive and strategic approach. Organizations that invest in robust compliance strategies, leverage technology, and prioritize ongoing education and collaboration are better equipped to address interpretation, harmonization, and resource constraints effectively. Compliance should not be seen as a burden but as an integral part of sustainable and responsible business practices.

STRATEGIES FOR ALIGNING EFFORTS ACROSS MULTIPLE REGULATORY FRAMEWORKS

Aligning compliance efforts across multiple regulatory frameworks is a complex but necessary endeavor for organizations operating in diverse jurisdictions. Adopting a unified approach to compliance involves several strategic considerations to ensure consistency, efficiency, and effectiveness.

STRATEGIES FOR ALIGNING COMPLIANCE EFFORTS

1. Regulatory Intelligence: Regularly monitor and analyze regulatory changes across all applicable jurisdictions. Leverage automated systems and services to stay informed about updates, ensuring a comprehensive understanding of evolving compliance requirements.

2. Cross-Functional Collaboration: Facilitate collaboration between legal, compliance, risk management, and operational teams. Create a cross-functional compliance team that can

collectively interpret and implement regulations while aligning with organizational objectives.

3. Centralized Governance, Risk, and Compliance (GRC) Platforms: Implement GRC platforms to centralize and streamline compliance processes. These platforms provide a unified view of compliance requirements, allow for real-time monitoring, and facilitate reporting across different regulatory frameworks.

4. Customized Compliance Programs: Develop customized compliance programs that incorporate the specific requirements of each regulatory framework. While maintaining consistency, tailor initiatives to address the unique nuances of each jurisdiction.

5. Continuous Training and Education: Invest in continuous training and education programs for employees. Ensure that staff members are well-informed about the regulatory landscape and equipped to navigate the complexities of compliance across various jurisdictions.

6. Engagement with Regulatory Authorities: Actively engage with regulatory authorities in each jurisdiction. Seek clarification on ambiguous regulations and participate in industry forums to stay connected with the evolving regulatory environment.

7. Risk-Based Approach: Adopt a risk-based approach to compliance by prioritizing efforts based on the severity of potential risks. This enables organizations to allocate resources more efficiently and focus on areas with the highest impact.

Benefits of a Unified Approach to Compliance

1. Consistency: A unified approach ensures consistency in compliance efforts across different regulatory frameworks. This consistency reduces the risk of conflicting interpretations and facilitates a cohesive organizational response.

2. Efficiency and Cost Savings: Streamlining compliance processes through a unified approach improves efficiency and reduces the costs associated with managing multiple, disparate compliance initiatives. Centralized reporting and monitoring further contribute to cost savings.

3. Enhanced Risk Management: A unified approach enables a more holistic view of risks across jurisdictions. By aligning compliance efforts, organizations can better identify, assess, and manage risks, enhancing overall risk management practices.

4. Improved Reputation and Stakeholder Trust: Demonstrating a commitment to compliance through a unified approach enhances the organization's reputation. Stakeholders, including customers, investors, and regulatory bodies, are more likely to trust an organization that can navigate complex regulatory landscapes with integrity.

5. Strategic Decision-Making: A unified approach allows for better strategic decision-making. Organizations can align compliance efforts with business objectives, ensuring that regulatory requirements support, rather than hinder, overall strategic goals.

6. Adaptability to Change: A unified compliance framework promotes adaptability to changes in the regulatory environment. Organizations can respond more efficiently to new regulations or modifications, minimizing disruption to operations.

EXPECTED CHANGES IN GLOBAL REGULATORY APPROACHES

The global regulatory landscape continuously evolves in response to emerging challenges, technological advancements, geopolitical shifts, and societal changes. While predicting specific changes is challenging, several trends and expectations are likely to shape the future of regulatory frameworks worldwide:

1. **Emphasis on Digital Transformation:**

   Expectation: Increased focus on regulating digital technologies, artificial intelligence, and data privacy.

   Rationale: The rapid advancement of technology necessitates regulatory frameworks that address ethical considerations, data protection, and the responsible use of emerging technologies.

2. **Strengthening Cybersecurity Regulations:**

   Expectation: Enhanced regulations around cybersecurity to address the growing threat landscape.

   Rationale: The escalation of cyber threats requires regulators to mandate robust cybersecurity measures to protect sensitive data and critical infrastructure.

3. **Climate Change and ESG Integration:**

   Expectation: Greater incorporation of Environmental, Social, and Governance (ESG) factors into regulatory frameworks.

   Rationale: Heightened awareness of climate change and sustainability issues is driving regulators to integrate ESG considerations into compliance requirements.

4. **Cross-Border Data Governance:**

    Expectation: Evolving regulations addressing cross-border data flows and data localization.

    Rationale: The global nature of data and concerns over data privacy are prompting regulators to establish clear guidelines for cross-border data transfers while addressing data sovereignty issues.

5. **Consumer Protection and Privacy:**

    Expectation: Stricter regulations to protect consumer rights and privacy.

    Rationale: Growing public concern about data privacy and the need to empower individuals with control over their personal information are likely to drive regulatory changes.

6. **Focus on Supply Chain Resilience:**

    Expectation: Regulations emphasizing supply chain resilience and risk management.

    Rationale: Disruptions such as the COVID-19 pandemic have underscored the importance of resilient supply chains, prompting regulators to address vulnerabilities and ensure business continuity.

7. **Regulatory Technology (RegTech) Advancements:**

    Expectation: Increased adoption and regulation of RegTech solutions.

    Rationale: Regulators are likely to embrace technology to enhance regulatory efficiency, automate compliance processes, and improve overall supervision.

8. **Integrated GRC Approaches:**

    Expectation: Encouragement of integrated Governance, Risk, and Compliance (GRC) frameworks.

    Rationale: Organizations and regulators recognize the need for holistic approaches that streamline compliance efforts, enhance risk management, and provide comprehensive governance oversight.

9. **Health and Pandemic Preparedness Regulations:**

    Expectation: Enhanced regulations related to public health and pandemic preparedness.

    Rationale: Global events like the COVID-19 pandemic have highlighted the need for regulatory frameworks that address public health emergencies and ensure resilience in healthcare systems.

10. **Sustainable Finance Standards:**

    Expectation: Development and implementation of standards for sustainable finance.

    Rationale: The rising focus on sustainable investments and environmental considerations is likely to lead to regulations that set standards for green finance and responsible investing.

THIRD-PARTY RISKS: MANAGING THE COMPLEXITIES IN VENDOR RELATIONSHIPS

A notable trend that has emerged in modern business is the increasing reliance on third-party vendors. Organizations, driven by the pursuit of efficiency, innovation, and global competitiveness, are expanding their networks of external partners to harness specialized expertise, access advanced technologies, and streamline operations. However, with this growing dependence on external collaborations comes a myriad of risks that demand careful consideration and proactive management.

This chapter delves into the intricacies of the contemporary business ecosystem, where third-party vendors play an integral role in shaping the operational fabric of organizations. From cloud service providers to logistics partners and technology developers, these external entities contribute significantly to the overall agility and capability of businesses. The chapter's primary focus is to unravel the complexities associated with these external partnerships and, more importantly, to equip organizations with strategies to understand, assess, and mitigate the inherent risks that accompany such collaborations.

As organizations intertwine their destinies with external vendors, a host of potential risks materializes, ranging from cybersecurity threats and data breaches to regulatory compliance lapses and reputational damage. Understanding the multifaceted nature of these risks is paramount for fostering resilience and sustaining a robust business foundation.

The subsequent sections will explore key dimensions of third-party risk management, shedding light on methodologies to assess the reliability, security, and compliance adherence of external partners. Drawing on real-world case studies and industry best practices, this chapter aims to provide actionable insights for organizations seeking to navigate the intricate terrain of external collaborations while safeguarding their operations, data, and reputation.

THE EXPANSIVE NETWORK OF THIRD-PARTY RELATIONSHIPS

The reach of third-party relationships has expanded to encompass a diverse array of partnerships, each playing a unique and critical role in the operations, growth, and innovation of organizations. Understanding the breadth and depth of these relationships is essential for organizations seeking to navigate the complexities of the modern business ecosystem.

Suppliers: Suppliers stand as the backbone of production, providing raw materials, components, or finished goods essential for creating products or delivering services. These relationships are pivotal, influencing product quality, cost-effectiveness, and the overall resilience of the supply chain.

Service Providers: Service providers bring specialized expertise to the table, offering services ranging from IT solutions and consulting to legal and marketing support. Organizations leverage these partnerships to streamline operations, access external know-how, and optimize efficiency in non-core functions.

Technology Partners: In the age of rapid technological advancement, organizations forge alliances with technology partners. These collaborations introduce innovative solutions, from cutting-edge software to state-of-the-art hardware, propelling organizations forward in their digital transformations.

Logistics and Distribution Partners: Efficient movement and delivery of products rely on logistics and distribution partners. These relationships are pivotal for ensuring timely delivery, minimizing lead times, and optimizing the overall supply chain efficiency.

Financial Institutions: Financial institutions play a critical role in providing banking services, financial advisory support, and investment opportunities. These relationships are instrumental in facilitating liquidity management, funding expansion initiatives, and maintaining financial health.

Collaborative Research and Development (R&D) Partners: Joint research initiatives and product development efforts often involve collaborative R&D partners. These alliances foster innovation, accelerate time-to-market, and allow organizations to tap into external creativity and expertise.

Regulatory and Compliance Partners: Navigating the intricate regulatory landscape requires collaboration with experts in the field. Regulatory and compliance partners assist organizations in ensuring adherence to legal requirements, mitigating risks, and navigating evolving regulatory frameworks.

Strategic Alliances and Joint Ventures: Formal partnerships, such as strategic alliances and joint ventures, are formed for mutual benefit and shared strategic goals. These collaborative efforts enable joint marketing, shared resources, and expanded market reach.

Outsourced Manufacturing Partners: Outsourced manufacturing partners take charge of the production processes on behalf of organizations. These relationships offer scalability, cost efficiency, and flexibility to adapt to market demands.

Environmental and Sustainability Partners: In an era where sustainability is paramount, organizations collaborate with partners focused on environmental and social responsibility. These partnerships contribute to eco-friendly practices, green supply chain management, and corporate social responsibility initiatives.

Each of these third-party relationships contributes uniquely to the fabric of an organization's operations, presenting both opportunities and challenges. Managing this diverse array requires strategic foresight, proactive risk management, and a commitment to fostering collaborative and mutually beneficial partnerships. As organizations continue to navigate the intricacies of the global business landscape, the optimization of these third-party relationships remains a linchpin for sustained success and adaptability.

Advantages and Vulnerabilities of An Interconnected Business Ecosystem

The interdependence among businesses, suppliers, service providers, and technology partners yields strategic advantages and introduces complexities that necessitate careful navigation. Let's look at a few worthy of note;

Strategic Advantages

1. Operational Efficiency: Interconnected ecosystems facilitate seamless data exchange and communication, optimizing operational efficiency. Real-time collaboration and information sharing streamline processes, reducing delays and enhancing productivity.

2. Innovation Acceleration: They have the access to tap into the collective expertise of partners, fostering a collaborative environment that accelerates innovation. Collaborative R&D efforts and technology partnerships drive the development of cutting-edge solutions.

3. Global Market Reach: Interconnected ecosystems enable organizations to expand their market reach by leveraging the capabilities of global partners. Strategic alliances and joint ventures provide access to new markets, customers, and distribution channels.

4. Cost Optimization: Shared resources and outsourcing to specialized partners contribute to cost optimization. Organizations can focus on their core competencies while leveraging the expertise of external partners for non-core functions.

5. Flexibility and Adaptability: An interconnected ecosystem enhances organizational flexibility, allowing businesses to adapt quickly to changing market conditions. Access to a diverse network of partners enables swift adjustments in response to evolving customer needs.

6. Enhanced Customer Experience: Collaboration with external partners, such as technology providers and service organizations, contributes to a more enriched customer experience. Seamless integration of services and technologies enhances overall satisfaction.

POTENTIAL VULNERABILITIES

1. Cybersecurity Risks: Increased connectivity amplifies the risk of cybersecurity threats. A breach in one part of the ecosystem can potentially impact the entire network, exposing sensitive data and disrupting operations.

2. Dependency Challenges: Overreliance on specific partners can create dependencies. If a key partner experiences financial instability, operational issues, or other challenges, it may have a cascading effect on the interconnected ecosystem.

3. Regulatory Compliance Complexity: Operating within an interconnected ecosystem often involves navigating complex regulatory landscapes. Ensuring compliance across various jurisdictions and industries becomes a considerable challenge.

4. Supply Chain Disruptions: The interconnected nature of supply chains makes them susceptible to disruptions. Events such as natural disasters, geopolitical tensions, or global crises can have a domino effect, impacting multiple interconnected businesses.

5. Data Privacy Concerns: The exchange of data within an interconnected ecosystem raises concerns about data privacy. Organizations must navigate stringent regulations and ensure the secure handling of sensitive information.

6. Reputational Risks: A crisis or controversy involving one entity within the interconnected ecosystem can tarnish the reputation of all associated partners. Maintaining a positive

brand image requires proactive risk management and crisis response.

7. Communication Breakdowns: The complexity of interconnected ecosystems introduces the risk of communication breakdowns. Miscommunication or lack of coordination among partners can lead to errors, delays, and operational inefficiencies.

THE DEPTH OF DEPENDENCE ON THIRD-PARTY ENTITIES AND POTENTIAL RISKS

The depth of dependence on third-party entities for critical business functions has significantly intensified in the contemporary business landscape. Organizations, driven by a pursuit of efficiency, specialization, and innovation, have increasingly outsourced key functions to external partners. This trend has led to a complex web of dependencies that spans various sectors and encompasses a wide range of critical business activities.

1. Supply Chain Dependency: Organizations heavily rely on third-party suppliers for the timely and reliable provision of raw materials, components, and finished goods. Disruptions in the supply chain, whether due to natural disasters, geopolitical tensions, or economic crises, can have cascading effects on production and delivery.

2. Technology Dependency: The integration of technology partners for software solutions, cloud services, and infrastructure has become integral to business operations. Organizations depend on these technology partners for innovation, security, and the smooth functioning of critical IT systems.

3. Service Provider Dependency: Outsourcing non-core functions to service providers, including legal, human resources, and marketing services, allows organizations to

focus on core competencies. However, reliance on these service providers introduces vulnerabilities related to service quality, data security, and regulatory compliance.

4. Financial Dependency: Financial institutions play a pivotal role in providing banking services, loans, and investment opportunities. Organizations often depend on these institutions for liquidity, capital for expansion, and financial advisory services.

5. Logistics Dependency: Efficient movement and distribution of goods rely on logistics partners. Organizations depend on these partners for timely and cost-effective transportation, warehousing, and delivery services.

6. Collaborative R&D Dependency: Collaborative R&D efforts with external partners contribute to innovation and product development. Organizations depend on these partnerships for accessing specialized expertise, sharing research costs, and accelerating time-to-market for new products.

7. Regulatory and Compliance Dependency: Organizations often collaborate with external regulatory and compliance partners to navigate complex legal landscapes. Dependencies on these partners arise from the need for accurate interpretation of regulations, adherence to compliance standards, and mitigation of legal risks.

8. Outsourced Manufacturing Dependency: Outsourced manufacturing partners handle the production of goods on behalf of organizations. Organizations depend on these partners for scalable and cost-effective manufacturing processes.

9. Environmental and Sustainability Dependency: Collaborating with partners focused on environmental and social responsibility is crucial for organizations committed to sustainable practices. Dependencies arise concerning

the adoption of eco-friendly processes, supply chain sustainability, and corporate social responsibility initiatives.

10. Strategic Alliances Dependency: Formal partnerships, such as strategic alliances and joint ventures, create dependencies on shared resources, joint marketing efforts, and mutual strategic goals.

CHALLENGES AND CONSIDERATIONS

1. Risk Management: The deepening dependence on third-party entities heightens the importance of robust risk management strategies. Organizations must proactively identify and mitigate risks associated with dependencies to ensure business continuity.

2. Resilience Building: Building resilience against disruptions in the interconnected ecosystem is essential. This involves contingency planning, diversifying sources, and establishing alternative solutions for critical functions.

3. Regulatory Compliance: Navigating complex regulatory environments becomes more challenging as organizations depend on external partners. Ensuring compliance across diverse jurisdictions requires meticulous attention to regulatory changes.

4. Continuous Monitoring: Continuous monitoring of the performance, reliability, and security of third-party entities is crucial. Regular assessments and audits help organizations stay informed and address potential vulnerabilities.

THE POTENTIAL RISKS

On the positive side, collaboration among vendors enhances operational efficiency, reduces costs, and fosters innovation, contributing to the overall competitiveness of the supply chain. However, this interdependence also magnifies risks that can reverberate throughout the entire network.

One critical risk lies in the potential for disruptions to propagate across the supply chain. Whether caused by natural disasters, geopolitical events, or financial instability, a disruption in one vendor's operations can have a cascading effect, impacting other interconnected vendors and leading to significant disruptions in the supply chain. This vulnerability is particularly pronounced when there is an over-reliance on a single vendor or a small group of tightly interconnected vendors. Such a concentration creates a single point of failure, where challenges faced by a critical vendor can send shockwaves throughout the supply chain.

Quality and compliance risks are heightened in an interconnected vendor ecosystem. If one vendor fails to meet quality standards or encounters compliance issues, the integrity of the entire supply chain is at stake. The collaborative nature of research and development efforts and technology partnerships introduces the risk of intellectual property compromise, potentially affecting the innovation pipeline and competitiveness of all interconnected vendors.

Cybersecurity threats pose a significant risk due to the exchange of sensitive information within the interconnected network. A breach in one vendor's systems can expose the entire supply chain to the risk of data theft, unauthorized access, and potential disruptions to digital operations. Additionally, navigating diverse regulatory landscapes across different jurisdictions becomes challenging, as non-compliance by one vendor can lead to regulatory scrutiny affecting other vendors in the supply chain.

Ethical and social responsibility considerations are also amplified in interconnected vendor relationships. If one vendor is involved in unethical practices or fails to meet social responsibility standards, the reputations of all interconnected vendors may suffer. Communication breakdowns among vendors introduce operational inefficiencies and errors that can disrupt the smooth functioning of the supply chain.

To address these challenges, organizations must adopt robust mitigation strategies. Diversifying the vendor base helps reduce dependence on a single source, enhancing resilience. Implementing advanced monitoring tools aids in early risk identification, while collaborative risk management fosters a collective approach to safeguarding the supply chain. Clear contractual safeguards define responsibilities and consequences, ensuring a framework for risk mitigation. Continuous communication and coordination among vendors are vital for preventing misunderstandings and resolving issues promptly.

RISK ASSESSMENT METHODOLOGIES APPLICABLE TO THIRD-PARTY RELATIONSHIPS

Various risk assessment methodologies are applicable to third-party relationships, reflecting the diverse nature of risks that organizations may encounter. The choice of a specific methodology depends on factors such as the complexity of the relationship, the industry, and the criticality of the services provided by the third party. Here are some commonly used risk assessment methodologies:

1. Due Diligence and Background Checks: Conducting thorough due diligence and background checks involves researching the third party's financial stability, reputation, compliance history, and overall business practices.

   Applicability: Suitable for assessing the reliability, integrity, and financial health of third-party entities.

2. Compliance Assessments: Evaluating third-party compliance with relevant laws, regulations, and industry standards.

   Applicability: Essential for industries with strict regulatory requirements, ensuring that third parties adhere to compliance standards.

3. Risk Profiling: Profiling third parties based on various risk factors, such as geographic location, industry, financial stability, and cybersecurity posture.

   Applicability: Provides a holistic view of potential risks associated with a diverse range of third-party relationships.

4. Cybersecurity Risk Assessments: Assessing the cybersecurity measures and practices of third-party entities to identify vulnerabilities and potential threats.

   Applicability: Crucial for evaluating the security posture of vendors handling sensitive data or involved in technology-related services.

5. Financial Risk Analysis: Analyzing the financial stability, creditworthiness, and overall fiscal health of third-party entities.

   Applicability: Important for assessing the risk of financial disruptions or insolvency that could impact the continuity of services.

6. Operational Risk Assessments: Examining the operational processes and controls of third parties to identify potential points of failure or inefficiencies.

   Applicability: Useful for understanding the operational risks that could affect the reliability and quality of services.

7. Contractual Risk Analysis: Reviewing and analyzing contractual agreements with third parties to identify obligations, responsibilities, and potential areas of legal or contractual risk.

   Applicability: Critical for understanding the legal implications of the relationship and ensuring alignment with organizational objectives.

8. Reputation Risk Assessment: Evaluating the reputation of third-party entities by considering factors such as past performance, client feedback, and industry perception.

    Applicability: Particularly relevant for industries where reputation is a critical asset.

9. 9. Strategic Risk Assessment: Assessing how the third-party relationship aligns with the organization's strategic goals and objectives.

    Applicability: Ensures that third-party engagements contribute positively to the organization's long-term strategy.

10. Continuous Monitoring and Audits: Implementing ongoing monitoring processes and periodic audits to track changes in the third-party's risk profile and performance.

    Applicability: Ensures that risk assessments remain current and responsive to evolving conditions.

11. Scenario Analysis: Conducting scenario-based assessments to evaluate how third parties would respond to specific risk scenarios, helping organizations prepare for potential disruptions.

12. Applicability: Provides insights into the resilience and preparedness of third-party entities.

13. Crisis Management Simulation: Simulating crisis scenarios to assess the third party's ability to manage and mitigate risks during emergencies.

14. Applicability: Evaluates the effectiveness of the third party's crisis management capabilities.

ELEVATING VENDOR RELATIONSHIPS THROUGH FRAMEWORKS

Globally recognized standards offer structured approaches to enhance the security posture and resilience of organizations, particularly when engaging with external partners. Let's delve into the applicability of ISO 27001 and NIST in the context of vendor relationships.

ISO 27001: STRENGTHENING INFORMATION SECURITY IN VENDOR PARTNERSHIPS

ISO 27001 APPLICABILITY:

ISO 27001, developed by the International Organization for Standardization, focuses on information security management systems. Its principles and requirements provide a versatile framework applicable to the complex landscape of vendor relationships. This framework is particularly relevant when entrusting third parties with sensitive data or critical business functions.

Key Aspects:

1. Risk Management: ISO 27001's emphasis on risk assessment and management aligns seamlessly with the need to evaluate and mitigate potential risks associated with vendor engagements. Organizations can apply these principles to identify, assess, and treat information security risks in their extended supply chain.

2. Security Controls: The standard's comprehensive catalog of security controls offers organizations a structured approach to defining and implementing measures that safeguard information assets. For vendor relationships, this translates into a systematic method for ensuring that external partners meet defined security standards.

3. Continuous Improvement: ISO 27001's commitment to a continuous improvement cycle fosters a dynamic security environment. When applied to vendor relationships, this means ongoing assessments and adjustments, ensuring that security measures evolve to meet changing threats and business requirements.

Benefits:

1. Uniform Security Standards: ISO 27001 facilitates the establishment of uniform security standards across vendors. This ensures a consistent and high level of information security throughout the vendor ecosystem.

2. Demonstrable Compliance: Achieving ISO 27001 certification enhances an organization's ability to demonstrate its commitment to information security to stakeholders, clients, and regulatory bodies. This can be a valuable differentiator in vendor selection processes.

NIST: Navigating Security Controls for Vendor Resilience

APPLICABILITY:

NIST's Special Publication 800-53 provides a comprehensive catalog of security controls for federal information systems and organizations. In the context of vendor relationships, organizations can leverage NIST's guidance to establish a robust security baseline, especially when dealing with vendors handling sensitive information or critical services.

Key Aspects:

1. Security Control Framework: NIST 800-53 offers a detailed and adaptable framework of security controls. This framework proves instrumental in defining security requirements for vendors and ensuring they align with organizational standards.

2. Continuous Monitoring: NIST emphasizes continuous monitoring of security controls, allowing organizations to actively track and respond to security events. This proactive approach is crucial in the context of vendor relationships to detect and address potential issues promptly.

3. Incident Response: The framework includes guidance on incident response planning and execution. In the vendor context, this prepares organizations to collaboratively respond to and recover from security incidents, minimizing potential impacts on operations.

Benefits:

1. Standardized Security Controls: NIST's standardized controls provide a common language for communicating security requirements with vendors. This clarity fosters mutual understanding and adherence to established security standards.

2. Adaptability to Risk Profiles: NIST's risk-based approach allows organizations to tailor security controls based on the specific risk profiles associated with different vendors. This adaptability ensures a nuanced and effective security strategy.

   By adopting these frameworks, organizations not only enhance the security posture of their vendor ecosystem but also instill a culture of continuous improvement and adaptability. The result is a resilient and secure collaboration that aligns with the ever-evolving challenges of the modern business landscape.

Best Practices For Onboarding Vendors

Onboarding vendors is a process that demands careful consideration and thorough due diligence to ensure that external partners align with an organization's values, standards, and operational requirements. Effective onboarding sets the stage for a collaborative and secure relationship. Below are some best practices, including comprehensive due diligence, for onboarding vendors:

1. Establish Clear Policies and Procedures: Develop comprehensive onboarding policies and procedures that clearly outline the steps, documentation requirements, and criteria for vetting potential vendors. This ensures consistency and transparency in the onboarding process.

2. Pre-Screening: Before initiating formal onboarding, conduct initial pre-screening to assess whether a vendor aligns with the organization's basic requirements, such as compliance, financial stability, and reputation.

3. Risk Categorization: Categorize vendors based on the level of risk they pose to the organization. High-risk vendors, such as those handling sensitive data or critical functions, require more in-depth due diligence.

4. Due Diligence Questionnaires: Utilize due diligence questionnaires to gather detailed information from vendors. These questionnaires should cover areas such as financial stability, compliance with laws and regulations, cybersecurity measures, and business continuity planning.

5. Financial Health Assessment: Evaluate the financial stability of vendors by reviewing financial statements, credit reports, and other relevant financial documentation. A financially stable vendor is more likely to provide consistent and reliable services.

6. Compliance Verification: Ensure vendors comply with relevant laws, industry regulations, and ethical standards. This may involve verifying certifications, licenses, and adherence to specific standards.

7. Security and Privacy Assessment: Assess the vendor's security and privacy practices, especially if they handle sensitive data. Review their information security policies, data protection measures, and any relevant certifications (e.g., ISO 27001).

8. Performance History Check: Investigate the vendor's performance history with other clients. Request references and, if possible, speak with organizations that have similar vendor relationships to gauge the vendor's reliability and responsiveness.

9. Contractual Clarity: Draft clear and comprehensive contracts that explicitly outline roles, responsibilities, service levels, compliance requirements, and termination clauses. Legal review is crucial to ensure the contract protects the organization's interests.

10. Ongoing Monitoring: Implement continuous monitoring mechanisms to track vendor performance, adherence to contractual terms, and any changes in their risk profile. Regularly reassess the vendor relationship to ensure it remains aligned with organizational needs.

11. Training and Communication: Train employees involved in vendor management on the onboarding process and the organization's expectations from vendors. Establish clear lines of communication to address issues promptly.

12. Contingency Planning: Develop contingency plans for potential disruptions in vendor services. This includes understanding the vendor's business continuity measures and having alternative plans in place to mitigate risks.

13. Legal and Regulatory Compliance: Ensure vendors comply with legal and regulatory requirements applicable to the organization's industry. Stay informed about changes in regulations that may impact the vendor relationship.

14. Cultural Alignment: Consider cultural alignment and shared values when onboarding vendors. A cultural fit can contribute to a smoother collaboration and foster a positive working relationship.

15. Periodic Audits: Conduct periodic audits of vendor operations to verify ongoing compliance, security measures, and overall performance. These audits should be part of a continuous improvement process.

CONTRACTUAL SAFEGUARDS TO INCORPORATE IN AGREEMENTS WITH THIRD-PARTY VENDORS

When drafting agreements with third-party vendors, it's crucial to include key clauses and contractual safeguards to protect the interests of your organization and establish clear expectations. Three vital aspects to focus on are indemnification, data protection clauses, and dispute resolution mechanisms. Let's explore each of these:

1. **Indemnification:**

   The indemnification clause is a crucial component that addresses the responsibility for certain types of losses or damages that may arise during the course of the vendor relationship. It specifies the circumstances under which the vendor agrees to compensate the organization for losses incurred.

   Key Elements:

   a. Scope of Indemnification: Clearly define the scope of indemnification, specifying the types of claims, losses, or damages for which the vendor is responsible. This could include breaches of contract, intellectual property infringement, or data breaches.

b. Limits of Liability: Set limits on the vendor's liability to ensure that indemnification is reasonable and aligned with the nature of the services provided. This prevents excessive financial burdens on the vendor.

c. Notification Requirements: Establish procedures for the prompt notification of potential claims. Timely notification is essential for both parties to assess and address issues efficiently.

d. Defense and Settlement: Outline whether the vendor has the responsibility to defend against legal claims and the extent to which they can settle claims without the organization's approval.

2. Data Protection Clauses:

Given the increasing importance of data protection and privacy, incorporating robust data protection clauses is essential to ensure that the vendor handles sensitive information appropriately.

Key Elements:

a. Data Handling Requirements: Specify how the vendor will handle, process, and protect any data provided by the organization. This includes requirements for data encryption, storage, and access controls.

b. Compliance with Laws: Ensure that the vendor complies with relevant data protection laws and regulations, such as GDPR, HIPAA, or other industry-specific requirements.

c. Data Breach Notification: Clearly define the vendor's obligations regarding the notification of data breaches. This should include the timeframe for reporting, the information to be provided, and the collaboration in resolving the breach.

d. Data Ownership and Return: Clarify the ownership of any data generated or processed during the engagement and establish procedures for data return or destruction at the end of the relationship.

3. Dispute Resolution Mechanisms:

Dispute resolution mechanisms are essential for addressing conflicts or disagreements that may arise during the course of the vendor relationship. Establishing clear procedures for dispute resolution helps prevent protracted legal battles and promotes timely resolution.

Key Elements:

a. Mediation and Arbitration: Specify whether disputes will be resolved through mediation, arbitration, or litigation. Mediation and arbitration are often preferred for their efficiency and confidentiality.

b. Governing Law: Clearly state the governing law that will apply to the agreement. This helps in determining the legal framework under which any dispute will be resolved.

c. Venue: Define the venue or jurisdiction for resolving disputes. This could be a specific city, state, or country agreed upon by both parties.

d. Costs and Attorney's Fees: Clarify how the costs associated with dispute resolution will be shared between the parties. Consider whether the prevailing party is entitled to recover attorney's fees.

Incorporating robust indemnification, data protection, and dispute resolution clauses in agreements with third-party vendors is essential for building a strong contractual foundation. These provisions not only protect the organization's interests but also foster clear communication and cooperation between both parties. Legal counsel should be involved in the drafting and review process to ensure that the clauses align with the specific needs and risks of the vendor relationship.

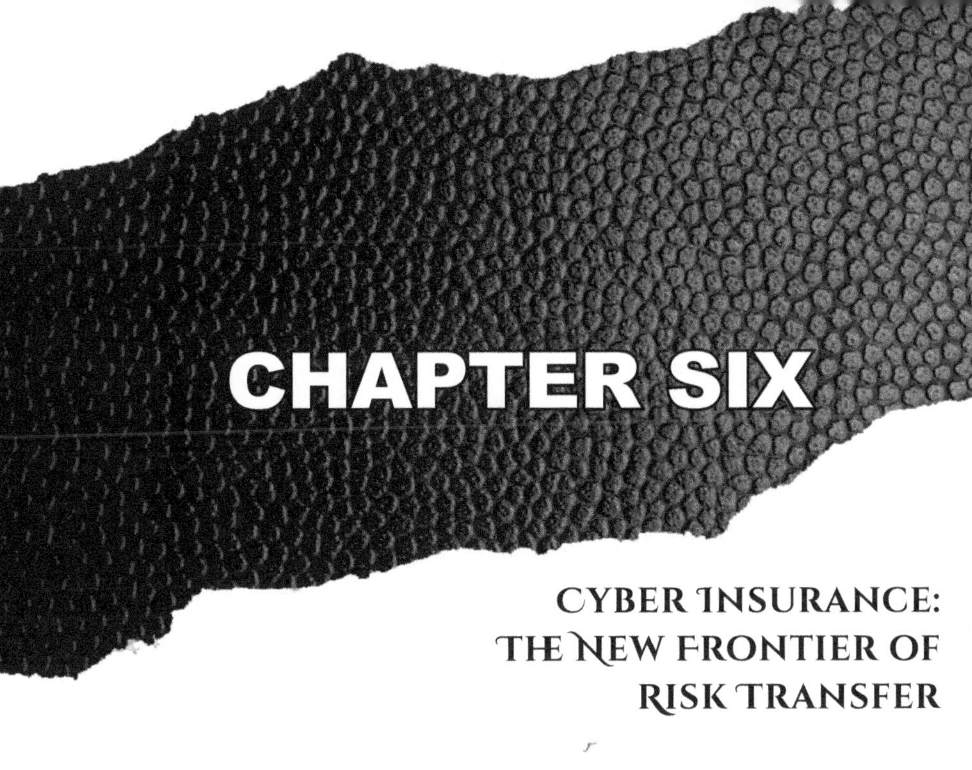

CHAPTER SIX

CYBER INSURANCE: THE NEW FRONTIER OF RISK TRANSFER

Cyber threats encompass a wide array of malicious activities, ranging from data breaches and ransomware attacks to phishing campaigns and sophisticated malware infiltrations. The perpetrators behind these threats, whether individual hackers, organized cybercrime groups, or state-sponsored actors, are leveraging cutting-edge techniques to exploit weaknesses in cybersecurity defenses. The motivations behind cyber attacks have also diversified, encompassing financial gain, political espionage, and ideological objectives.

The consequences of falling victim to cyber threats are multifaceted. Beyond the immediate financial losses resulting from data breaches and business interruptions, organizations face reputational damage, regulatory scrutiny, and legal liabilities. The interconnected nature of global business ecosystems further amplifies the impact of cyber incidents, as disruptions can cascade through supply chains and industry sectors.

Against this backdrop, the upcoming chapter places a spotlight on the imperative for organizations to comprehend and proactively manage cyber risks. It delves into the multifaceted nature of contemporary cyber threats, providing insights into the evolving tactics employed by cyber adversaries. The chapter aims to equip readers with a comprehensive understanding of the dynamic and complex landscape in which cybersecurity operates, emphasizing the need for strategic approaches to risk mitigation.

As a central theme, the chapter shifts focus to the strategic tool of cyber insurance as a means of transferring and mitigating the financial ramifications of cyber risks. In acknowledging the inevitability of cyber threats and the challenges organizations face in completely eliminating these risks, the chapter underscores the importance of adopting a holistic risk management strategy. By harnessing cyber insurance, organizations can strategically transfer the financial burden associated with cyber incidents, thereby fortifying their resilience against the uncertainties of the digital age.

The exploration of cyber insurance as a risk transfer mechanism becomes a pivotal aspect of the chapter, offering readers insights into the nuanced world of policy considerations, market dynamics, and the evolving role of cyber insurance within broader cybersecurity frameworks. By framing cyber insurance as a proactive and strategic tool, the chapter seeks to empower organizations to navigate the complexities of the digital frontier with resilience and adaptability.

PREVALENT CYBER THREATS

Organizations face an array of sophisticated threats that can disrupt operations and compromise sensitive information. Among these threats, data breaches, ransomware attacks, and phishing campaigns stand out as pervasive challenges.

DATA BREACHES:

A data breach, a pervasive menace, occurs when unauthorized entities gain access to confidential information. Whether through system vulnerabilities or targeted attacks, the exposure of personal data, financial records, or intellectual property poses substantial risks. The fallout includes compromised customer trust, regulatory penalties for insufficient data protection, and lasting reputational damage.

RANSOMWARE ATTACKS:

Ransomware, a malicious software, infiltrates systems through deceptive means, encrypting files and demanding payment for their release. These attacks cause operational disruptions, financial extortion through ransom demands often in cryptocurrency, and significant reputational harm. The public revelation of a ransomware incident can undermine an organization's perceived security resilience.

PHISHING ATTACKS:

Phishing, a subtle but potent threat, involves deceptive attempts to extract sensitive information by masquerading as trustworthy entities. Whether through fraudulent emails, messages, or deceptive websites, phishing compromises credentials, leads to financial fraud, and inflicts reputational harm by exploiting the trust of unsuspecting individuals.

FINANCIAL AND REPUTATIONAL IMPLICATIONS OF CYBER INCIDENTS

FINANCIAL IMPLICATIONS:

The fallout of a cyber incident extends into the financial realm with direct losses incurred through incident response efforts, recovery initiatives, and potential ransom payments. Operational downtime resulting from attacks like ransomware inflicts further financial strain, disrupting regular business operations and causing productivity losses. Regulatory fines and legal costs may compound the financial toll, particularly in cases of non-compliance with data protection regulations.

REPUTATIONAL IMPLICATIONS:

The damage to an organization's reputation following a cyber incident can be profound. The erosion of trust among customers, partners, and stakeholders is a direct consequence, triggered by the organization's perceived failure to safeguard sensitive information. Brand damage, often intensified by negative media coverage, can lead to a decline in market value. Moreover, customer churn may occur as individuals affected by data breaches opt to sever ties with the compromised organization, and the long-term impact can persist, affecting customer loyalty, investor confidence, and overall market standing.

EXPLORING LATEST TRENDS IN CYBER THREATS

Staying abreast of the latest trends is crucial for organizations seeking to fortify their defenses. Several contemporary threats have emerged, shaping the dynamic nature of cybersecurity challenges.

1. **Supply Chain Attacks:**

   Supply chain attacks have surged to the forefront as a sophisticated strategy employed by cyber adversaries. Instead of directly targeting a company's systems, attackers exploit vulnerabilities in the supply chain, compromising software, hardware, or services before they reach the intended organization. This approach, often challenging to detect, can have far-reaching consequences, impacting multiple entities across the supply chain.

2. Zero-Day Vulnerabilities:

Zero-day vulnerabilities refer to undiscovered or undisclosed software vulnerabilities that malicious actors exploit before developers can create a patch. These vulnerabilities provide attackers with a window of opportunity to launch targeted attacks without the knowledge of the software vendor or the affected organization. The rapid weaponization of zero-day vulnerabilities underscores the need for proactive security measures.

3. Advanced Persistent Threats (APTs):

Advanced Persistent Threats (APTs) represent a category of highly sophisticated and targeted cyber attacks. APTs involve persistent, long-term campaigns orchestrated by well-funded and organized threat actors. These attacks often span various tactics, techniques, and procedures (TTPs), with the primary aim of infiltrating and exfiltrating sensitive information without detection.

THE DYNAMIC NATURE OF CYBER RISKS AND THE NEED FOR ADAPTIVE RISK MANAGEMENT STRATEGIES

The landscape of cyber risks is inherently dynamic, marked by continuous evolution in the tactics employed by cyber adversaries. As new technologies emerge, threat actors adapt, seeking innovative ways to exploit vulnerabilities. This dynamic nature necessitates a shift from traditional, static risk management approaches to adaptive strategies that can respond to the fluidity of the cyber threat environment.

1. **Continuous Threat Intelligence:**

    To effectively counter the dynamic nature of cyber risks, organizations must engage in continuous threat intelligence gathering. This involves staying informed about the latest tactics, vulnerabilities, and threat actor behaviors. Proactive monitoring enables organizations to identify emerging threats and vulnerabilities, allowing for timely and targeted risk mitigation.

2. **Adaptive Security Frameworks:**

    Adaptive security frameworks emphasize flexibility and responsiveness. Unlike rigid, one-size-fits-all approaches, adaptive frameworks enable organizations to adjust their security postures based on real-time threat intelligence. This approach ensures that security measures align with the evolving threat landscape, offering a more resilient defense against dynamic cyber risks.

3. **Incident Response Planning:**

    Given the inevitability of cyber incidents, organizations must prioritize robust incident response planning. This involves developing and regularly testing response plans to address a variety of cyber threats. An adaptive incident response

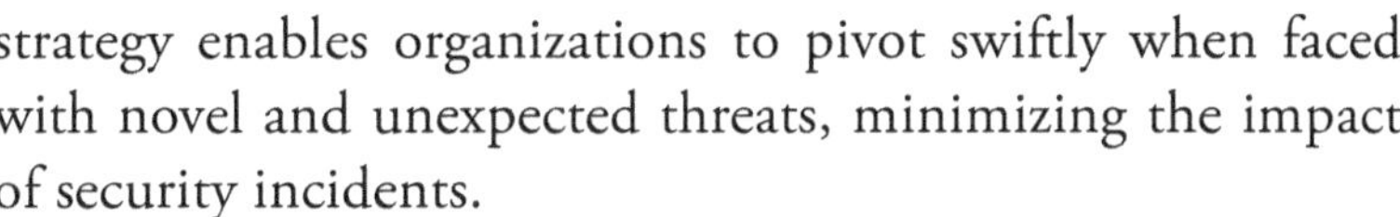

strategy enables organizations to pivot swiftly when faced with novel and unexpected threats, minimizing the impact of security incidents.

4. **Collaboration and Information Sharing:**

    In the face of dynamic cyber threats, collaboration and information sharing among industry peers, government agencies, and security communities become paramount. Collective intelligence enhances the ability of organizations to anticipate and respond to emerging threats, fostering a community-driven defense against cyber adversaries.

Understanding Cyber Insurance

Cyber insurance, also known as cyber risk insurance or cyber liability insurance, is a specialized form of insurance designed to provide financial protection to organizations in the event of cyber incidents. These incidents may include data breaches, ransomware attacks, business interruptions due to cyber events, and other forms of cyber threats. Cyber insurance policies are tailored to address the unique risks and challenges posed by the digital landscape, offering coverage for both first-party and third-party losses.

Purpose in Mitigating Financial Losses

The primary purpose of cyber insurance is to mitigate the financial impact of cyber incidents on organizations. It serves as a strategic risk management tool by offering financial compensation to cover the costs associated with responding to and recovering from a cyber incident. The specific financial losses that cyber insurance aims to address include:

1. Incident Response Costs: Expenses related to investigating the incident, notifying affected parties, and implementing immediate remediation measures.

2. Data Breach Costs: Costs associated with recovering and restoring compromised data, including forensic analysis and data restoration.

3. Business Interruption Losses:

4. Compensation for income losses and additional expenses incurred during the period of business interruption caused by a cyber event.

5. Ransom Payments: Coverage for ransom payments made to threat actors in the event of a ransomware attack, although some policies may have limitations or exclusions in this regard.

6. Legal and Regulatory Costs: Coverage for legal fees and regulatory fines that may result from non-compliance with data protection laws or other cybersecurity regulations.

7. Third-Party Liability: Protection against lawsuits and legal expenses arising from third parties, such as customers or partners, affected by a cyber incident.

8. Reputation Management Costs: Assistance in covering costs related to public relations efforts and reputation management following a cyber incident.

    By providing financial support for these aspects, cyber insurance helps organizations recover more swiftly and effectively from cyber incidents, ultimately minimizing the long-term financial impact on their operations.

Broader Risk Management Landscape

Cyber insurance operates within the broader risk management landscape, complementing other risk mitigation strategies and measures. In the context of the broader risk management framework, cyber insurance interacts with:

1. Cybersecurity Measures: Cyber insurance is not a substitute for robust cybersecurity measures. Instead, it works in conjunction with preventative strategies such as firewalls, encryption, antivirus software, and employee training to reduce the likelihood of a cyber incident.

2. Risk Assessments: Organizations conduct risk assessments to identify and evaluate potential vulnerabilities and threats. Cyber insurance aligns with these assessments by providing coverage for the risks identified during the evaluation process.

3. Incident Response Planning: Cyber insurance dovetails with incident response planning by offering financial support for the execution of response plans. This synergy ensures a comprehensive approach to handling cyber incidents.

4. Compliance and Governance: Cyber insurance aligns with compliance efforts by assisting organizations in meeting regulatory requirements and covering costs associated with legal and regulatory actions.

5. Enterprise Risk Management (ERM): Cyber insurance contributes to the broader enterprise risk management strategy by addressing specific risks within the digital realm, offering a more holistic approach to overall risk mitigation.

Exploring Components of Cyber Insurance Coverage

Cyber insurance is a comprehensive risk management tool that encompasses various components to provide financial protection to organizations in the event of a cyber incident. These components can be broadly categorized into first-party and third-party coverages.

First-Party Coverages

This kind of coverage applies to;

1. Data Breach Response Costs: Coverage for expenses related to investigating a data breach, notifying affected parties, and providing credit monitoring services.

2. Data Restoration Costs: Reimbursement for the costs associated with restoring or recovering lost or compromised data.

3. Business Interruption Losses: Compensation for income losses and additional expenses incurred during a period of business interruption caused by a cyber event.

4. Ransomware Payments: Some policies may provide coverage for ransom payments made to threat actors in the event of a ransomware attack. However, coverage for this may vary, and certain policies may have limitations or exclusions.

5. Cyber Extortion Costs: Coverage for expenses related to cyber extortion attempts, including payments made to prevent or mitigate an imminent threat.

6. Reputational Harm: Compensation for costs associated with public relations efforts and reputation management to mitigate reputational damage resulting from a cyber incident.

THIRD-PARTY COVERAGES

Third-party coverage applies to;

1. Liability to Third Parties: Coverage for legal liabilities arising from a cyber incident, including lawsuits filed by customers, partners, or other third parties affected by the breach.

2. Regulatory Fines and Penalties: Reimbursement for fines and penalties imposed by regulatory bodies due to non-compliance with data protection laws or other cybersecurity regulations.

3. Legal Defense Costs: Coverage for legal fees and expenses incurred in defending against lawsuits related to a cyber incident.

4. Media Liability: Protection against claims of intellectual property infringement, defamation, or other media-related liabilities arising from a cyber event.

COVERAGE FOR SPECIFIC CYBER RISKS

1. Social Engineering Fraud: Protection against losses resulting from fraudulent schemes that manipulate individuals into transferring funds or providing sensitive information.

2. System Failure: Coverage for losses incurred due to a failure in computer systems or networks, which may result in business interruption.

3. Crisis Management Costs: Reimbursement for expenses related to crisis management, including public relations efforts and communication strategies to address the aftermath of a cyber incident.

4. Notification Costs: Coverage for costs associated with notifying affected parties about a data breach, including communication expenses and credit monitoring services.

Importance of Conducting a Comprehensive Cyber Risk Assessment

Before purchasing cyber insurance, conducting a comprehensive cyber risk assessment is paramount. This assessment serves as the foundation for understanding an organization's unique cybersecurity landscape, identifying vulnerabilities, and determining the appropriate level of coverage needed. The importance of this assessment lies in:

1. Tailoring Coverage to Specific Risks: A cyber risk assessment allows organizations to identify and prioritize their specific cybersecurity risks. This insight enables the customization of insurance coverage to address the most relevant threats, ensuring that the policy aligns with the organization's risk profile.

2. Avoiding Underinsurance or Over insurance: Without a thorough understanding of the cyber risks an organization faces, there is a risk of either underestimating or overestimating the coverage needed. Underinsurance can leave an organization exposed to financial vulnerabilities, while over insurance may result in unnecessary premium costs.

3. Enhancing Risk Mitigation Strategies: A cyber risk assessment provides insights into existing cybersecurity measures and their effectiveness. This information helps organizations strengthen their risk mitigation strategies by identifying areas for improvement and guiding investments in cybersecurity measures.

4. Meeting Insurance Requirements: Some insurers may require organizations to demonstrate a certain level of cybersecurity maturity before providing coverage. A comprehensive risk assessment helps organizations meet these requirements and may even lead to more favorable insurance terms.

5. Identifying Critical Assets and Data: Understanding the organization's critical assets and sensitive data is crucial for determining the appropriate coverage. A cyber risk assessment helps identify what needs protection, allowing organizations to focus on safeguarding their most valuable assets.

METHODOLOGIES FOR EVALUATING AN ORGANIZATION'S CYBER RISK PROFILE:

1. Asset Inventory: Conduct a thorough inventory of digital assets, including hardware, software, and data. Identify critical assets that, if compromised, could significantly impact the organization.

2. Vulnerability Assessments: Regularly assess vulnerabilities in the organization's systems and networks. This involves identifying weaknesses that could be exploited by cyber threats and prioritizing them based on their potential impact.

3. Threat Intelligence: Leverage threat intelligence sources to understand the current threat landscape. This includes staying informed about emerging cyber threats and tactics employed by threat actors.

4. Incident History Analysis: Analyze past cybersecurity incidents, if any, to understand the organization's historical risk exposure. Learning from previous incidents helps in fortifying defenses against similar future threats.

5. Regulatory Compliance: Evaluate the organization's compliance with relevant cybersecurity regulations. Compliance requirements often serve as a baseline for cybersecurity maturity and may impact insurance eligibility and terms.

6. Business Impact Analysis: Assess the potential financial and operational impact of cyber incidents on the organization. This analysis helps prioritize risk mitigation efforts and determine appropriate coverage levels.

7. Cybersecurity Culture and Training: Evaluate the organization's cybersecurity culture and the effectiveness of employee training programs. Human factors are a significant contributor to cyber risks, and a well-trained workforce can be a valuable defense against threats.

8. Third-Party Risk Management: Consider the risks introduced by third-party vendors and partners. Assess the cybersecurity practices of third parties with access to the organization's systems or data, as their vulnerabilities can impact the overall risk profile.

    By employing these methodologies, organizations can gain a comprehensive understanding of their cyber risk landscape. This knowledge forms the basis for informed decision-making when selecting cyber insurance coverage, ensuring that the policy aligns with the organization's specific needs and vulnerabilities.

COMMON COVERAGE GAPS IN STANDARD CYBER INSURANCE POLICIES:

While standard cyber insurance policies provide valuable protection, they may have coverage gaps that organizations need to be aware of. Some common coverage gaps include:

1. Inadequate Business Interruption Coverage: Standard policies may not sufficiently cover the full extent of financial losses and operational disruptions during a business interruption caused by a cyber incident.

2. Limited or No Coverage for Social Engineering Fraud: Some policies may not adequately cover losses resulting from fraudulent schemes that manipulate employees into transferring funds or providing sensitive information.

3. Exclusions for Certain Types of Cyber Attacks: Policies may have exclusions for specific types of cyber attacks, such as nation-state-sponsored attacks or attacks originating from certain geographic regions.

4. Insufficient Coverage for Regulatory Fines: In cases of non-compliance with data protection regulations, standard policies may not provide enough coverage for regulatory fines and penalties.

5. Exclusions for Pre-Existing Conditions: Some policies may exclude coverage for cyber incidents related to pre-existing vulnerabilities or breaches that occurred before the policy's inception.

6. Limited Coverage for Third-Party Liabilities: Standard policies may have limitations in covering legal liabilities arising from third-party claims, such as lawsuits filed by customers or business partners.

STRATEGIES FOR CUSTOMIZING COVERAGE TO ADDRESS SPECIFIC ORGANIZATIONAL VULNERABILITIES:

To address these coverage gaps and tailor cyber insurance to specific organizational vulnerabilities, organizations can adopt the following strategies:

1. Risk Profiling and Assessment: Conduct a thorough risk assessment to identify and prioritize specific cyber risks faced by the organization. This includes understanding the industry-specific threats and vulnerabilities relevant to the business.

2. Collaboration with Insurers: Work closely with insurers to customize coverage based on the organization's unique risk profile. This collaboration may involve negotiating terms, adjusting coverage limits, and addressing specific concerns.

3. Endorsements and Add-Ons: Consider adding endorsements or add-ons to the policy to address specific vulnerabilities. For example, organizations can add coverage for social engineering fraud or tailor coverage for specific types of cyber attacks.

4. Customized Business Interruption Coverage: Work with insurers to develop a business interruption coverage plan that accurately reflects the potential financial impact of a cyber incident on the organization's operations.

5. Review and Negotiate Policy Language: Carefully review the language of the policy to understand exclusions and limitations. Negotiate with insurers to modify policy language to ensure coverage aligns with organizational needs.

6. Benchmarking Against Industry Standards: Benchmark the organization's cyber insurance coverage against industry standards and best practices. This helps ensure that the policy meets or exceeds the expectations set by the industry.

7. Continuous Monitoring and Policy Adjustments: Regularly reassess the organization's cyber risk landscape and adjust the policy accordingly. Cyber threats evolve, and continuous monitoring allows for proactive adjustments to coverage as the risk profile changes.

8. Engagement with Cybersecurity Experts: Seek input from cybersecurity experts when customizing coverage. Their insights can help identify nuanced vulnerabilities and potential areas of exposure that may not be immediately apparent.

By adopting these strategies, organizations can go beyond standard coverage and create a cyber insurance policy that aligns closely with their specific risk landscape. Customizing coverage ensures that the organization is adequately protected against the unique cyber threats and challenges it faces.

CURRENT LANDSCAPE OF THE CYBER INSURANCE MARKET

The cyber insurance market has experienced significant growth and evolution as organizations recognize the increasing threats posed by cyber incidents. Several key factors shape the current landscape:

1. Growing Demand: The escalating frequency and severity of cyber attacks have fueled a surge in demand for cyber insurance. Organizations across industries are recognizing the need for financial protection against the potential fallout of cyber incidents.

2. Increasing Awareness: Awareness of cyber risks has grown, prompting businesses to prioritize cybersecurity measures. This heightened awareness has contributed to the understanding that cyber insurance is a crucial component of a comprehensive risk management strategy.

3. Diverse Product Offerings: Insurers now offer a range of cyber insurance products tailored to meet the diverse needs of organizations. Coverage options include first-party coverages (e.g., data breach response, business interruption) and third-party coverages (e.g., liability for third-party claims).

4. Market Competition: The market has witnessed increased competition among insurers, leading to innovation in policy features, coverage options, and pricing structures. Insurers are striving to differentiate their offerings to attract clients in a competitive landscape.

5. Rising Premiums: As the frequency and severity of cyber attacks grow, premiums for cyber insurance have risen. Insurers are adjusting pricing models to account for the evolving threat landscape and the increasing costs associated with cyber incidents.

KEY PLAYERS IN THE CYBER INSURANCE MARKET

Several key players dominate the cyber insurance market, offering a wide range of products and services. Some prominent players include:

CHUBB LIMITED

Chubb is a global insurance leader offering various insurance products, including comprehensive cyber insurance solutions.

AIG (AMERICAN INTERNATIONAL GROUP)

AIG is a multinational insurance company providing cyber insurance coverage with a focus on risk mitigation and tailored solutions.

AXA XL

AXA XL is a subsidiary of AXA Group, offering cyber insurance products and risk management services for businesses worldwide.

ZURICH INSURANCE GROUP

Zurich is a leading global insurer that provides cyber insurance coverage to businesses, addressing the financial impact of cyber incidents.

ALLIANZ SE

Allianz is a major player in the insurance industry, offering cyber insurance solutions to help organizations manage cyber risks effectively.

Market Trends

1. Parametric Insurance: Parametric insurance models, which provide predefined payouts based on specific triggers, are gaining traction in the cyber insurance market. This approach aims to simplify claims processing and enhance transparency.

2. Risk Quantification Services: Insurers are increasingly offering risk quantification services to help organizations assess and understand their cyber risk exposure. This involves using data analytics and modeling to estimate potential financial losses.

3. Collaboration with Cybersecurity Firms: Insurers are forming partnerships with cybersecurity firms to enhance their risk assessment capabilities. By leveraging the expertise of cybersecurity experts, insurers can better evaluate and mitigate cyber risks.

4. Focus on Incident Response: Cyber insurance policies are placing a greater emphasis on incident response services. This includes providing access to cybersecurity experts, legal support, and crisis management resources to help organizations respond effectively to cyber incidents.

5. Continuous Monitoring and Underwriting: Insurers are increasingly adopting continuous monitoring and underwriting practices. This involves real-time monitoring of an insured's cybersecurity posture and adjusting coverage based on the organization's evolving risk profile.

IMPACT OF INDUSTRY-SPECIFIC REGULATIONS

Industry-specific regulations play a significant role in shaping the cyber insurance market. The impact can be observed in several ways:

DATA PROTECTION LAWS

Regulations such as the General Data Protection Regulation (GDPR) in the European Union and the California Consumer Privacy Act (CCPA) in the United States have heightened the importance of cyber insurance. Non-compliance with these regulations can result in substantial fines, driving organizations to seek insurance coverage for potential liability.

INDUSTRY COMPLIANCE REQUIREMENTS

Certain industries, such as healthcare and finance, have specific cybersecurity and data protection regulations. Cyber insurance becomes a critical component for these industries to meet compliance requirements and manage the financial implications of regulatory penalties.

INSURABILITY CRITERIA

Some industry-specific regulations may influence insurers' underwriting criteria. Insurers may evaluate an organization's adherence to industry-specific cybersecurity standards when determining insurability and coverage terms.

EVOLVING REGULATORY LANDSCAPE

The evolving nature of cybersecurity regulations globally influences insurers to adapt their offerings. Insurers must stay abreast of regulatory changes to ensure that their policies remain compliant and provide relevant coverage.

CRITICAL CONSIDERATIONS WHEN SELECTING A CYBER INSURANCE POLICY

Choosing the right cyber insurance policy is a strategic decision that requires careful consideration of various factors. Here are critical considerations when selecting a cyber insurance policy:

1. Coverage Limits: Evaluate the coverage limits offered by the policy. Ensure that the limits align with the potential financial impact of a cyber incident on the organization. Coverage limits should be adequate to cover response costs, business interruption losses, legal liabilities, and other associated expenses.

2. Deductibles: Examine the deductible structure of the policy. A deductible is the amount the insured must pay before the insurance coverage kicks in. Consider how deductible amounts may impact the organization's ability to manage the financial burden of a cyber incident.

3. Retroactive Dates: Pay attention to retroactive dates, which define the period during which a covered incident must have occurred to be eligible for a claim. Understanding the retroactive date is crucial, as it can impact coverage for past incidents and potentially affect the insurability of pre-existing conditions.

4. Scope of Coverage: Carefully review the scope of coverage provided by the policy. Ensure that the policy covers a broad range of cyber risks, including data breaches, ransomware attacks, business interruption, and other relevant threats. Tailor the coverage to align with the organization's specific risk profile.

5. Exclusions and Limitations: Understand the exclusions and limitations outlined in the policy. Identify any specific types of cyber incidents or scenarios that may not be covered.

Work with insurers to negotiate policy language and address any concerns related to exclusions.

6. Incident Response Services: Assess the incident response services provided by the policy. This includes access to cybersecurity experts, legal support, and crisis management resources. Strong incident response services are essential for effective and efficient recovery from a cyber incident.

7. Third-Party Liability Coverage: Evaluate the extent of third-party liability coverage. This includes coverage for legal liabilities arising from third-party claims, such as lawsuits filed by customers, partners, or other affected parties. Adequate third-party liability coverage is crucial for managing legal and financial consequences.

8. Regulatory Compliance Coverage: Consider whether the policy provides coverage for regulatory fines and penalties resulting from non-compliance with data protection laws or other cybersecurity regulations. This is particularly important for industries subject to specific regulatory requirements.

ROLE OF ENDORSEMENTS AND ADD-ONS

Endorsements and add-ons play a vital role in tailoring cyber insurance policies to specific organizational needs. These additional features can enhance coverage and address unique risk factors:

1. Social Engineering Fraud Coverage: Add coverage for social engineering fraud, which protects against losses resulting from deceptive schemes that manipulate individuals into transferring funds or providing sensitive information.

2. System Failure Coverage: Consider adding coverage for losses incurred due to a failure in computer systems or networks. This can include coverage for business interruption and income losses resulting from system failures.

3. Crisis Management Services: Include endorsements that provide access to crisis management services. These services assist with public relations efforts, reputation management, and communication strategies following a cyber incident.

4. Media Liability Coverage: Consider endorsements that offer protection against claims of intellectual property infringement, defamation, or other media-related liabilities arising from a cyber event.

5. Cyber Extortion Coverage: Add coverage for expenses related to cyber extortion attempts, including payments made to prevent or mitigate an imminent threat.

6. Privacy Notification and Credit Monitoring: Include coverage for privacy notification costs and credit monitoring services to address the financial and reputational impact of data breaches.

7. Business Interruption Enhancements: Explore endorsements that enhance business interruption coverage, ensuring that the policy adequately addresses the potential financial losses during a disruption caused by a cyber incident.

8. Network Security Liability: Consider endorsements that provide additional coverage for network security liabilities, addressing legal expenses associated with cybersecurity-related lawsuits.

   Tailoring a cyber insurance policy through endorsements and add-ons allows organizations to customize coverage to their specific needs and risk landscape. Collaboration with insurers is essential to negotiate and implement these additions effectively.

Principles That Highlight Successful Claim Handling

While specific details of cyber insurance claims are often confidential, there are general examples and principles that highlight successful claims handling in the context of cyber incidents. Effective communication and collaboration between insured parties and insurers play a crucial role in navigating the claims process.

Examples of Successful Cyber Insurance Claims Handling

Swift Incident Response: In successful cases, insured parties have demonstrated a swift and well-coordinated incident response. This includes promptly identifying and containing the cyber incident, engaging cybersecurity experts, and initiating the necessary steps to mitigate further damage.

1. Transparent Communication: Insured parties that communicate openly and transparently with their insurers tend to experience smoother claims handling. Providing detailed information about the incident, its impact, and the steps taken for remediation helps insurers assess the situation accurately.

2. Collaboration with Experts: Organizations that collaborate effectively with cybersecurity experts recommended by the insurer often achieve better outcomes. This collaboration ensures a thorough assessment of the incident, helps in implementing effective remediation measures, and provides valuable insights for the claims process.

3. Documentation of Costs: Successful claims handling involves meticulous documentation of all costs incurred due to the cyber incident. This includes expenses related to incident response, legal services, notification to affected parties, public relations efforts, and any other direct or indirect costs.

4. Compliance with Policy Terms: Adhering to the terms and conditions specified in the insurance policy is crucial. Successful claims handling often involves a clear understanding of policy terms, ensuring that the organization complies with any requirements outlined by the insurer.

Importance of Effective Communication and Collaboration:

1. Timely Reporting: Prompt communication of a cyber incident to the insurer is essential. Delays in reporting may impact the claims process and could potentially result in coverage issues. Timely reporting allows insurers to assess the situation and provide guidance on next steps.

2. Clear and Comprehensive Information: Providing clear and comprehensive information about the incident is vital. This includes details about the nature of the attack, the extent of data compromise, and any potential regulatory implications. Clear communication enables insurers to better understand the situation and make informed decisions.

3. Collaboration in Risk Mitigation: Effective collaboration involves working closely with the insurer to implement risk mitigation measures. This may include recommendations for strengthening cybersecurity defenses, improving incident response protocols, and enhancing overall resilience to future cyber threats.

4. Understanding Policy Coverage: Insured parties and insurers should work collaboratively to ensure a mutual understanding of the policy coverage. This involves clarifying coverage limits, deductibles, and any specific conditions that may impact the claims process. Clear communication helps avoid misunderstandings during the claims handling.

5. Negotiation and Resolution: In cases where there are uncertainties or disputes, effective communication and collaboration are key to negotiating and resolving issues. A collaborative approach can lead to fair and equitable resolutions that benefit both the insured party and the insurer.

6. Post-Incident Review: After the incident is resolved, conducting a post-incident review with the insurer can provide valuable insights. This collaborative assessment helps identify lessons learned, areas for improvement, and adjustments that can be made to enhance future cybersecurity and claims readiness.

STRATEGIES FOR INTEGRATING CYBER INSURANCE INTO BROADER CYBERSECURITY PROGRAMS:

Integrating cyber insurance into broader cybersecurity programs is essential for a comprehensive and proactive approach to managing cyber risks. Here are strategies to achieve effective integration:

1. Risk Assessment and Coverage Alignment: Conduct a thorough risk assessment to identify potential cyber risks and vulnerabilities. Align the coverage provided by cyber insurance with the specific risks identified, ensuring that the policy addresses the organization's unique threat landscape.

2. Policy Customization: Customize cyber insurance policies to match the organization's cybersecurity posture and risk tolerance. Work closely with insurers to adjust policy terms, coverage limits, and endorsements based on the organization's specific needs and risk profile.

3. Incident Response Planning: Integrate cyber insurance considerations into incident response planning. Clearly define the steps to be taken in the event of a cyber incident, including how to engage with insurers, report incidents promptly, and leverage the coverage effectively.

4. Collaboration with Insurers: Establish open lines of communication with insurers. Regularly engage with insurers to discuss cybersecurity measures, risk mitigation efforts, and any changes in the organization's threat landscape. This collaboration helps insurers better understand the organization's risk profile and may lead to more favorable terms.

5. Employee Training and Awareness: Include information about cyber insurance in employee training programs. Ensure that employees are aware of the organization's cyber insurance coverage, the importance of reporting incidents promptly, and their role in the overall cybersecurity program.

6. Regular Policy Reviews: Conduct regular reviews of cyber insurance policies to ensure that they remain aligned with the organization's cybersecurity strategy. As the threat landscape evolves, policy reviews help identify any gaps or areas where adjustments may be necessary.

7. Benchmarking Against Industry Standards: Benchmark the organization's cybersecurity practices and insurance coverage against industry standards and best practices. This ensures that the organization is keeping pace with evolving cybersecurity requirements and staying competitive in terms of coverage.

8. Crisis Management Integration: Integrate cyber insurance considerations into crisis management plans. Clearly outline how the organization will communicate with stakeholders, manage public relations, and address reputational damage in the aftermath of a cyber incident.

CONCEPT OF CYBER RESILIENCE AND ITS CONNECTION TO INSURANCE

Cyber resilience refers to an organization's ability to prepare for, respond to, and recover from cyber threats or incidents. It goes beyond traditional cybersecurity measures and emphasizes the organization's capacity to adapt and maintain critical functions during and after a cyber attack. Cyber resilience and insurance are interconnected components of a comprehensive risk management strategy. Here's how they relate:

Cyber resilience involves proactive planning and preparedness to minimize the impact of cyber incidents. Insurance complements this by providing financial protection in the event of a significant incident, enabling organizations to implement response plans without severe financial strain.

RISK MITIGATION AND INSURANCE PREMIUMS

A strong cyber resilience program, which includes effective risk mitigation measures, can influence insurance premiums positively. Insurers may view organizations with robust cyber resilience as lower risk, potentially leading to more favorable premium terms.

1. Incident Response and Recovery: Cyber resilience emphasizes the ability to respond swiftly and recover from cyber incidents. Insurance supports this by providing coverage for response costs, business interruption losses, and other expenses incurred during the recovery process.

2. Adaptability and Continuous Improvement: Both cyber resilience and insurance require organizations to adapt to evolving threats. A culture of continuous improvement in cybersecurity practices, incident response capabilities, and insurance coverage contributes to overall organizational resilience.

3. Collaboration with Insurers: Organizations with a strong cyber resilience framework are likely to collaborate more effectively with insurers. This collaboration involves transparent communication, regular risk assessments, and a shared commitment to reducing cyber risk. This partnership contributes to a more robust overall risk management strategy.

Influence of Technological Advancements on the Future of Cyber Insurance:

Technological advancements, particularly in the realms of artificial intelligence (AI) and machine learning, are significantly influencing the future of cyber insurance. These advancements bring several transformative elements to the industry:

1. Risk Assessment and Underwriting: AI and Machine Learning enable insurers to analyze vast amounts of data quickly and accurately. This is particularly valuable in risk assessment and underwriting, allowing insurers to better understand an organization's cybersecurity posture and set more precise premium rates.

2. Behavioral Analytics: Advanced analytics, powered by AI, can analyze user behavior within an organization's network. By establishing a baseline of normal behavior, these systems can detect anomalies that may indicate potential security threats. Insurers can use such insights to assess an organization's risk more comprehensively.

3. Claims Processing and Fraud Detection: AI streamlines claims processing by automating routine tasks and accelerating the assessment of damages. Machine learning algorithms can detect patterns associated with fraudulent claims, enhancing fraud prevention measures within the cyber insurance sector.

4. Cybersecurity Monitoring: Insurers can leverage AI-driven cybersecurity monitoring tools to continuously assess the security posture of insured organizations. These tools can provide real-time insights into emerging threats, allowing insurers to proactively engage with clients to mitigate risks.

5. Automation in Incident Response: AI can facilitate automated incident response by rapidly identifying and containing cyber threats. Insurers may integrate AI-driven incident response tools into their offerings, helping organizations minimize the impact of a cyber incident and potentially reducing claims costs.

6. Predictive Analytics for Loss Modeling: Predictive analytics, fueled by machine learning, can assist insurers in developing sophisticated loss models. By analyzing historical data and identifying correlations, insurers can better predict the likelihood and severity of future cyber incidents, influencing pricing and risk management strategies.

7. Customization of Policies: AI enables insurers to tailor cyber insurance policies more precisely to individual organizations. By understanding the unique risks and needs of each client, insurers can use AI-driven analytics to customize coverage, ensuring a more accurate alignment between policy terms and organizational risk profiles.

POTENTIAL FOR PREDICTIVE ANALYTICS IN RISK ASSESSMENT

Predictive analytics, empowered by AI and machine learning, holds immense potential in revolutionizing the risk assessment process in cyber insurance:

1. Identifying Emerging Threats: Predictive analytics can analyze historical data to identify emerging cyber threats and attack patterns. This forward-looking approach enables insurers to assess the potential impact of new threats on

insured organizations and adjust coverage and premiums accordingly.

2. Quantifying Vulnerabilities: By assessing an organization's cybersecurity vulnerabilities and historical data on similar vulnerabilities, predictive analytics can quantify the potential impact of these weaknesses. Insurers can use this information to guide risk mitigation efforts and set appropriate coverage levels.

3. Continuous Monitoring and Adjustment: Predictive analytics allows for continuous monitoring of an organization's cyber risk profile. As the risk landscape evolves, insurers can use real-time data and predictive models to adjust coverage, ensuring that policies remain aligned with the dynamic nature of cyber threats.

4. Data-Driven Decision-Making: Leveraging predictive analytics enables insurers to make data-driven decisions. This includes determining optimal pricing, identifying trends in claims data, and understanding the factors that contribute to successful risk management practices.

5. Enhancing Underwriting Precision: Predictive models can enhance underwriting precision by evaluating a multitude of factors, such as an organization's industry, security measures, and historical cyber incidents. This results in more accurate risk assessments, allowing insurers to offer competitive pricing and coverage terms.

6. Proactive Risk Mitigation: Predictive analytics can provide insights into potential future risks, allowing insurers to work proactively with clients on risk mitigation strategies. This collaboration can lead to a reduction in the frequency and severity of cyber incidents, ultimately benefiting both insurers and insured organizations.

The integration of AI, machine learning, and predictive analytics into the sphere of cyber insurance represents a transformative shift. These technologies not only streamline traditional processes but also offer innovative approaches to risk assessment, policy customization, and proactive risk management. As the cyber insurance landscape continues to evolve, the adoption of advanced technologies will play a pivotal role in shaping the industry's future.

ANTICIPATED REGULATORY DEVELOPMENTS IN CYBER INSURANCE

As the cyber insurance landscape continues to evolve, several anticipated regulatory developments are expected to shape the industry's future. These regulatory initiatives are driven by the increasing importance of cyber insurance in mitigating financial risks associated with cyber incidents. Here are key areas of anticipated regulatory developments:

STANDARDIZATION OF CYBERSECURITY REQUIREMENTS

Regulatory bodies may move towards establishing standardized cybersecurity requirements that organizations must meet to qualify for cyber insurance coverage. This could involve defining baseline security measures, incident response protocols, and risk management practices that insurers use to assess an organization's eligibility for coverage.

DATA BREACH NOTIFICATION STANDARDS

Anticipated regulations may establish uniform standards for data breach notifications. Insurers might be required to follow specific guidelines when notifying affected parties, and there could be increased transparency regarding the reporting of cyber incidents to regulatory authorities.

INSURER SOLVENCY AND CAPITAL ADEQUACY REQUIREMENT

As the demand for cyber insurance grows, regulatory bodies may introduce specific solvency and capital adequacy requirements for insurers offering cyber coverage. This ensures that insurers have sufficient financial reserves to cover potential large-scale cyber events without compromising their overall stability.

CLARIFICATION OF POLICY TERMS AND CONDITIONS

Regulators may play a role in clarifying and standardizing policy terms and conditions within cyber insurance contracts. This could include guidelines on language used in policies, transparency in coverage details, and ensuring that policyholders have a clear understanding of what is covered and what is excluded.

REGULATION OF CYBER INSURANCE PRICING

There may be increased scrutiny on the pricing of cyber insurance policies. Regulators might assess whether premiums accurately reflect an organization's risk profile and whether there is potential for discriminatory pricing practices. This could involve ensuring that pricing models are fair, transparent, and based on objective risk assessments.

ENHANCED CONSUMER PROTECTION MEASURES

Regulatory developments may focus on enhancing consumer protection within the cyber insurance sector. This could involve measures to ensure that policyholders are treated fairly during the claims process, have access to clear and understandable policy documents, and are informed about potential coverage limitations.

INTERNATIONAL COORDINATION AND COOPERATION

Given the global nature of cyber threats, there may be increased efforts towards international coordination and cooperation in cyber insurance regulation. This involves aligning regulatory frameworks across jurisdictions to facilitate the efficient functioning of the global cyber insurance market.

GUIDANCE ON RISK MITIGATION PRACTICES

Regulatory bodies may issue guidance on best practices for risk mitigation within cyber insurance. This could include recommendations on cybersecurity measures, incident response planning, and ongoing risk management strategies that organizations should adopt to qualify for favorable insurance terms.

OVERSIGHT OF THIRD-PARTY SERVICE PROVIDERS

With the reliance on third-party vendors for various cyber risk management services, regulators may introduce oversight measures to ensure that these service providers adhere to appropriate cybersecurity standards. This is particularly relevant for cybersecurity firms providing risk assessments and incident response services to insured organizations.

FOCUS ON EMERGING TECHNOLOGIES

As new technologies emerge, such as quantum computing and artificial intelligence, regulatory developments may address their implications for cyber insurance. This could involve guidance on assessing the impact of emerging technologies on cybersecurity risks and incorporating them into risk models.

The anticipated regulatory developments in the cyber insurance landscape reflect the growing recognition of the sector's importance in managing and mitigating cyber risks. These regulations aim to enhance transparency, fairness, and overall effectiveness in the cyber insurance market, fostering a resilient and well-regulated environment for organizations seeking protection against the evolving threat landscape. As organizations navigate the cyber seas of governance, risk, and compliance, staying informed about these regulatory developments will be crucial for effective risk management.

CHAPTER SEVEN

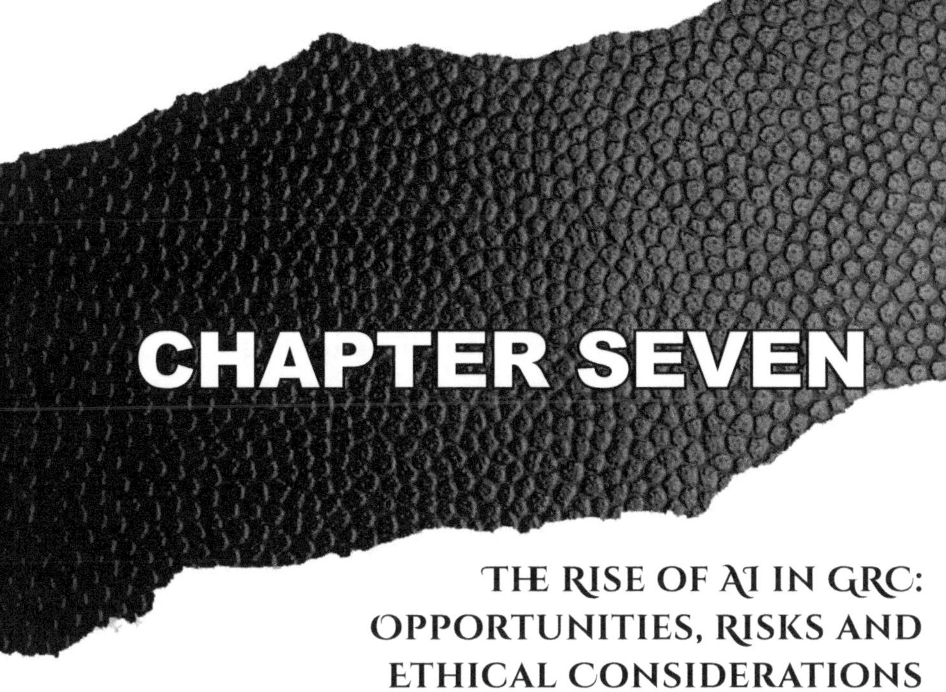

THE RISE OF AI IN GRC: OPPORTUNITIES, RISKS AND ETHICAL CONSIDERATIONS

The integration of Artificial Intelligence (AI) has become an unmistakable and transformative force across various business domains. Its unprecedented ability to analyze vast datasets, recognize patterns, and make data-driven predictions has led to significant advancements in sectors ranging from finance and healthcare to manufacturing and beyond. This surge in AI adoption is not merely a technological trend but a paradigm shift in how businesses operate, make decisions, and manage complex processes.

In the context of Governance, Risk, and Compliance (GRC), the influence of AI is particularly noteworthy. This chapter delves into the multifaceted role of AI within the GRC landscape, exploring its applications, opportunities, and challenges. AI brings a wealth of possibilities for organizations seeking to enhance their governance structures, fortify risk management strategies, and ensure compliance with an ever-expanding array of regulations.

AI's Role in Governance

Within the realm of governance, AI introduces a new era of efficiency and precision. Automated systems powered by AI can analyze governance frameworks, streamline decision-making processes, and facilitate more informed strategic planning. Boards and executives can harness the analytical capabilities of AI to gain deeper insights into organizational performance, anticipate potential governance issues, and optimize decision workflows.

AI's Impact on Risk Management

The utilization of AI in risk management is a game-changer. Traditional risk assessments are often constrained by manual processes and limited data analysis capabilities. AI, on the other hand, enables organizations to conduct more sophisticated risk analyses by processing vast datasets in real-time. This facilitates the identification of emerging risks, enhances risk prediction accuracy, and ultimately empowers organizations to proactively address potential challenges.

AI's Contribution to Compliance

In the ever-evolving landscape of compliance, where regulations are numerous, intricate, and subject to constant updates, AI emerges as a valuable ally. Automated compliance management systems driven by AI can efficiently monitor regulatory changes, interpret complex legal texts, and ensure that organizations adhere to compliance requirements. This not only reduces the risk of non-compliance but also enhances the adaptability of organizations in navigating the dynamic regulatory environment.

However, the integration of AI in GRC is not without its complexities. The chapter will critically examine the risks associated with AI adoption, including potential biases, security concerns, and the ethical implications of relying on algorithmic decision-making. It will also explore best practices for implementing AI in GRC, strategies for mitigating associated risks, and the ethical considerations that organizations must navigate to strike a balance between innovation and responsibility. Through a comprehensive exploration of AI's role in GRC, this chapter aims to equip organizations with the insights needed to harness the transformative power of AI while effectively managing its associated challenges.

Opportunities Presented by AI in GRC

Automating Routine GRC Tasks with AI for Improved Operational Efficiency

The fusion of AI into GRC is a union that has birthed many positive outcomes. The integration of Artificial Intelligence (AI) stands out as a revolutionary force, particularly in automating routine tasks. This application of AI brings forth a multitude of benefits, primarily focused on enhancing operational efficiency within organizations.

1. **Automating Risk Assessment:**

    AI-powered systems can automate the process of risk assessment by analyzing historical data, identifying patterns, and predicting potential risks. Routine risk evaluations, which traditionally consume significant time and resources, can be streamlined through AI algorithms, allowing organizations to allocate resources more strategically.

2. **Dynamic Policy Management:**

    AI enables organizations to automate the management of policies by continuously monitoring changes in regulations and updating internal policies accordingly. This ensures that policies are always up-to-date, reducing the risk of non-compliance and providing a more agile response to evolving regulatory landscapes.

3. **Incident Response Automation:**

   AI-driven tools can automate incident response processes by rapidly detecting and categorizing incidents based on predefined criteria. This not only accelerates the response time but also ensures consistency in handling incidents, reducing the likelihood of human error.

4. **Data Classification and Monitoring:**

   AI can automate the classification and monitoring of sensitive data, ensuring compliance with data protection regulations. By continuously scanning and categorizing data, organizations can minimize the risk of data breaches and improve overall data governance.

   5. Internal Control Testing:

   AI can streamline the testing of internal controls by automating the identification of control points and assessing their effectiveness. This reduces the reliance on manual testing processes, allowing auditors to focus on more complex tasks that require human judgment.

STREAMLINING COMPLIANCE PROCESSES WITH AI TO REDUCE MANUAL WORKLOADS

1. **Regulatory Change Management:**

   AI-powered tools can monitor and analyze regulatory changes, automatically updating compliance requirements. This reduces the manual effort required to track and interpret regulatory updates, ensuring that compliance programs remain current.

2. **Automated Compliance Audits:**

   AI can facilitate automated compliance audits by continuously assessing adherence to regulatory standards and internal policies. This not only expedites the audit process but also provides a more comprehensive and real-time view of an organization's compliance status.

3. **Contract Review and Management:**

   AI-driven contract management systems can review contracts for compliance with legal and regulatory requirements. This reduces the time and resources needed for manual contract reviews, allowing legal teams to focus on higher-value tasks.

4. **Anti-Money Laundering (AML) and Know Your Customer (KYC) Compliance:**

   AI applications can automate AML and KYC compliance processes by analyzing vast amounts of customer data.

   This improves the accuracy of customer due diligence and reduces the manual workload associated with compliance checks.

5. **Training and Awareness Programs:**

   AI can personalize and automate compliance training programs based on individual employee needs and risk profiles. This ensures that employees receive targeted training, reducing the time and effort required for generic training sessions.

Harnessing AI-Driven Analytics for Enhanced Risk Prediction and Decision-Making

Through advanced analytics, AI empowers organizations to move beyond traditional risk management practices, offering real-time insights and predictive capabilities that significantly elevate their ability to navigate complex risk landscapes.

1. **Data Analysis at Scale:**

   AI-driven analytics excels in processing vast datasets at unprecedented speeds, allowing organizations to analyze diverse sources of information simultaneously. This capability enables a more comprehensive understanding of risk factors, incorporating both structured and unstructured data.

2. **Pattern Recognition and Anomaly Detection:**

   AI excels at recognizing patterns and anomalies within data, providing a nuanced view of historical trends and deviations. By identifying unusual patterns, organizations can proactively detect potential risks that may go unnoticed in traditional risk analysis approaches.

3. **Predictive Modeling for Risk Identification:**

   Through predictive modeling, AI can identify emerging risks in real-time by analyzing historical data and extrapolating future trends. This allows organizations to move beyond reactive risk management and adopt a proactive stance, anticipating potential challenges before they materialize.

4. **Scenario Analysis and Sensitivity Testing:**

   AI-powered analytics facilitates sophisticated scenario analysis and sensitivity testing, allowing organizations to simulate the impact of various risk scenarios on their operations.

   This proactive approach enables decision-makers to assess the potential consequences of different risk events and formulate more resilient strategies.

5. **Dynamic Risk Profiling:**

   AI continuously updates risk profiles based on evolving data, ensuring that risk assessments remain current in the face of changing circumstances. This dynamic risk profiling enhances the agility of organizations in responding to emerging risks and adapting their risk management strategies accordingly.

6. Natural Language Processing (NLP) for Unstructured Data:

AI's proficiency in Natural Language Processing enables the analysis of unstructured data, such as news articles, social media, and industry reports. By extracting valuable insights from unstructured sources, organizations can enhance their understanding of external factors that may impact risk.

7. Machine Learning Algorithms for Risk Prediction:

Machine Learning algorithms within AI systems can learn from historical data patterns, enabling them to predict future risks based on evolving trends. This predictive capability enhances the accuracy of risk assessments, providing decision-makers with a data-driven foundation for strategic planning.

8. Real-Time Monitoring and Alerts:

AI-driven analytics allows for real-time monitoring of key risk indicators, triggering alerts when predefined thresholds are breached. This instantaneous feedback loop enables swift responses to emerging risks, minimizing potential negative impacts.

9. Continuous Learning and Adaptation:

AI systems, powered by continuous learning algorithms, adapt to changing risk landscapes by incorporating new data and refining predictive models. This adaptability ensures that risk predictions remain relevant and effective over time.

INHERENT RISKS OF HANDLING SENSITIVE GRC DATA WITH AI

The integration of Artificial Intelligence (AI) in Governance, Risk, and Compliance (GRC) processes brings about transformative advantages, but it also introduces inherent risks associated with the handling of sensitive data. Understanding and mitigating these risks are crucial to ensuring the ethical and secure deployment of AI in GRC.

1. Data Privacy Concerns: AI systems often require access to large datasets, including sensitive GRC information. The extensive use of such data raises concerns about privacy breaches and unauthorized access.

   Mitigation: Implement robust encryption and access controls, ensuring that only authorized personnel and AI algorithms can access sensitive data.

2. Algorithmic Bias: AI algorithms can inadvertently perpetuate biases present in historical data, leading to biased decision-making in GRC processes.

   Mitigation: Regularly audit and retrain AI models, employing techniques to identify and correct biases. Ensure transparency in AI decision-making to promote fairness.

3. Security of AI Models: Malicious actors may attempt to manipulate or compromise AI models to gain unauthorized access to sensitive GRC data.

   Mitigation: Implement robust security measures, conduct regular vulnerability assessments, and employ techniques like model encryption to safeguard AI models.

4. Data Quality and Integrity: AI models heavily rely on the quality and integrity of input data. Inaccurate or manipulated GRC data can lead to flawed predictions and decisions.

Mitigation: Implement data validation processes, regularly audit data sources, and establish mechanisms for detecting and correcting anomalies.

IMPACT OF AI ON DATA SECURITY AND PRIVACY COMPLIANCE

1. Enhanced Security Measures: AI can strengthen data security by automating threat detection, rapidly identifying and responding to security incidents.

   Consideration: Organizations must ensure that AI itself is secure, avoiding situations where AI becomes a vulnerability rather than an asset.

2. Privacy-Preserving Techniques: AI introduces privacy-preserving techniques, such as federated learning and homomorphic encryption, allowing data analysis without exposing raw data.

   Consideration: Organizations should assess the applicability of these techniques to their GRC processes and ensure compliance with privacy regulations.

3. Regulatory Compliance Challenges: The complexity of AI systems may pose challenges in ensuring compliance with data protection regulations, such as the General Data Protection Regulation (GDPR).

   Consideration: Organizations must conduct thorough assessments to align AI implementations with regulatory requirements, implementing measures like privacy impact assessments.

4. Data Subject Rights: AI's use in processing personal data may impact individuals' rights, such as the right to access, rectify, or erase their data.

   Consideration: Organizations must establish processes for handling data subject requests and ensure that AI systems are designed to respect and uphold these rights.

5. Transparency and Explainability: AI models may operate as "black boxes," making it challenging to explain their decisions. Lack of transparency can pose challenges in demonstrating compliance.

   Consideration: Emphasize the importance of transparency in AI decision-making. Choose AI models that provide explainability, especially in contexts where regulatory compliance requires it.

6. Cross-Border Data Flows: The use of AI may involve cross-border data transfers, potentially complicating compliance with data protection laws that restrict such transfers.

   Consideration: Organizations must be cognizant of data sovereignty and implement measures to comply with regulations governing cross-border data flows.

THE PERILS OF OVERDEPENDENCE ON AI IN GRC FUNCTIONS

The incorporation of Artificial Intelligence (AI) undoubtedly introduces efficiencies and advancements and definitely a few pitfalls as well. The allure of technological prowess comes with inherent risks when organizations lean too heavily on AI for their GRC functions.

Much like in anything else, over dependence on AI as a tool for elevating GRC functions can come at a cost. From loss of human expertise to the limitations inherent in AI itself, it is worth discussing a few of the disadvantages that professionals may face when the right balance is not found in the application of AI in the practice of GRC. Some downsides to over-application include

1. **Loss of Human Expertise:**

   Over Reliance on AI systems may usher in a disconcerting erosion of human expertise. The nuanced insights, intuition, and ethical considerations that human professionals bring to the table could find themselves relegated, potentially leading to incomplete risk assessments and strategic oversights.

2. **Algorithmic Limitations:**

    While AI excels in processing vast datasets, its prowess encounters limits in the face of complex, context-dependent risk scenarios. Relying exclusively on algorithmic analyses might result in oversights or inaccuracies, particularly in industries where a deep understanding of nuanced environments is paramount.

3. **Ethical and Cultural Blind Spots:**

    AI, being a product of algorithms and historical data, may falter in comprehending the intricacies of ethical and cultural considerations. The absence of a human touch could inadvertently pave the way for ethical lapses or cultural insensitivity in risk assessments, jeopardizing an organization's reputation.

4. **Overlooked Contextual Factors:**

    AI's struggle to interpret contextual nuances poses a substantial risk. Critical factors that require a human touch, such as industry-specific intricacies or region-specific compliance requirements, may be overlooked, resulting in suboptimal decision-making.

5. **Inflexibility in Unforeseen Scenarios:**

    AI systems, rooted in historical data, face challenges in adapting to unforeseen or unprecedented scenarios. In rapidly changing environments, an overdependence on AI might lead to an inability to respond effectively to emerging risks, leaving organizations exposed.

Preserving the Human Touch: The Importance of Human Oversight and Trust in AI-Driven Processes

Amid the rapid ascent of AI in GRC, the role of human oversight stands as a cornerstone for responsible and effective decision-making.

1. **Ethical Decision-Making:**

    Human oversight injects a crucial ethical dimension into AI-driven processes. While algorithms operate on data patterns, humans navigate the moral landscape, ensuring that AI aligns with an organization's ethical compass and societal norms.

2. **Contextual Understanding:**

    Human experts bring an unparalleled depth of contextual understanding to GRC functions. Their ability to interpret nuances, cultural intricacies, and industry-specific factors allows for a more holistic and accurate risk assessment, complementing the quantitative capabilities of AI.

3. **Adaptability to Change:**

    In the face of unforeseen risks and changing environments, human oversight provides a dynamic adaptability that AI systems may lack. The ability to dynamically respond to emerging risks ensures that GRC strategies remain agile and relevant.

4. **Trust Building:**

    Trust is the bedrock of effective GRC processes. Human oversight fosters trust by providing transparency, accountability, and the assurance that decisions are made with a comprehensive understanding of risks and compliance requirements.

5. **Mitigating Bias and Discrimination:**

   Humans play a crucial role in identifying and rectifying biases in AI algorithms. Through ongoing monitoring and intervention, they ensure that AI-driven decisions are fair, unbiased, and compliant with ethical standards, mitigating the risk of discriminatory outcomes.

6. **Complex Decision-Making:**

   Certain GRC decisions demand a level of complexity that extends beyond algorithmic capabilities. Human expertise shines in scenarios where legal, ethical, and business considerations converge in intricate ways, ensuring nuanced and well-balanced decisions.

7. **Stakeholder Engagement:**

   Effective communication with stakeholders is an art that requires the human touch. Humans can address concerns, explain decisions, and engage stakeholders in a way that builds trust and ensures a shared understanding of GRC processes.

ETHICAL IMPERATIVE OF TRANSPARENCY AND EXPLAINABILITY IN AI ALGORITHMS

The ethical underpinning of transparency and explainability is of significance, particularly in Governance, Risk, and Compliance (GRC) processes. Understanding how AI algorithms arrive at decisions is not just a technical necessity but a moral imperative that shapes trust, accountability, and the responsible deployment of these powerful technologies.

1. **Transparency as a Pillar of Trust:**

   Transparency acts as a cornerstone in building trust between organizations, stakeholders, and the AI-driven GRC systems they rely upon. When the inner workings of algorithms are laid bare, stakeholders gain insight into decision-making processes, fostering confidence in the fairness and reliability of AI-driven assessments.

2. **Explainability for Accountability:**

Explainability complements transparency by providing a comprehensible narrative of how AI arrives at specific decisions. This not only enhances accountability but also empowers stakeholders to contest or seek clarification on decisions that may have significant ramifications.

3. **Guarding Against Bias and Discrimination:**

Transparent and explainable AI algorithms serve as a bulwark against biases that may inadvertently seep into the decision-making process. By shedding light on the factors influencing decisions, organizations can proactively identify and rectify biases, mitigating the risk of discriminatory outcomes.

4. **Empowering Stakeholders:**

A transparent and explainable AI framework empowers stakeholders, including employees, customers, and regulatory bodies, with a deeper understanding of GRC decisions. This empowerment cultivates a culture of collaboration, where stakeholders can actively participate in refining AI models to align with ethical standards.

Ensuring Transparency in AI-Powered GRC Processes:

1. Algorithm Documentation: Organizations should comprehensively document the design, training data, and functionality of AI algorithms. This documentation should be accessible to relevant stakeholders, providing a clear roadmap of how the AI system operates.

2. Plain-Language Explanations: AI-driven decisions should be translated into plain-language explanations that non-experts can understand. This promotes transparency and ensures that stakeholders with varying degrees of technical expertise can grasp the reasoning behind GRC decisions.

3. Auditable Decision Trails: Implementing auditable decision trails allows organizations to trace back and scrutinize the decision-making process of AI algorithms. This auditability reinforces transparency, enabling stakeholders to verify the legitimacy of decisions and identify potential areas of improvement.

4. Stakeholder Engagement: Actively involve stakeholders in the development and validation of AI models. Soliciting feedback and insights from diverse perspectives enhances transparency, as it incorporates a broader understanding of ethical considerations into the AI framework.

5. Regular Audits and Assessments: Conduct regular audits and assessments of AI algorithms to ensure ongoing transparency. This involves evaluating the impact of AI decisions, identifying any biases, and making necessary adjustments to maintain ethical standards in GRC processes.

6. Ethical AI Guidelines: Establish clear ethical guidelines for the development and deployment of AI in GRC. These guidelines should emphasize the importance of transparency, fairness, and accountability, serving as a framework for ethical AI practices within the organization.

7. Regulatory Compliance: Stay abreast of relevant regulatory frameworks governing AI in GRC. Adhering to regulatory requirements not only ensures legal compliance but also underscores the organization's commitment to ethical and transparent AI practices.

There must be a maintained commitment to openness in technology to safeguard against unintended consequences, enhance accountability, and pave the way for the responsible integration of AI into the complex realm of Governance, Risk, and Compliance.

THE NECESSITY FOR ROBUST GOVERNANCE IN AI-ENHANCED GRC

As organizations across the globe move towards the integration of Artificial Intelligence (AI) into the GRC field of practice, it necessitates the establishment of robust governance structures to ensure checks and balances.

These structures are crucial not only for maximizing the benefits of AI but also for ensuring ethical, transparent, and accountable decision-making within the complex realms of GRC.

1. Ethical and Legal Compliance: Robust governance structures serve as the bedrock for ensuring that AI-enhanced GRC aligns with ethical principles and legal compliance. Establishing clear ethical guidelines within the governance framework helps organizations navigate the complex landscape of ethical considerations.

2. Risk Management: Governance structures provide a systematic approach to risk management. By outlining protocols for identifying, assessing, and mitigating risks associated with AI deployment in GRC, organizations can safeguard against unintended consequences and enhance decision-making resilience.

3. Transparency and Accountability: Transparency and accountability are integral components of ethical AI deployment. Governance structures define mechanisms for transparent decision-making processes, accountability frameworks, and avenues for stakeholders to seek explanations, contributing to a culture of trust.

4. Data Privacy and Security: In the age of AI, data privacy and security are paramount. Governance structures ensure that organizations implement robust measures to protect sensitive information, establishing guidelines for ethical data usage, storage, and disposal within the context of GRC.

5. Stakeholder Trust: Building and maintaining trust among stakeholders is a core function of governance structures. When organizations can demonstrate a commitment to ethical AI practices through transparent governance, stakeholders, including customers and regulatory bodies, are more likely to trust the GRC processes.

ESTABLISHING OVERSIGHT MECHANISMS AND ETHICAL GUIDELINES

1. Board-Level Oversight: Organizations should designate a governance body, possibly at the board level, responsible for overseeing AI implementation in GRC. This body ensures alignment with organizational values, regulatory compliance, and ethical standards.

2. Cross-Functional Collaboration: Foster collaboration between technical and non-technical teams. A cross-functional approach ensures that AI implementation considers both the technical aspects and the ethical, legal, and societal implications of GRC decisions.

3. Ethical Guidelines Development: Develop comprehensive ethical guidelines explicitly tailored to AI deployment in GRC. These guidelines should address issues such as bias mitigation, data privacy, transparency, and the responsible use of AI within the organization's unique GRC context.

4. Continuous Training and Education: Provide ongoing training and education for personnel involved in AI-driven GRC processes. This ensures that individuals are equipped to

navigate ethical considerations, understand the limitations of AI, and contribute to the responsible use of technology.

5. Auditable Decision Trails: Incorporate mechanisms for creating auditable decision trails. This allows organizations to trace back and scrutinize the decision-making process of AI algorithms, promoting transparency and accountability in GRC practices.

6. External Audits and Certification: Consider engaging external auditors or seeking certification for AI-driven GRC practices. External assessments add an additional layer of scrutiny and validation, demonstrating a commitment to ethical governance in the eyes of stakeholders and regulators.

7. Regulatory Compliance Monitoring: Stay abreast of evolving regulations related to AI in GRC. Governance structures should include mechanisms for monitoring regulatory changes, ensuring ongoing compliance and adapting ethical guidelines to evolving legal landscapes.

8. Stakeholder Engagement: Actively involve stakeholders in the development and validation of ethical guidelines. Soliciting feedback and engaging with stakeholders foster a collaborative approach to governance, incorporating diverse perspectives and building a foundation of trust.

These efforts must be consistent and emphasized because not only are they procedural necessities but they are also strategically beneficial to all concerned. When executed properly, organizations stand to reap the benefits long into the future.

Anticipated Advancements in AI Technology and Their Impact on GRC

The continuous evolution of Artificial Intelligence (AI) technology holds profound implications for Governance, Risk, and Compliance (GRC) practices. As AI advances, its impact on risk management and compliance is poised to reshape the landscape, introducing new capabilities and efficiencies.

ANTICIPATED ADVANCEMENTS

1. Advanced Predictive Analytics: Anticipated advancements in AI technology include more sophisticated predictive analytics. AI algorithms will evolve to better anticipate risks by analyzing vast datasets, enabling organizations to proactively identify and address potential compliance issues before they escalate.

2. Explainable AI Models: The drive towards more explainable AI models is expected to gain prominence. As AI becomes more integral to GRC decision-making, the ability to understand and interpret the rationale behind AI-driven decisions will become crucial for transparency and accountability.

3. Natural Language Processing (NLP) Enhancements: Improvements in Natural Language Processing will enable AI systems to better understand and interpret complex regulatory language. This advancement will enhance the extraction of insights from legal documents, facilitating more accurate compliance assessments and reducing the risk of misinterpretation.

4. AI-Enhanced Cybersecurity: AI's role in cybersecurity is expected to expand. Advanced AI algorithms will play a critical role in identifying and mitigating cyber risks, enhancing organizations' ability to safeguard sensitive data

and maintain compliance with evolving data protection regulations.

5. Automated Compliance Monitoring: Automation of compliance monitoring will reach new levels. AI technologies will continuously monitor regulatory changes, automatically updating compliance protocols and alerting organizations to potential non-compliance issues in real-time.

6. Ethical AI Governance: Anticipated advancements include the development of frameworks for ethical AI governance. As AI becomes more autonomous in decision-making, organizations will prioritize the establishment of ethical guidelines and governance structures to ensure responsible and fair AI use in GRC.

HOW AI WILL CONTINUE TO SHAPE THE FUTURE OF RISK MANAGEMENT AND COMPLIANCE

There are several instances where Artificial Intelligence is expected to impact risk management and compliance in the future based on prevalent trends. A few of them are;

1. **Enhanced Risk Prediction**

   AI's evolution will significantly enhance risk prediction capabilities. By analyzing historical data, market trends, and emerging patterns, AI algorithms will provide organizations with more accurate and timely predictions, enabling proactive risk management strategies.

2. **Dynamic Compliance Adaptability:**

   AI will enable organizations to dynamically adapt to changing compliance landscapes. AI algorithms will continuously monitor regulatory updates, assess their impact on existing compliance frameworks, and autonomously recommend adjustments to ensure ongoing adherence.

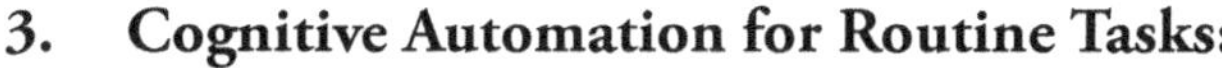

3. Cognitive Automation for Routine Tasks:

Routine GRC tasks will witness increased cognitive automation. AI will handle repetitive, rule-based tasks, allowing human professionals to focus on more complex and nuanced aspects of risk management and compliance, such as ethical considerations and strategic decision-making.

4. Integrated Risk and Performance Management:

AI's integration with performance management systems will become more seamless. This integration will enable organizations to view risk management and compliance not merely as regulatory obligations but as integral components of overall business performance.

5. Continuous Monitoring and Adaptive Controls:

Continuous monitoring capabilities will be augmented by AI-driven adaptive controls. AI systems will not only identify risks in real-time but also autonomously implement adaptive controls, offering a dynamic and responsive approach to risk management.

6. Human-AI Collaboration for Complex Decision-Making:

As AI evolves, the collaboration between humans and AI in complex decision-making will deepen. AI will assist human professionals in analyzing vast datasets, identifying patterns, and providing insights, fostering a symbiotic relationship that leverages the strengths of both.

7. Evolving Ethical Considerations:

The evolution of AI will necessitate ongoing considerations of ethical implications. Organizations will need to address questions of bias, transparency, and accountability in AI-driven decision-making, shaping ethical guidelines that evolve alongside technological advancements.

REGULATORY RESPONSES TO THE INTEGRATION OF AI IN GRC

Regulatory bodies worldwide are actively responding to the challenges and opportunities posed by the technological evolution birthing the permeation of Artificial Intelligent into Governance, Risk and Compliance. The responses encompass a spectrum of efforts, including the development of regulatory frameworks, guidelines, and standards aimed at ensuring responsible and ethical AI integration in the GRC domain.

REGULATORY RESPONSES

1. **Guidance Documents:**

   Regulatory bodies are issuing guidance documents to assist organizations in navigating the integration of AI into GRC. These documents provide insights into regulatory expectations, ethical considerations, and best practices for deploying AI responsibly in compliance and risk management.

2. **Risk-Based Approaches:**

   Some regulatory bodies are adopting risk-based approaches to AI in GRC. This involves assessing the potential risks associated with AI deployment, emphasizing the importance of robust risk management strategies, and encouraging organizations to align AI practices with existing compliance frameworks.

3. **Transparency Requirements:**

   Many regulatory bodies are emphasizing transparency as a key requirement for AI in GRC. Organizations are encouraged to disclose how AI algorithms operate, the data used for training, and the decision-making processes. This promotes accountability and enables stakeholders to understand and trust AI-driven GRC outcomes.

4. **Ethical Guidelines:**

    Regulatory bodies are increasingly integrating ethical considerations into AI governance. Guidelines address issues such as bias mitigation, fairness, and the responsible use of AI. These guidelines serve as a foundation for organizations to align their AI-driven GRC practices with societal and ethical norms.

POTENTIAL REGULATORY FRAMEWORKS AND STANDARDS

1. International Organization for Standardization (ISO): ISO is actively developing standards related to AI governance. ISO/IEC JTC 1/SC 42, the subcommittee on artificial intelligence, is working on standards that cover ethical considerations, explainability, and data privacy, providing a comprehensive framework for organizations implementing AI in GRC.

2. European Union: The EU is at the forefront of shaping AI regulations. The proposed AI Act aims to establish a harmonized regulatory framework, outlining requirements for high-risk AI systems. This includes GRC applications, emphasizing transparency, accountability, and risk management.

3. United States: In the U.S., regulatory initiatives focus on sector-specific approaches. Agencies like the Federal Trade Commission (FTC) are developing guidelines for AI applications, addressing issues such as algorithmic transparency and data privacy, which have implications for AI in GRC.

4. Singapore: Singapore has introduced guidelines through the Monetary Authority of Singapore (MAS) for the responsible adoption of AI and data analytics in the financial sector. These guidelines stress the importance of governance,

explainability, and ethical considerations in deploying AI for risk management and compliance.

5. United Kingdom: The UK's Information Commissioner's Office (ICO) provides guidance on the use of AI in data protection. The guidance emphasizes accountability, transparency, and fairness, considerations that are directly relevant to AI applications in GRC, particularly concerning data privacy.

6. Global Partnership on Artificial Intelligence (GPAI): The GPAI, an international initiative which focuses on fostering responsible AI innovation. Its work includes developing policies and standards to guide the development and deployment of AI, with an emphasis on aligning AI practices with human rights, inclusion, and ethical considerations in GRC.

KEY PRINCIPLES IN REGULATORY FRAMEWORKS

1. Transparency and Explainability: Regulatory frameworks emphasize the need for transparency in AI systems and the ability to explain AI-driven decisions, ensuring that organizations can articulate and stakeholders can comprehend the reasoning behind GRC outcomes.

2. Accountability and Governance: Regulatory bodies stress the importance of establishing robust governance structures, placing accountability on organizations to manage the risks associated with AI in GRC. This includes defining roles, responsibilities, and ethical considerations within the governance framework.

3. Risk Management: Risk-based approaches guide organizations in assessing and managing the risks introduced by AI applications in GRC. This involves identifying potential risks, implementing mitigation strategies, and

continuously monitoring the impact of AI on compliance and risk management.

ETHICAL CONSIDERATIONS

Ethical guidelines embedded in regulatory frameworks underscore the significance of ethical AI deployment. Organizations are encouraged to consider issues of bias, fairness, and societal impact when integrating AI into GRC processes.

DATA PRIVACY AND SECURITY:

Regulatory bodies stress the need for organizations to uphold data privacy and security standards when deploying AI in GRC. Compliance with existing data protection regulations is a fundamental aspect of responsible AI practices.

From all indications, regulatory responses to the integration of AI in GRC are diverse, reflecting a global effort to strike a balance between fostering innovation and safeguarding ethical and compliant use of AI. Organizations are encouraged to stay informed about evolving regulations, standards, and guidelines to ensure that their AI-driven GRC practices align with legal and ethical expectations in this rapidly evolving landscape.

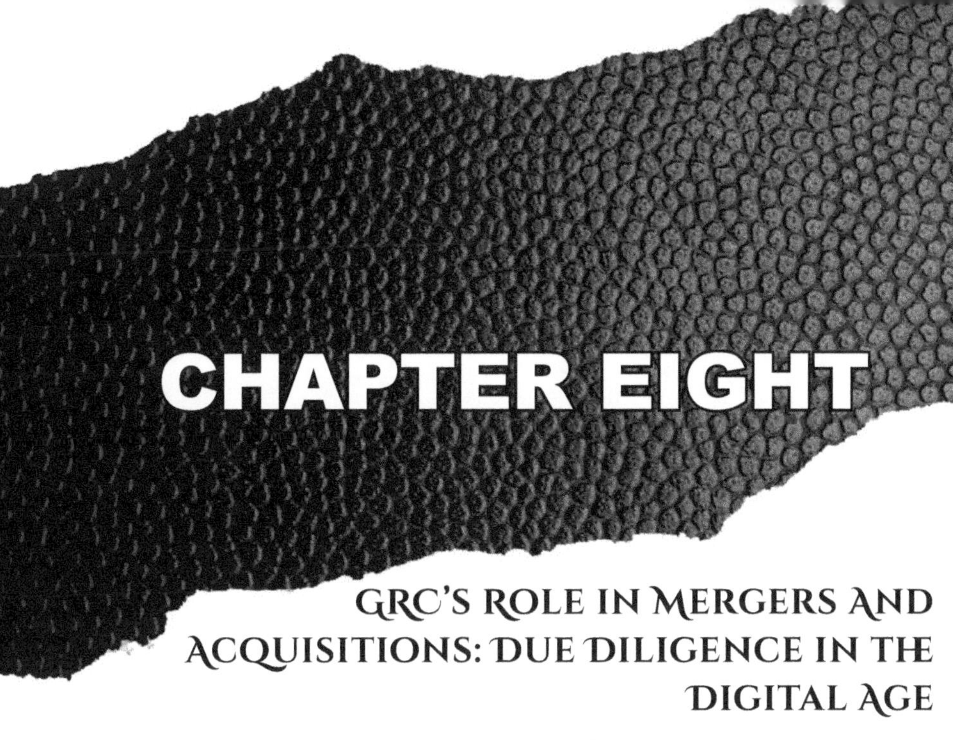

GRC'S ROLE IN MERGERS AND ACQUISITIONS: DUE DILIGENCE IN THE DIGITAL AGE

WHAT ARE MERGERS AND ACQUISITIONS?

Most organization aspire to a bold narrative of transformation and one of the surest ways to do this is through a merger and acquisition. Coincidentally, mergers are quite risky to delve into. Negotiating a merger is like orchestrating a symphony; the key is to harmonize different notes into a successful composition, but watch out for the occasional dissonance in the balance sheet

These strategic maneuvers unfold in various forms, each a distinctive brushstroke on the canvas of business evolution – from the intricate dance of mergers to the deliberate acquisitions, the strategic sell-offs in divestitures, and the collaborative ventures in joint ventures.

Mergers, at their essence, embody a coming together, where disparate entities decide to harmonize their operations, strengths, and corporate destinies. It's a symphony of shared objectives and synergies, seeking to create a corporate entity greater than the sum of its parts.

On the other hand, acquisitions cast a different narrative, where one company takes the lead, acquiring another with the aim of unlocking strategic assets, technologies, or market footholds. The acquired may either maintain its identity or find itself seamlessly integrated into the acquiring force. M&A deals vary in terms of the complexity and sophistication of the legal operation implemented to carry them out (LII 2021).

Then there are the strategic divestitures, a deliberate act of shedding corporate skin to focus on the core, to streamline operations, or perhaps to generate capital for future endeavors. And in the realm of collaboration, joint ventures emerge as strategic partnerships, allowing companies to join forces temporarily, sharing risks, resources, and opportunities without a full embrace.

Why embark on these strategic journeys? Market expansion is a common refrain, with companies seeking broader horizons either geographically or within specific industries. The allure of synergy beckons, promising increased efficiency, reduced costs, and an enhanced overall performance born from shared resources, technologies, or operational prowess.

Access to talent and innovation propels others forward, as companies look beyond their walls to secure specialized skills, intellectual capital, or groundbreaking technologies. Strategic realignment is a familiar motive, where businesses reshape their portfolios, shedding non-core assets or embracing ventures more aligned with their long-term aspirations.

Yet, for all the promises of M&A, challenges and risks lurk in the shadows. Integration, that elusive alchemy of combining corporate cultures, technologies, and operational processes, demands careful orchestration. Regulatory compliance, a stringent gatekeeper, ensures fair competition and safeguards consumers, requiring adept navigation of intricate regulatory landscapes.

Financial risks cast their shadows, with the perils of overpayment, unforeseen liabilities, and the hurdles in achieving projected synergies threatening the financial equilibrium of the combined entity. And then there's the delicate dance of managing expectations – of employees, customers, and stakeholders – a ballet of communication and transparency crucial for maintaining trust during the metamorphosis.

M&A is a narrative of transformation, written in the language of strategy, governance, and adaptability. It's a saga where corporate destinies entwine, where challenges and triumphs shape the course of industry landscapes. For companies bold enough to script their M&A narratives, success hinges on the ability to weave a story of effective integration, sound governance, and resilience in the face of challenges inherent in reshaping corporate identities and strategies.

EVOLUTION OF DUE DILIGENCE IN THE DIGITAL AGE AND THE SIGNIFICANCE OF GOVERNANCE, RISK, AND COMPLIANCE (GRC) IN M&A

Due diligence has undergone a profound evolution, transforming from a traditional checklist of financial and legal assessments to a dynamic, technology-driven process. As businesses navigate the complexities of mergers and acquisitions (M&A) in this digital landscape, the role of Governance, Risk, and Compliance (GRC) has become increasingly pivotal, acting as the compass that steers these strategic endeavors toward success.

EVOLUTION OF DUE DILIGENCE IN THE DIGITAL AGE

The digital age has ushered in an era of unprecedented access to information, analytics, and technological tools, fundamentally reshaping the due diligence landscape. Traditional due diligence, which primarily focused on financial statements and legal contracts, now extends its reach to the digital realm. Key elements of this evolution include:

TECHNOLOGICAL ASSESSMENTS

1. Digital Infrastructure: Due diligence now involves a meticulous examination of a company's digital infrastructure. This includes assessing the robustness of IT systems, cybersecurity measures, and the overall technological resilience of the organization.

2. Data Privacy Audits: With the rising importance of data, privacy assessments have become integral. Companies engaging in M&A now evaluate data protection measures, compliance with privacy regulations, and potential vulnerabilities in handling sensitive information.

AI AND DATA ANALYTICS:

1. Predictive Analytics: The integration of AI and data analytics has enabled predictive modeling in due diligence. Organizations can anticipate future risks and opportunities by analyzing vast datasets, providing a more forward-looking perspective.

2. Real-time Monitoring: AI-driven tools offer real-time monitoring capabilities, allowing for continuous assessment of operational performance, potential risks, and compliance issues during the due diligence process.

CYBERSECURITY AUDITS:

1. Comprehensive Cybersecurity Checks: Due diligence now includes comprehensive cybersecurity audits. This involves evaluating a company's resilience to cyber threats, assessing the effectiveness of security protocols, and identifying potential vulnerabilities.

DIGITAL FOOTPRINT ANALYSIS:

1. Online Reputation and Presence: Companies scrutinize the digital footprint of potential M&A targets, assessing their online reputation, customer reviews, and social media presence. This analysis provides insights into brand perception and potential risks.

2. 2. Significance of Governance, Risk, and Compliance (GRC) in M&A: GRC plays a central and multifaceted role in the success of M&A transactions in the digital age. Its significance extends across various dimensions:

CULTURAL ALIGNMENT

GRC frameworks facilitate an assessment of corporate culture, ensuring that the values and ethical considerations of both entities align. M&A success hinges on cultural harmony, and GRC provides the tools to navigate these intangible but crucial aspects.

1. Ethical Considerations: In an era where ethical considerations are paramount, GRC ensures that M&A activities adhere to ethical standards. This includes evaluating the ethical implications of business practices, ensuring transparency, and maintaining integrity throughout the transaction.

2. Risk Management: GRC frameworks are instrumental in identifying, assessing, and mitigating risks associated with M&A. This includes financial risks, cybersecurity threats, regulatory compliance risks, and other potential pitfalls that could impact the success of the transaction.

3. Regulatory Compliance: The digital age brings forth an intricate web of regulatory requirements. GRC ensures that M&A activities comply with these regulations, reducing the risk of legal complications and financial penalties.

4. Data Security and Privacy Compliance: With data becoming a cornerstone of business operations, GRC ensures that M&A activities adhere to data security and privacy regulations. This is critical in safeguarding sensitive information and maintaining the trust of stakeholders.

5. Adaptability to Change: GRC frameworks enable organizations to adapt to the dynamic changes triggered by M&A. Whether it's changes in regulatory landscapes or shifts in risk profiles, GRC provides the adaptability needed to navigate the evolving business environment.

IMPACT OF DIGITAL TRANSFORMATION ON BUSINESS PROCESSES

Digital transformation has reshaped the way organizations carry out their activities today from how they operate to how they interact, and deliver value. The impact spans across various dimensions, fundamentally altering traditional business processes. Here's a comprehensive exploration of how digital transformation has left an indelible mark on these critical aspects:

1. **Operational Efficiency:**

   Automation: Digital transformation introduces automation to mundane and rule-based tasks, freeing up human resources to focus on more complex, strategic activities. This leads to streamlined processes, reduced errors, and increased overall operational efficiency.

   Data-Driven Decision-Making: Businesses harness the power of data analytics to inform decision-making processes. Real-time insights derived from data contribute to informed, agile decision-making, optimizing operational processes.

2. **Customer Experience:**

   Personalization: Digital transformation enables businesses to tailor products and services to individual customer preferences. Through data analytics and AI, organizations create personalized customer experiences, fostering loyalty and satisfaction.

   Multi-Channel Engagement: Organizations leverage digital channels to engage with customers across multiple touchpoints. From social media to mobile apps, businesses connect with their audience in diverse ways, enhancing the overall customer experience.

3. **Supply Chain Management:**

   Visibility and Transparency: Digital tools provide end-to-end visibility into supply chain processes. This transparency helps in tracking products, optimizing inventory management, and mitigating risks associated with disruptions.

   IoT Integration: Internet of Things (IoT) devices enhance supply chain efficiency by providing real-time data on the movement and condition of goods. This data is invaluable for making proactive decisions and reducing inefficiencies.

4. **Collaboration and Communication:**

   Digital Collaboration Tools: The advent of collaboration tools, cloud-based platforms, and project management software has transformed how teams collaborate. Remote work, real-time collaboration, and virtual meetings are now integral to modern business processes.

   Unified Communication: Integrated communication platforms streamline interactions within and outside organizations. From emails to instant messaging, businesses adopt unified communication tools for seamless and efficient communication.

5. **Innovation and Product Development:**

   Rapid Prototyping: Digital technologies facilitate rapid prototyping and iterative product development. This accelerates the innovation cycle, allowing businesses to bring new products and services to market faster.

   AI in Research and Development: Artificial Intelligence is employed in research and development processes, aiding in data analysis, pattern recognition, and predictive modeling. This contributes to more informed decision-making in the innovation phase.

6. **Human Resources and Talent Management:**

   Digital Recruitment: Businesses utilize digital platforms for recruitment, leveraging social media and online job portals. AI-driven tools assist in candidate screening, making the hiring process more efficient.

   Employee Experience: Digital transformation focuses on enhancing the employee experience through HR technologies. From onboarding processes to performance management, digital tools contribute to a more engaging and productive work environment.

7. **Data Security and Compliance:**

   Cybersecurity Measures: As businesses digitize processes, the importance of cybersecurity becomes paramount. Digital transformation initiatives include robust cybersecurity measures to safeguard sensitive data and ensure compliance with regulations.

   Blockchain for Transparency: In industries where transparency is critical, such as finance and supply chain, blockchain technology is employed to secure and authenticate transactions, enhancing data integrity and compliance.

8. **Marketing and Sales:**

Digital Marketing Strategies: Traditional marketing has evolved into a digital realm. Social media, content marketing, and data analytics are integral to modern marketing strategies, allowing businesses to target audiences with precision.

E-Commerce and Online Sales: The rise of e-commerce platforms has transformed how products and services are bought and sold. Businesses leverage online channels for sales, reaching global markets with ease.

9. **Regulatory Compliance:**

Digital Compliance Management: Digital tools assist organizations in navigating complex regulatory landscapes. Compliance management systems ensure that business processes adhere to industry-specific regulations, minimizing the risk of legal issues.

10. **Agile and Adaptive Strategies:**

Digital Platforms for Strategy Execution: Businesses adopt digital platforms for strategic planning and execution. This facilitates agile methodologies, allowing organizations to adapt quickly to changing market conditions and consumer demands.

Continuous Improvement: Digital transformation encourages a culture of continuous improvement. Through data analytics and feedback mechanisms, businesses can identify areas for enhancement and refine processes iteratively.

TECHNOLOGICAL CONSIDERATIONS IN M&A DUE DILIGENCE

In mergers and acquisitions, we often assume that only the buyer should be performing due diligence. However, the company being acquired also must do their own due diligence. In this instance, technology due diligence.

Also known as Technical due diligence, this is the analysis of the technology products, architecture, and processes of an organization. It is one of the most important types of due diligence in M&A. This aspect of due diligence allows the acquiring company to evaluate IT structures and identify any potential security risks.

A typical M&A technical often involves the following:

1. **Assessment of Digital Infrastructure:**

   Hardware and Software Evaluation: A meticulous examination of the target company's hardware and software infrastructure is essential. This includes assessing the condition, capacity, and compatibility of servers, computers, and other technology assets.

   Network Architecture: Understanding the target's network architecture is crucial. This involves evaluating the scalability, security, and efficiency of the existing network infrastructure to ensure it aligns with the acquiring company's needs.

2. **Cybersecurity and Data Privacy Audits:**

   Cybersecurity Measures: Evaluating the cybersecurity posture of the target company is paramount. This includes assessing the effectiveness of firewalls, encryption protocols, and intrusion detection systems to identify potential vulnerabilities.

   Data Privacy Compliance: Due diligence must delve into the target's data privacy practices. This includes an examination of data handling procedures, compliance with regulations such as GDPR or HIPAA, and measures taken to protect sensitive information.

3. **Integration of IT Systems:**

Compatibility Assessment: In cases where integration of IT systems is planned post-acquisition, compatibility assessments are crucial. This involves evaluating the compatibility of software, databases, and other IT systems to ensure a smooth integration process.

Data Migration Strategies: Understanding how data will be migrated between systems is vital. Assessing the feasibility, risks, and potential challenges associated with data migration ensures a seamless transition without loss or compromise of critical information.

4. **Digital Transformation Readiness:**

Technological Alignment with Strategy: Due diligence includes an examination of how well the target company's technological capabilities align with its strategic objectives. This assessment helps in determining the readiness for digital transformation.

Innovation and R&D Capabilities: Understanding the target's approach to innovation and research and development (R&D) provides insights into its technological adaptability. This is crucial for anticipating future technological trends and staying competitive.

5. **Software and Licensing Audits:**

Software Asset Management: A thorough audit of software assets is essential to ensure compliance with licensing agreements. Non-compliance can lead to legal and financial repercussions post-acquisition.

Open Source Software Usage: Identifying the usage of open-source software is critical. Understanding how such software is utilized, and ensuring compliance with associated licenses, mitigates risks associated with open-source code.

6. **Digital Resilience and Disaster Recovery:**

Resilience Planning: Evaluating the target's resilience to digital disruptions is vital. This includes assessing the existence and effectiveness of disaster recovery plans, business continuity strategies, and measures taken to mitigate the impact of cyber threats.

Incident Response Protocols: Understanding how the target responds to cybersecurity incidents is crucial. This involves evaluating the incident response protocols, communication strategies, and the overall cybersecurity resilience posture.

7. **Regulatory Compliance in Technology:**

Technology-Specific Regulations: Depending on the industry, there may be specific technology-related regulations. Due diligence must ensure that the target is compliant with such regulations to avoid legal complications post-acquisition.

Intellectual Property Rights: Assessing the target's intellectual property portfolio and ensuring compliance with intellectual property laws is crucial. This includes software patents, trademarks, and other technology-related intellectual assets.

8. **Digital Talent and Skill Set Analysis:**

Assessment of IT Workforce: Evaluating the capabilities of the target company's IT workforce is essential. This includes assessing the skill sets, expertise, and experience of IT professionals who will play a key role in the technological transition.

Leadership in Technology Roles: Understanding the leadership in technology-related roles provides insights into the strategic direction and vision of the target company in the digital realm.

9. Vendor and Third-Party Technology Dependencies:

Vendor Contracts and Relationships: Due diligence must explore the target's relationships with technology vendors and third-party service providers. This includes an assessment of existing contracts, service level agreements, and potential dependencies.

Risk Mitigation Strategies: Identifying risks associated with technology dependencies is crucial. This involves understanding how the target manages and mitigates risks related to third-party technology solutions.

10. Technology Lifecycle Management:

Assessment of Technology Assets: A thorough examination of the target's technology assets throughout their lifecycle is crucial. This includes understanding the depreciation schedule, upgrade plans, and the overall health of technology assets.

Legacy System Considerations: Assessing the presence of legacy systems and their impact on the target's technological landscape is essential. Understanding the plans for modernization or replacement of legacy systems is crucial for long-term strategic planning.

Importance of Robust Governance Structures in M&A

The foundation of robust governance structures is akin to a well-crafted choreography. Governance serves as the guiding force that ensures transparency, accountability, and strategic alignment throughout the M&A process. Here's an exploration of why robust governance structures are of paramount importance:

1. **Alignment with Strategic Objectives:**

   Clear Direction: Robust governance structures provide a clear direction for M&A activities aligned with the overall strategic objectives of the organization. This ensures that each step in the M&A process contributes to the long-term vision and goals.

   Stakeholder Expectations: Governance frameworks consider the expectations of various stakeholders, including shareholders, employees, and customers. This alignment fosters confidence and trust during the M&A journey.

2. **Risk Mitigation and Compliance:**

   Identification of Risks: Governance structures facilitate the identification and assessment of risks associated with M&A. This includes financial risks, regulatory compliance risks, and operational risks, allowing for proactive mitigation strategies.

   Adherence to Regulations: M&A governance ensures compliance with regulatory frameworks. Adhering to legal requirements not only avoids legal complications post-transaction but also enhances the reputation and credibility of the involved entities.

3. **Transparent Decision-Making:**

Board Accountability: Governance structures define roles and responsibilities, ensuring that decision-makers, particularly the board, are held accountable for their actions. Transparent decision-making processes foster trust among stakeholders.

Communication Protocols: A well-defined governance framework establishes communication protocols, ensuring that key decisions are communicated effectively to internal and external stakeholders. This transparency minimizes uncertainty and speculation.

4. **Cultural Alignment and Integration:**

Assessment of Corporate Culture: Robust governance includes mechanisms for assessing the corporate culture of both the acquiring and target companies. This assessment is crucial for anticipating potential challenges in cultural alignment and integration.

Leadership in Cultural Integration: Governance structures guide leadership in facilitating cultural integration. This involves creating a shared vision, fostering open communication, and addressing cultural differences that may arise during the M&A process.

5. **Financial Prudence:**

Financial Due Diligence: Governance frameworks emphasize the importance of thorough financial due diligence. This includes evaluating the financial health of both entities, assessing liabilities, and ensuring that the transaction is financially sound.

Post-Merger Financial Management: Governance structures extend beyond the pre-transaction phase, guiding post-merger financial management. This involves monitoring financial performance, implementing cost synergies, and optimizing resources.

6. **Ethical Considerations:**

   Ethical Decision-Making: Governance structures embed ethical considerations into decision-making processes. This is particularly important in M&A, where ethical practices ensure fair treatment of employees, customers, and other stakeholders.

   Compliance with Ethical Standards: Governance frameworks guide the assessment of ethical practices in both the acquiring and target companies. This includes evaluating corporate social responsibility initiatives and ethical behavior within the business ecosystem.

ROLE OF BOARDS AND LEADERSHIP IN M&A GOVERNANCE:

The boards and leadership teams play a central role in shaping and implementing governance structures during M&A. Their involvement is instrumental in steering the M&A ship toward success:

1. **Strategic Oversight:**

   Strategic Decision-Making: Boards provide strategic oversight, guiding decision-making processes related to M&A. Leadership teams, in turn, execute these strategies, ensuring that each step aligns with the overarching goals.

   Long-Term Vision: Boards contribute to the development of a long-term vision for the merged entity. This involves setting clear objectives, defining success criteria, and ensuring that the M&A activities contribute to sustained value creation.

2. Risk Management:

Risk Oversight: Boards are responsible for overseeing the identification and management of risks associated with M&A. They work closely with leadership teams to implement risk mitigation strategies and ensure that risk profiles align with organizational tolerance.

Due Diligence Leadership: Leadership teams, under the guidance of boards, lead the due diligence process. This includes comprehensive assessments of financial, operational, and cultural risks associated with the M&A activities.

3. Stakeholder Communication:

Transparent Communication: Boards are instrumental in establishing transparent communication channels with stakeholders. This includes shareholders, employees, customers, and regulatory bodies. Leadership teams execute communication strategies to maintain transparency.

Managing Expectations: Leadership plays a key role in managing stakeholder expectations. Clear and timely communication about the M&A process, its impact, and the anticipated benefits helps build trust among stakeholders.

4. Ethical Leadership:

Setting Ethical Standards: Boards set the ethical standards for M&A activities. Leadership teams are responsible for embodying these standards, fostering an ethical culture, and ensuring that ethical considerations are embedded in decision-making processes.

Addressing Ethical Concerns: If ethical concerns arise during the M&A process, leadership teams, guided by the board, take prompt and decisive actions to address and rectify issues, demonstrating a commitment to ethical behavior.

5. **Post-Merger Integration:**

Integration Planning: Boards play a pivotal role in shaping integration strategies. Leadership teams are tasked with developing detailed integration plans, ensuring that the post-merger phase is executed smoothly and that synergies are realized.

Cultural Leadership: Leadership teams lead the way in cultural integration. Boards provide guidance on aligning organizational cultures, and leadership teams actively foster a collaborative and inclusive culture within the merged entity.

6. **Financial Stewardship:**

Financial Oversight: Boards exercise financial stewardship, ensuring that M&A activities align with financial goals. Leadership teams implement financial strategies, monitor performance, and make data-driven decisions to optimize financial outcomes.

Cost Synergy Implementation: Leadership teams, under the guidance of boards, implement cost synergies outlined in the M&A strategy. This involves aligning financial resources, optimizing operational efficiency, and maximizing value for stakeholders.

7. **Continuous Evaluation and Adaptation:**

Performance Evaluation: Boards play a role in evaluating the performance of M&A activities. Leadership teams conduct regular assessments, seeking feedback, and adapting strategies to address challenges and capitalize on opportunities.

Agile Decision-Making: Leadership teams are tasked with agile decision-making. Boards support this agility by providing a framework that allows for flexibility in adapting to changing market conditions, unforeseen challenges, or shifts in strategic priorities.

Aligning Corporate Cultures in M&A

Picture two distinct organizational frameworks, each with its unique set of values, norms, and practices. The challenge lies in navigating the convergence of these distinct cultures into a cohesive and integrated whole.

Before the M&A process begins, leadership undertakes a comprehensive analysis of the existing organizational cultures. This involves understanding the prevailing values, communication styles, and work approaches of both entities. The objective is not to eliminate differences but to find a common ground that can form the basis of a shared organizational culture.

As the M&A progresses, leadership becomes responsible for orchestrating the alignment of corporate cultures. This entails identifying areas of commonality and potential divergence. Clear and transparent communication becomes the tool for conveying the vision of a unified culture. Open dialogue facilitates understanding and collaboration, enabling employees to contribute to the evolving cultural landscape.

Employee engagement becomes a pivotal aspect of this alignment process. Leadership encourages the active participation of employees in shaping the integrated culture. The goal is to create a collective identity that reflects the strengths of both organizations, fostering a sense of belonging and shared purpose.

The process of aligning corporate cultures is ongoing. Leadership continually monitors and adjusts the integration efforts, ensuring that the cultural convergence remains in harmony with the strategic goals of the organization. The aim is not uniformity but a synthesis that respects the unique contributions of each organizational culture.

ADDRESSING ETHICAL CONSIDERATIONS

In tandem with cultural alignment, addressing ethical considerations is a crucial aspect of the M&A journey. Leadership takes on the responsibility of establishing ethical standards that will govern the conduct of the merged entity. This involves setting a framework that prioritizes integrity, transparency, and accountability.

Ethical due diligence becomes a meticulous examination of the ethical practices within both organizations. The focus is on identifying potential ethical risks and areas that may require improvement. Transparency in communication is key, with leaders openly addressing ethical expectations, challenges, and the steps taken to mitigate them.

When ethical concerns arise, leadership responds promptly and decisively. Ethical considerations are not treated as isolated incidents but as integral components of the overall business conduct. Investigations are conducted, corrective measures are implemented, and a commitment to upholding ethical standards is communicated to all stakeholders.

Leadership actively embeds ethical values into the evolving organizational culture. The goal is to create an environment where ethical behavior is not just encouraged but becomes an inherent part of the organizational DNA. This involves incorporating ethical considerations into decision-making processes and fostering a culture of integrity at every level.

In the pragmatic landscape of M&A, aligning corporate cultures and addressing ethical considerations are essential components for building a cohesive and sustainable merged entity. Leadership's role is that of a facilitator, ensuring that these processes are approached with transparency, sensitivity, and a commitment to long-term ethical business practices.

Identifying And Evaluating Risks in M&A

The ability to identify and evaluate risks is a critical skill that can make the difference between a successful integration and potential pitfalls. This process involves a thorough examination of various facets, from financial considerations to operational intricacies, aiming to anticipate challenges and develop mitigation strategies. Here's a practical exploration of the steps involved:

1. **Financial Risks:**

    Due Diligence: The cornerstone of risk identification in M&A is financial due diligence. This involves a meticulous examination of the financial health of both the acquiring and target companies. It includes scrutinizing financial statements, assessing liabilities, and uncovering potential hidden risks.

    Valuation Risks: Valuation risks must be carefully assessed. Fluctuations in market conditions, unexpected liabilities, or overestimated synergies can impact the overall financial health post-transaction. A realistic valuation ensures a more accurate understanding of the financial landscape.

2. **Operational Risks:**

    Cultural Alignment: M&A involves the integration of not just operations but also cultures. The risk of cultural misalignment can significantly impact employee morale and productivity. Identifying cultural nuances early allows for strategic planning to bridge potential gaps.

    Technology Integration: Merging different technological infrastructures can pose operational challenges. Risks associated with data migration, system integration, and potential disruptions to daily operations need to be thoroughly evaluated and addressed.

3. **Regulatory and Compliance Risks:**

Legal Due Diligence: Understanding the legal landscape is crucial. This includes compliance with industry regulations, environmental standards, and any potential legal disputes. Legal due diligence unveils hidden legal risks that might affect the smooth transition of the M&A.

Regulatory Changes: Anticipating changes in regulations, especially in industries prone to frequent updates, is essential. This proactive approach allows for adjustments to business strategies and operations to remain compliant with evolving regulatory frameworks.

4. **Human Capital Risks:**

Employee Retention: Losing key talent during an M&A can impact the continuity and success of the integrated entity. Identifying key personnel and implementing retention strategies helps mitigate the risk of talent drain.

Communication Breakdown: Poor communication can lead to uncertainty and anxiety among employees. Risks associated with communication breakdowns, such as misinformation or lack of transparency, need to be addressed to maintain employee morale and confidence.

5. **Market and Competitive Risks:**

Market Dynamics: External factors such as changes in market trends, consumer behavior, or economic conditions can pose risks. Conducting a thorough market analysis helps identify potential challenges and opportunities in the post-merger market landscape.

Competitive Landscape: Assessing the competitive environment is vital. Understanding how the merged entity will position itself in the market, potential reactions from competitors, and any shifts in market dynamics is essential for strategic planning.

6. **Integration Risks:**

Post-Merger Integration Planning: The process of integrating operations, technologies, and cultures carries inherent risks. Developing a comprehensive integration plan that anticipates potential roadblocks and includes contingency measures is crucial for a smooth transition.

Timeline Risks: Delays in the integration process can incur additional costs and disrupt operations. Identifying potential bottlenecks and establishing realistic timelines helps manage the risk of prolonged integration periods.

7. **Financial Market Risks:**

Economic Fluctuations: The broader economic landscape can impact the success of an M&A. Economic downturns, currency fluctuations, or interest rate changes can affect the financial stability of the merged entity. Considering these external factors is vital in risk evaluation.

Financing Risks: If the M&A involves significant financing, risks associated with interest rates, debt covenants, and credit ratings must be carefully evaluated. Assessing the financial market conditions ensures a realistic understanding of the financing risks involved.

8. **Reputation Risks:**

Brand Perception: M&A activities can influence how the merged entity is perceived in the market. Risks associated with changes in brand perception, customer loyalty, and stakeholder trust need to be actively managed through strategic communication and brand management.

Ethical Considerations: Unethical practices or perceived ethical lapses during M&A can damage the reputation of the integrated entity. Identifying potential ethical risks and establishing a strong ethical framework is vital for long-term reputation management.

Cybersecurity Risks and Data Breach in M&A

As organizations integrate their operations and IT infrastructures, the potential vulnerabilities and threats to sensitive information multiply. Understanding and mitigating these risks is crucial for safeguarding not only the organizations involved but also the trust of stakeholders and the integrity of the merged entity.

1. **Data Sensitivity and Privacy Risks:**

   Data Inventory: Conducting a comprehensive inventory of sensitive data is the first step. Identifying what data is collected, processed, and stored allows organizations to understand the potential impact of a data breach on both parties involved in the M&A.

   Compliance Assessment: Assessing compliance with data protection regulations, such as GDPR or HIPAA, is essential. Differences in compliance levels between the merging entities can lead to regulatory complications and financial penalties.

2. **Third-Party and Supply Chain Risks:**

   Vendor Security Assessment: If either party relies on third-party vendors, assessing the cybersecurity measures of these vendors is crucial. Weak links in the supply chain can expose the merged entity to additional cybersecurity risks.

   Contractual Obligations: Reviewing existing contracts and agreements with third parties to ensure they align with cybersecurity standards is important. Clearly defining each party's responsibilities in terms of data protection helps establish a robust framework.

3. **Technology Integration Challenges:**

   System Compatibility: Merging different IT infrastructures may pose challenges in terms of system compatibility. Ensuring that all systems are updated, secure, and compatible is vital to prevent vulnerabilities that could be exploited by cyber threats.

Incident Response Planning: Developing a unified incident response plan that accounts for the merged entity's technology landscape is crucial. This plan should outline the steps to be taken in the event of a cybersecurity incident, minimizing potential damage.

4. Employee Training and Insider Threats:

Security Awareness Programs: Both parties should invest in ongoing cybersecurity training for employees. Human error remains a significant factor in data breaches, and educating employees on best practices enhances the overall security posture.

Insider Threat Detection: Implementing monitoring systems to detect unusual activities or behavior among employees helps mitigate insider threats. This includes unauthorized access to sensitive information or attempts to compromise cybersecurity measures.

5. Due Diligence in Cybersecurity:

Cybersecurity Due Diligence: Integrating cybersecurity due diligence into the overall due diligence process is essential. This involves assessing the historical security performance of both organizations, identifying past incidents, and understanding how they were addressed.

Risk Assessment: Conducting a comprehensive risk assessment specific to cybersecurity helps identify potential vulnerabilities and threats. This assessment should be part of the broader risk evaluation during the M&A process.

6. **Post-Merger Security Planning:**

Unified Security Policy: Developing a unified cybersecurity policy for the merged entity is crucial. This policy should outline security measures, acceptable use of technology, and incident response protocols that align with the organization's overall risk appetite.

Integration of Security Teams: Integrating cybersecurity teams from both organizations ensures a cohesive approach to managing and mitigating cybersecurity risks. Collaboration between security professionals facilitates a unified response to potential threats.

7. **Legal and Regulatory Implications:**

Notification Obligations: Understanding the legal and regulatory obligations in the event of a data breach is critical. Clear communication and timely reporting to regulatory authorities and affected individuals can mitigate legal repercussions.

Contractual Protections: Including cybersecurity clauses in M&A agreements can provide legal protections. Clearly defining responsibilities related to cybersecurity and data protection in contractual agreements sets expectations for both parties.

8. **Continuous Monitoring and Adaptation:**

Threat Intelligence: Incorporating threat intelligence into the cybersecurity strategy allows organizations to stay abreast of emerging threats. Continuous monitoring of the threat landscape enables a proactive approach to cybersecurity.

Adaptive Security Measures: Recognizing that cybersecurity is an ever-evolving field, the merged entity should adopt adaptive security measures. This includes regularly updating security protocols, investing in advanced cybersecurity technologies, and staying informed about industry best practices.

ENSURING COMPLIANCE WITH REGULATORY STANDARDS IN M&A TRANSACTIONS

The complexity of regulatory environments requires a meticulous approach to avoid legal complications, financial penalties, and reputational damage. Here's an exploration of key considerations:

1. Regulatory Due Diligence: Conduct a thorough regulatory due diligence process to identify and understand the regulatory landscape applicable to both the acquiring and target companies. Assess compliance with industry-specific regulations and standards, ensuring a comprehensive understanding of the regulatory obligations and potential risks involved.

2. Compliance Integration Planning: Develop a detailed integration plan that specifically addresses the compliance aspects of the M&A. This plan should outline how the merged entity will harmonize its operations to meet regulatory requirements seamlessly.

    Assign responsibilities for compliance oversight within the integrated organization to ensure accountability in meeting regulatory standards.

3. Post-Merger Regulatory Reporting: Establish a clear protocol for regulatory reporting in the post-merger phase. This includes timely and accurate reporting to regulatory authorities, ensuring transparency and adherence to compliance obligations. Implement systems and processes to monitor ongoing compliance and generate reports as required by regulatory standards.

Industry-Specific Compliance Considerations in M&A

Each industry comes with its unique set of compliance considerations, and M&A transactions within specific sectors require a tailored approach to navigate these complexities. Here's a closer look at industry-specific compliance considerations:

1. **Healthcare Industry:**

   Address compliance with healthcare regulations, such as the Health Insurance Portability and Accountability Act (HIPAA). Ensure that patient data protection measures are in place, and assess the compliance history of both entities in handling sensitive health information.

2. **Financial Services Industry:**

   Navigate the complex regulatory landscape of financial services, including compliance with the Sarbanes-Oxley Act (SOX) and the Dodd-Frank Wall Street Reform and Consumer Protection Act. Evaluate the financial stability of both parties to ensure compliance with regulatory capital requirements.

3. **Technology and Data-Driven Industries:**

   Assess compliance with data protection regulations, such as the General Data Protection Regulation (GDPR). Address cybersecurity considerations, ensuring that both entities have robust measures in place to protect sensitive data.

Assessing Legal and Ethical Compliance in M&A Transactions:

In addition to regulatory standards, legal and ethical compliance considerations play a pivotal role in M&A transactions. A failure to uphold legal and ethical standards can lead to legal challenges, damage to reputation, and erosion of stakeholder trust. Here's how to approach these aspects:

1. **Legal Due Diligence:**

    Conduct thorough legal due diligence to identify any ongoing legal proceedings, potential liabilities, or unresolved legal issues within the acquiring and target companies.

    Assess contractual obligations and potential legal risks associated with the M&A, including the review of intellectual property rights, licensing agreements, and employment contracts.

2. **Ethical Compliance Assessment:**

    Evaluate the ethical culture and practices of both organizations. Consider implementing ethical compliance assessments to gauge the commitment to ethical conduct.

    Establish a code of ethics for the merged entity, outlining expected standards of behavior and conduct for employees at all levels.

MITIGATING COMPLIANCE RISKS IN M&A TRANSACTIONS

Mitigating compliance risks in M&A transactions requires a proactive and strategic approach. Key strategies to effectively manage and mitigate compliance risks include:

1. **Continuous Monitoring and Adaptation:**

    Implement systems for continuous monitoring of regulatory changes, industry standards, and legal requirements. Adapt compliance strategies based on emerging regulatory trends, ensuring that the merged entity remains resilient to evolving compliance landscapes.

2. **Robust Compliance Training:**

Provide comprehensive compliance training for employees at all levels, emphasizing the importance of adherence to regulatory, legal, and ethical standards. Incorporate ongoing training programs to keep employees informed about any changes in compliance requirements.

3. **Engage Legal and Compliance Experts:**

Seek guidance from legal and compliance experts who specialize in the industry and regulatory environments relevant to the M&A. Utilize the expertise of legal professionals to navigate complex compliance issues, ensuring a thorough understanding of legal implications.

4. **Establish Clear Policies and Procedures:**

Develop and communicate clear policies and procedures that outline compliance expectations for employees. Ensure that all employees are aware of the established protocols for reporting potential compliance violations and provide mechanisms for anonymous reporting.

5. **Collaboration with Regulatory Authorities:**

Foster open communication and collaboration with regulatory authorities. Proactively engage with relevant agencies to address any concerns, seek clarification on compliance matters, and demonstrate a commitment to regulatory adherence.

6. **Integration of Compliance Teams:**

Integrate compliance teams from both entities to create a cohesive and unified approach to compliance management. Facilitate collaboration between compliance professionals to share best practices, align processes, and ensure a consistent compliance culture.

The Evolving Regulatory Landscape

Regulatory changes and updates significantly impact how organizations operate, manage risks, and ensure compliance. The following aspects highlight the dynamics of this evolving landscape:

1. **Increasing Complexity:**

   Regulatory frameworks are becoming more intricate, reflecting the complexity of modern business environments. Cross-border operations often expose organizations to diverse regulatory requirements, necessitating a comprehensive understanding of global compliance standards.

2. **Emphasis on Transparency:**

   Regulators are placing a growing emphasis on transparency, requiring organizations to disclose more information about their operations, financial health, and governance practices.

   Enhanced transparency is aimed at building trust among stakeholders and enabling better-informed decision-making.

3. **Digitalization and Data Protection:**

   With the digital transformation of business processes, data protection regulations, such as GDPR, are gaining prominence. Regulators are addressing the challenges posed by data breaches, privacy concerns, and the responsible use of emerging technologies.

4. **Focus on Cybersecurity:**

   The increasing frequency and sophistication of cyber threats have prompted regulators to prioritize cybersecurity. Organizations are required to implement robust cybersecurity measures and report incidents promptly to regulatory authorities.

5. **Sustainable Finance Regulations:**

   The financial industry is witnessing a surge in regulations related to sustainable finance.

   Regulators are encouraging environmentally responsible investments and integrating Environmental, Social, Governance (ESG) factors into financial decision-making.

INTEGRATION OF ESG FACTORS

The integration of ESG factors into GRC practices reflects a paradigm shift in how organizations approach sustainability and social responsibility. ESG considerations are gaining prominence across industries, influencing decision-making and shaping corporate strategies.

1. **Environmental Considerations:**

   Organizations are increasingly focusing on environmental sustainability, addressing issues such as climate change, carbon emissions, and resource conservation. ESG integration involves assessing the environmental impact of operations and implementing measures to minimize negative effects.

2. **Social Responsibility:**

   Social factors, including diversity and inclusion, employee well-being, and community engagement, are becoming integral to organizational governance.

   Companies are recognizing the importance of fostering positive social impacts and addressing societal challenges.

3. **Governance Practices:**

   Effective governance, including ethical leadership, transparent decision-making, and shareholder engagement, is a core aspect of ESG integration. Organizations are expected to demonstrate strong governance structures that align with ethical standards and promote accountability.

4. **Investor Expectations:**

Investors are increasingly factoring ESG performance into their investment decisions.

Companies with strong ESG profiles are often perceived as more resilient and better positioned for long-term success.

5. **Regulatory Mandates:**

Some jurisdictions are introducing regulatory mandates that require companies to disclose ESG-related information. Compliance with these mandates is crucial for organizations operating in regions where ESG reporting is a legal requirement.

6. **Risk Management and Resilience:**

Integrating ESG factors into risk management processes helps organizations identify and mitigate risks associated with environmental, social, and governance issues. Building resilience against ESG-related risks contributes to long-term sustainability and organizational stability.

7. **Stakeholder Engagement:**

ESG integration emphasizes the importance of engaging with a broad range of stakeholders, including investors, employees, customers, and communities. Collaborative efforts with stakeholders are essential for addressing ESG challenges and fostering positive impacts.

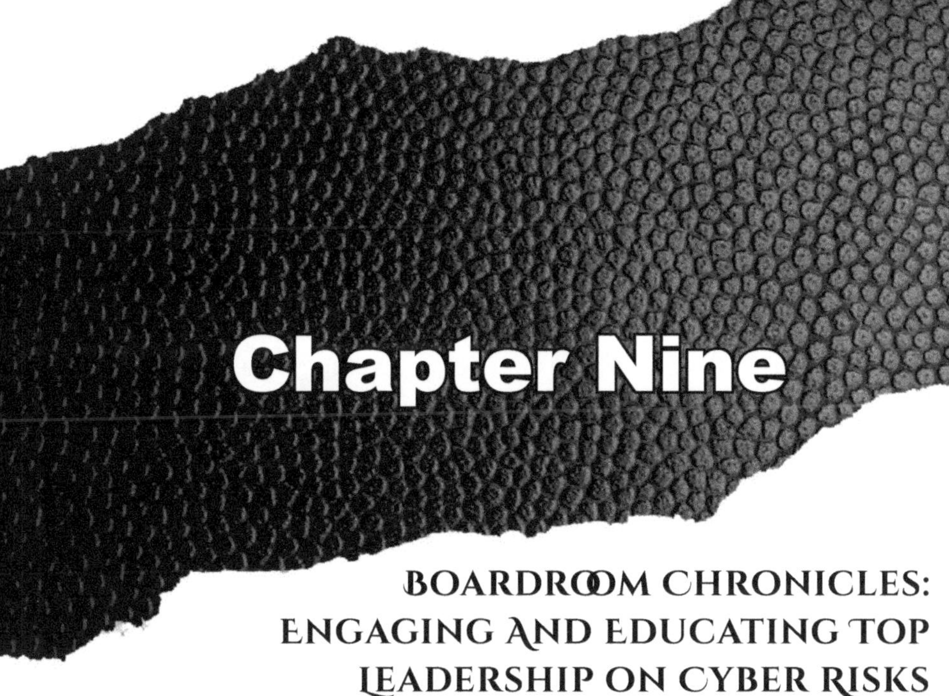

Chapter Nine

BOARDROOM CHRONICLES: ENGAGING AND EDUCATING TOP LEADERSHIP ON CYBER RISKS

In recent times, boardrooms around the world have had a major point of discussion in common; the ever-increasing threats that emanate from interconnected technology and cybersecurity.

According to a Wall Street Journal publication, "the many high-profile breaches in recent years have shown business leaders that efforts to prevent, detect, respond to, and recover from cyber incidents require the collective wisdom and authority of executives across a range of functions."

Cyber threats, ranging from data breaches to ransomware attacks, pose substantial risks to organizations, necessitating a strategic and proactive approach to cybersecurity governance.

Key aspects of the growing significance of cybersecurity in the boardroom include:

1. **Strategic Imperative:**

   Cybersecurity is no longer solely an IT concern; it is a strategic imperative that directly impacts an organization's reputation, financial stability, and overall resilience. Boards recognize the need to align cybersecurity strategies with business objectives to protect brand value and sustain long-term success.

2. **Reputational Risks:**

   High-profile cyber incidents have highlighted the potential for severe reputational damage. Boards are acutely aware of the importance of safeguarding customer trust and brand reputation. Cybersecurity discussions in the boardroom center on minimizing reputational risks and ensuring a swift and effective response to incidents.

3. **Regulatory Compliance:**

   Increasingly stringent data protection regulations and cybersecurity compliance requirements place boards under scrutiny. Boards must ensure organizational compliance with these regulations, addressing legal and financial consequences of non-compliance.

4. **Financial Impact:**

   Cybersecurity incidents can have significant financial repercussions, from direct financial losses to increased insurance premiums and legal costs. Boards are focusing on understanding and quantifying the financial impact of cyber risks to make informed risk management decisions.

5. **Board Expertise:**

   Boards are recognizing the need for cybersecurity expertise within their ranks. Some organizations are appointing dedicated cybersecurity experts or establishing technology committees. Cybersecurity discussions in the boardroom often involve assessing the board's current level of expertise and identifying areas for improvement.

Purpose of the Chapter: Bridging the Knowledge Gap:

The purpose of dedicating a chapter to bridging the knowledge gap in cybersecurity within the boardroom is to address the critical need for board members to be well-informed and proactive in managing cyber risks. This chapter aims to:

1. **Educate Board Members:**

   Provide essential knowledge on the current cybersecurity landscape, including emerging threats, attack vectors, and evolving regulatory requirements and enhance board members' understanding of the potential impact of cyber risks on the organization's overall risk profile.

2. **Establish a Common Language:**

   Facilitate communication between cybersecurity experts and board members by establishing a common language. This involves translating technical jargon into strategic business terms and foster collaboration between IT professionals and the board by creating a shared understanding of cybersecurity priorities.

3. **Outline Board Responsibilities:**

   Clearly define the responsibilities of the board in cybersecurity governance. This includes oversight, setting risk appetite, and ensuring adequate resources are allocated to cybersecurity initiatives. Also, to address the board's role in creating a cybersecurity aware culture throughout the organization.

4. **Case Studies and Practical Examples:**

    Present real-world case studies and practical examples to illustrate the impact of cybersecurity incidents on organizations. To also highlight successful cybersecurity strategies and lessons learned from organizations that effectively navigated cyber challenges.

5. **Encourage Continuous Learning:**

    Emphasize the dynamic nature of cybersecurity and the need for continuous learning. Boards should be proactive in staying informed about evolving threats and industry best practices. To encourage board members to participate in cybersecurity training and educational programs to enhance their expertise.

THE BOARD'S ROLE IN CYBER RISK MANAGEMENT

The chapter further delves into the specific role of the board in cyber risk management. This involves:

1. **Setting Cybersecurity Strategy:**

    Boards play a crucial role in setting the organization's cybersecurity strategy in alignment with its overall business objectives. Define strategic priorities, risk appetite, and resource allocation for cybersecurity initiatives.

2. **Oversight and Governance:**

    Provide effective oversight of the organization's cybersecurity governance structure.

    Establish governance mechanisms to ensure accountability, risk reporting, and compliance with cybersecurity policies.

3. **Aligning Cybersecurity with Business Goals:**

   Ensure that cybersecurity initiatives align with the organization's broader business goals and risk management strategy. Incorporate cybersecurity considerations into strategic planning and decision-making processes.

4. **Incident Response Planning:**

   Oversee the development and testing of a robust incident response plan.

   Define the board's role in the event of a cybersecurity incident, including communication strategies and collaboration with executive leadership.

5. **Talent and Resource Allocation:**

   Assess and ensure the adequacy of cybersecurity talent within the organization.

   Approve budget allocations for cybersecurity resources, including technology, training, and personnel.

6. **Regular Reporting and Metrics:**

   Require regular reporting on cybersecurity metrics and key performance indicators (KPIs).

   Establish a framework for measuring the effectiveness of cybersecurity initiatives and monitoring progress over time.

SHIFTING BOARDROOM PERCEPTION ON CYBERSECURITY

No longer relegated to the realm of technical concerns, cybersecurity is now recognized as a fundamental pillar of overall business strategy. As organizations embrace a proactive approach to cybersecurity, viewing it not merely as a defensive measure but as a strategic enabler, they position themselves to navigate the digital landscape with resilience and foresight.

Key factors driving this shift include:

1. **Recognition of Cyber Risks:**

    Boards increasingly acknowledge the severity and sophistication of cyber threats. High-profile data breaches and cyber-attacks have demonstrated the potential for severe financial, reputational, and operational consequences.

2. **Strategic Imperative:**

    Cybersecurity is now viewed as a strategic imperative rather than a standalone IT concern. Boards recognize that effective cybersecurity measures are essential for safeguarding brand reputation, customer trust, and long-term business viability.

3. **Regulatory Compliance Pressures:**

    The ever-expanding landscape of data protection regulations and compliance standards places immense pressure on organizations to prioritize cybersecurity. Boards understand the legal and financial ramifications of non-compliance.

4. **Reputational Impact:**

    Reputational damage resulting from cyber incidents can be profound. Boards recognize that the trust of customers, partners, and stakeholders is closely tied to the organization's ability to protect sensitive data.

5. **Boardroom Expertise:**

    There's a growing recognition of the need for cybersecurity expertise within the boardroom. Boards are actively seeking members with a deep understanding of cybersecurity to enhance their collective decision-making.

6. **Strategic Oversight:**

   Boards are moving beyond a reactive approach to cybersecurity, taking on a more proactive and strategic oversight role. This involves setting clear expectations, defining risk appetites, and aligning cybersecurity efforts with overall business objectives.

7. **Cybersecurity as a Boardroom Agenda Item:**

   Cybersecurity discussions are now a regular agenda item in board meetings. Boards engage in in-depth conversations about cyber risk assessments, incident response plans, and the organization's overall cybersecurity posture.

THE LINK BETWEEN CYBERSECURITY AND BUSINESS STRATEGY:

Recognizing the integral connection between cybersecurity and business strategy is pivotal for organizations navigating the complexities of the digital era. The convergence of these two realms is evident in several key aspects:

1. **Strategic Alignment:**

   Cybersecurity strategies are aligning closely with overall business strategies. Organizations recognize that cybersecurity is an enabler of business goals, not a hindrance.

2. **Risk Management Integration:**

   Cyber risk is integrated into the broader risk management framework. Boards understand that effective risk management requires a comprehensive approach that includes cyber risk considerations.

3. **Innovation and Digital Transformation:**

   Boards understand that innovation and digital transformation initiatives must be accompanied by robust cybersecurity measures. The pursuit of technological advancements is balanced with the need to safeguard against emerging cyber threats.

4. **Customer Trust and Brand Reputation:**

   Cybersecurity is viewed as integral to building and maintaining customer trust. Boards understand that a strong cybersecurity posture enhances brand reputation and fosters customer confidence in the organization.

5. **Business Continuity Planning:**

   Cybersecurity is woven into business continuity planning. Boards recognize that cyber incidents can disrupt operations, and strategic resilience requires robust cybersecurity measures to ensure continuous business operations.

6. **Strategic Investments in Cybersecurity:**

   Boards approve strategic investments in cybersecurity, viewing them as essential components of the organization's overall risk management and business resilience strategies.

7. **Competitive Advantage:**

   Cybersecurity is increasingly seen as a competitive advantage. Boards understand that customers and partners prioritize working with organizations that demonstrate a commitment to cybersecurity and data protection.

8. **Metrics and Key Performance Indicators (KPIs):**

   Boards establish metrics and KPIs to measure the effectiveness of cybersecurity initiatives. Key performance indicators are aligned with broader business goals, emphasizing the strategic impact of cybersecurity efforts.

Boardroom Culture And Its Impact on Cyber Risk Awareness

A strong boardroom culture that prioritizes cyber risk awareness fosters a proactive stance towards mitigating threats and ensures the organization is well-prepared to navigate the complexities of the digital landscape. Here's an exploration of the key dynamics:

1. **Leadership Tone and Commitment:**

    The tone set by board leadership is instrumental in influencing the overall approach to cybersecurity. When board members demonstrate a genuine commitment to cybersecurity, it sends a powerful message throughout the organization. A culture of leadership commitment encourages proactive measures, investment in cybersecurity resources, and a sense of urgency in addressing cyber risks.

2. **Board Composition and Expertise:**

    The composition of the board, including the presence of members with cybersecurity expertise, significantly impacts cyber risk awareness. Boards that include members with a deep understanding of cybersecurity can more effectively assess risks and guide strategic decisions. A culture that values and actively seeks cybersecurity expertise contributes to a more informed and vigilant boardroom.

3. **Education and Training:**

    A culture that emphasizes continuous education and training on cybersecurity issues is crucial. Board members need to stay informed about evolving cyber threats, regulatory changes, and best practices. Regular training sessions and educational programs create a boardroom culture that prioritizes staying ahead of the curve in understanding cyber risks.

4. **Integration with Strategic Discussions:**

Boardroom culture influences the integration of cybersecurity discussions into broader strategic conversations. A culture that recognizes cybersecurity as integral to business strategy ensures that it is not treated as a siloed function.

When cybersecurity considerations are seamlessly woven into strategic discussions, the organization is better equipped to align security measures with overarching business goals.

5. **Risk Appetite and Communication:**

Boardroom culture shapes the organization's risk appetite concerning cybersecurity. A culture that encourages open communication about cyber risks, vulnerabilities, and potential impacts fosters a proactive risk management approach. A willingness to discuss and address cyber risks openly contributes to an informed and vigilant boardroom culture.

6. **Incident Response Preparedness:**

The level of preparedness for cyber incidents reflects the boardroom culture. A proactive culture ensures the establishment of robust incident response plans, which include clear roles, responsibilities, and communication strategies. A culture of readiness acknowledges that cyber incidents are not a matter of "if" but "when," and the organization is well-prepared to respond effectively.

7. **Metrics and Reporting:**

Boardroom culture influences the emphasis placed on cybersecurity metrics and reporting. A culture that values data-driven decision-making encourages the establishment of key performance indicators (KPIs) related to cybersecurity. Regular reporting on cybersecurity metrics ensures that the board is continuously informed about the organization's security posture and the effectiveness of risk mitigation efforts.

8. **Crisis Simulation Exercises:**

Conducting crisis simulation exercises is indicative of a proactive boardroom culture. Simulations help test the organization's response capabilities and identify areas for improvement. A culture that embraces crisis simulations demonstrates a commitment to continuous improvement and readiness for cyber threats.

9. **Collaboration with Executive Leadership:**

Boardroom culture shapes the level of collaboration between board members and executive leadership on cybersecurity matters. A collaborative culture fosters a shared understanding of cyber risks and a unified approach to addressing them. When board members actively engage with executive leadership on cybersecurity, it contributes to a culture of collective responsibility.

10. **Incentives for Cybersecurity Excellence:**

The existence of incentives for cybersecurity excellence reflects the boardroom culture. Recognizing and rewarding efforts to enhance cybersecurity awareness and resilience create a culture that values and prioritizes security measures. A culture of incentives reinforces the importance of individual and collective contributions to cybersecurity.

Adapting Cybersecurity Education For The Board: A Strategic Approach

Tailoring cybersecurity education to the board involves a nuanced approach, blending diverse learning methods to cater to the unique dynamics of board members. Workshops serve as immersive forums, delving into intricacies such as the cyber threat landscape, regulatory frameworks, and risk management strategies. For instance, a workshop might involve interactive discussions on recent cyber incidents, fostering a deep understanding of the potential impacts on the organization.

Complementary to workshops, training programs act as foundational pillars. These initiatives equip board members with essential cybersecurity knowledge, covering fundamentals, legal considerations, and incident response planning. Imagine a scenario where board members engage in structured training modules, gaining insights into cybersecurity best practices and legal obligations, laying the groundwork for informed decision-making.

Simulations, akin to strategic rehearsals, provide hands-on experience. Through simulated cyber incidents and crisis communication exercises, board members can navigate the complexities of incident response in a risk-free environment. Picture a tabletop simulation where the board is faced with a simulated ransomware attack, prompting them to make real-time decisions and assess the efficacy of their response strategies.

Scenario-based learning augments this approach by presenting real-world cases and industry-specific scenarios. Analyzing historical cyber breaches or dissecting industry-relevant incidents, board members glean practical insights. These scenarios offer a tangible grasp of the consequences of cyber threats, fostering a proactive mindset within the boardroom.

Continuous awareness programs keep the board abreast of evolving threats. Regular updates on the threat landscape, industry trends, and interactive learning platforms serve as ongoing resources.

Consider board members participating in webinars or accessing tailored online content, ensuring they stay informed in a rapidly evolving cybersecurity landscape.

Engagement with external experts brings specialized perspectives into the boardroom. Guest speakers, industry forums, and collaborations with cybersecurity partners expose board members to diverse viewpoints. Envision a scenario where a renowned cybersecurity expert addresses the board, providing in-depth insights into emerging threats and best practices.

Metrics and reporting form a crucial aspect, providing tangible indicators of cybersecurity effectiveness. Key performance indicators (KPIs), regular reporting, and trend analysis enable the board to gauge the organization's cybersecurity posture. Picture a boardroom discussion where metrics are dissected, facilitating informed decision-making based on measurable cybersecurity outcomes.

Governance guidelines ensure clarity in the board's role. Defining governance frameworks, reviewing policies, and ensuring compliance with regulations contribute to a robust cybersecurity governance structure. Imagine a board actively engaging in the review and adoption of cybersecurity policies, underscoring their commitment to governance.

Feedback and improvement mechanisms close the loop. Post-training surveys, incident post-mortems, and adaptation to emerging threats enable continuous enhancement. Picture a scenario where feedback from simulated incidents leads to adjustments in education content, ensuring its relevance and effectiveness.

Designating a board champion for cybersecurity adds a personal touch to the educational approach. This champion leads and advocates for cybersecurity initiatives within the board, embodying a commitment to continuous learning and proactive cybersecurity governance. Envision a cybersecurity champion actively championing the cause, fostering a culture of cyber resilience at the highest echelons of leadership.

In this comprehensive approach, the board becomes not only informed but actively engaged in cybersecurity governance. Tailored education, combining workshops, training, simulations, and various examples, transforms the boardroom into a proactive hub for navigating the complex cyber landscape with resilience and foresight.

THE ROLE OF CHIEF INFORMATION SECURITY OFFICERS (CISO) IN BOARD EDUCATION

The role of Chief Information Security Officers (CISOs) in board education is instrumental in bridging the gap between technical cybersecurity intricacies and the strategic decision-making processes of the boardroom. As guardians of an organization's cybersecurity posture, CISOs play a pivotal role in shaping the awareness, understanding, and proactive engagement of board members in the realm of cybersecurity.

1. **Translation of Technical Jargon:**

   CISOs serve as translators, converting complex technical jargon into clear, concise language that resonates with board members. By articulating the implications of cybersecurity in business terms, CISOs enable the board to make well-informed decisions without getting entangled in technical complexities.

   Risk Communication:

   They are adept at conveying cybersecurity risks in a language that aligns with the board's risk appetite. They facilitate a nuanced understanding of the potential impact of cyber threats on the organization's overall risk landscape, helping the board prioritize and allocate resources effectively.

2. Educational Workshops and Training Programs:

CISOs often spearhead educational workshops and training programs tailored for the board. These initiatives delve into critical cybersecurity concepts, emerging threats, and best practices. Through interactive sessions, CISOs enhance the board's cybersecurity literacy, empowering them to contribute meaningfully to strategic discussions.

Incident Response Simulations:

They orchestrate incident response simulations that mimic real-world cyber incidents. By involving board members in these simulations, CISOs enable them to experience the challenges of responding to a cyber crisis. This hands-on approach fosters a proactive mindset, ensuring the board is well-prepared for potential cybersecurity incidents.

3. Regular Reporting and Metrics Presentation:

CISOs provide regular reports to the board, presenting key cybersecurity metrics and performance indicators. These reports offer insights into the organization's security posture, the effectiveness of implemented measures, and trends in the threat landscape. CISOs ensure that these reports are comprehensible and relevant to the strategic goals of the organization.

4. Industry Trends and Benchmarking:

CISOs keep the board abreast of industry trends, benchmarking the organization's cybersecurity practices against industry standards. By contextualizing cybersecurity measures within the broader industry landscape, CISOs enable the board to gauge the organization's competitiveness and resilience.

5. **Regulatory Compliance Guidance:**

   Given the ever-evolving regulatory landscape, CISOs guide the board on compliance requirements related to cybersecurity. They explain the implications of regulations, assist in developing compliance strategies, and ensure the board is aware of its role in overseeing regulatory adherence.

6. **Engagement with External Experts:**

   CISOs facilitate engagements with external cybersecurity experts and thought leaders. By organizing guest speakers, forums, or collaborations, CISOs provide the board with diverse perspectives and insights into emerging threats and best practices, enriching their understanding.

7. **Continuous Education Initiatives:**

   CISOs champion continuous education within the board, ensuring that members stay informed about evolving cyber threats. They recommend and facilitate participation in relevant conferences, webinars, and training programs, fostering a culture of ongoing learning.

8. **Strategic Advisory Role:**

   CISOs serve as strategic advisors to the board on cybersecurity matters. They actively participate in board meetings, offering insights into the organization's cybersecurity strategy, aligning it with business objectives, and contributing to the formulation of risk-aware strategic decisions.

9. **Governance and Policy Guidance:**

   CISOs guide the board in establishing robust governance structures and cybersecurity policies. They ensure that the board's oversight role is defined, policies are comprehensive, and governance mechanisms are in place to support effective cybersecurity management.

Transparent Communication during Incidents:

In the event of a cybersecurity incident, CISOs play a crucial role in transparently communicating with the board. They provide timely and accurate information, outline response strategies, and facilitate a clear understanding of the incident's impact on the organization.

10. Board Collaboration on Cybersecurity Roadmap:

CISOs collaborate with the board to develop a comprehensive cybersecurity roadmap aligned with the organization's strategic goals. They actively engage in discussions about budget allocation, resource planning, and the prioritization of cybersecurity initiatives.

OVERSIGHT VS. MANAGEMENT : DEFINING BOARD RESPONSIBILITIES

The distinction between oversight and management is a fundamental concept in corporate governance, delineating the roles and responsibilities of boards of directors and executive management. Understanding this difference is crucial for effective governance, ensuring that each entity operates within its designated sphere of influence. Let's explore the definitions and implications of oversight and management within the context of board responsibilities:

OVERSIGHT: THE BOARD'S ROLE

Oversight refers to the board's duty to monitor, evaluate, and guide the overall direction and performance of the organization. It involves a high-level review of management's activities to ensure alignment with the organization's mission, strategy, and stakeholder interests.

Responsibilities:

* **Setting Strategy:** The board is responsible for approving the organization's strategic direction and ensuring that it aligns with its mission and long-term goals.

* **Risk Management:** Boards oversee the identification, assessment, and mitigation of risks, ensuring that the organization operates within acceptable risk parameters.

* **Performance Evaluation:** Regularly assessing the performance of the CEO and executive team to ensure they are effectively managing the organization.

* **Financial Oversight:** Monitoring financial health, approving budgets, and ensuring financial transparency and accountability.

* **Compliance:** Ensuring the organization complies with relevant laws, regulations, and ethical standards.

* **Stakeholder Relations:** Oversight includes representing and balancing the interests of various stakeholders, including shareholders, employees, customers, and the broader community.

Key Principle:

The board's oversight role emphasizes a strategic and forward-looking perspective. It involves asking critical questions, providing guidance, and holding management accountable for achieving the organization's objectives.

MANAGEMENT: THE EXECUTIVE'S ROLE

Management involves the day-to-day operations, implementation of strategy, and execution of plans to achieve the organization's goals. This responsibility lies with the CEO and executive team.

Responsibilities:

* **Operational Execution:** Managing day-to-day activities to implement the strategic direction set by the board.

* Resource Allocation: Making decisions on resource allocation, budgeting, and prioritizing initiatives to achieve organizational goals.

* Team Leadership: Leading and managing the executive team, as well as overseeing the broader workforce.

* Execution of Strategy: Implementing the strategic plan approved by the board and adapting tactics as needed.

* Performance Measurement: Monitoring key performance indicators and reporting on operational performance to the board.

* Risk Management Implementation: Executing risk management strategies based on board guidance.

Key Principle:

Management involves the tactical and operational aspects of running the organization. It requires a focus on efficiency, effectiveness, and the day-to-day tasks necessary for achieving the organization's strategic objectives.

HARMONIZING OVERSIGHT AND MANAGEMENT:

1. Clear Communication: Open and transparent communication between the board and management is essential. This ensures alignment on strategic goals, risk tolerance, and organizational priorities.

2. Delegation and Trust: The board delegates authority to the executive team to manage daily operations. Trust is a critical component, and boards should provide guidance without micromanaging.

3. Regular Reporting: Management provides regular updates to the board on key performance indicators, strategic initiatives, and any significant developments. This reporting facilitates informed oversight.

4. Strategic Planning Sessions: Periodic strategic planning sessions involving both the board and management help align long-term goals and ensure that both entities are on the same page regarding the organization's future.

5. Adaptability: The board and management must remain adaptable to changing circumstances. A dynamic and collaborative relationship allows for effective responses to emerging challenges and opportunities.

THE ROLE OF THE BOARD DURING CYBER INCIDENTS

While day-to-day cybersecurity management falls under the purview of executive leadership and IT professionals, the board plays a strategic and oversight role during times of crisis. In the event of a cyber incident, the board assumes a crucial role in navigating the organization through the challenges posed by cybersecurity threats. The responsibilities and actions undertaken by the board during such incidents can be outlined as follows:

1. **Notification and Activation:**

    The board is promptly notified of the cyber incident, and a meeting is convened to assess the situation.

2. **Understanding the Impact:**

    The board seeks to comprehend the nature and potential impact of the cyber incident on the organization through briefings from cybersecurity experts.

3. **Decision-Making on Incident Response Strategy:**

    Participating in strategic decision-making with executive leadership, the board determines the organization's response strategy, including containment and communication plans.

4. **Legal and Regulatory Compliance:**

    Ensuring compliance with legal and regulatory obligations, the board oversees efforts to report the incident to relevant authorities.

5. **Communication and Stakeholder Relations:**

    Managing external and internal communication to protect the organization's reputation, the board approves communication plans.

6. **Resource Allocation and Budget Approval:**

    Allocating resources, including approving budget adjustments, for incident response efforts is a responsibility of the board.

7. **Long-Term Cybersecurity Strategy Review:**

    Evaluating the effectiveness of the organization's cybersecurity strategy, the board reviews the incident to identify weaknesses and revises the strategy accordingly.

8. **Engaging External Experts and Counsel:**

    Based on the nature of the incident, the board may engage external cybersecurity firms, legal counsel, or public relations experts.

9. **Post-Incident Review and Lessons Learned:**

    Conducting a thorough post-incident review, the board identifies lessons learned and incorporates them into future cybersecurity planning.

10. **Updating and Testing Incident Response Plans:**

    Ensuring incident response plans are updated and regularly tested, the board oversees revisions and testing to validate their effectiveness.

11. **Ensuring Accountability and Oversight:**

   Holding executive leadership accountable, the board ensures the implementation of corrective measures and maintains ongoing oversight to prevent recurrence.

12. **Advisory Role for Cybersecurity Culture:**

   Encouraging a cybersecurity-aware culture within the organization, the board plays an advisory role in promoting security best practices.

   The board, as the steward of the organization's well-being, stands as a bulwark against the uncertainties of the digital realm. In a world where cyber threats loom large, the board's vigilance, adaptability, and commitment to cybersecurity principles become the cornerstones for building a robust defense against evolving risks. This chapter underscores the imperative for boards to not only react effectively to incidents but also proactively shape a cybersecurity culture that permeates every facet of the organization, ensuring a steadfast and resilient response to the ever-evolving cyber landscape.

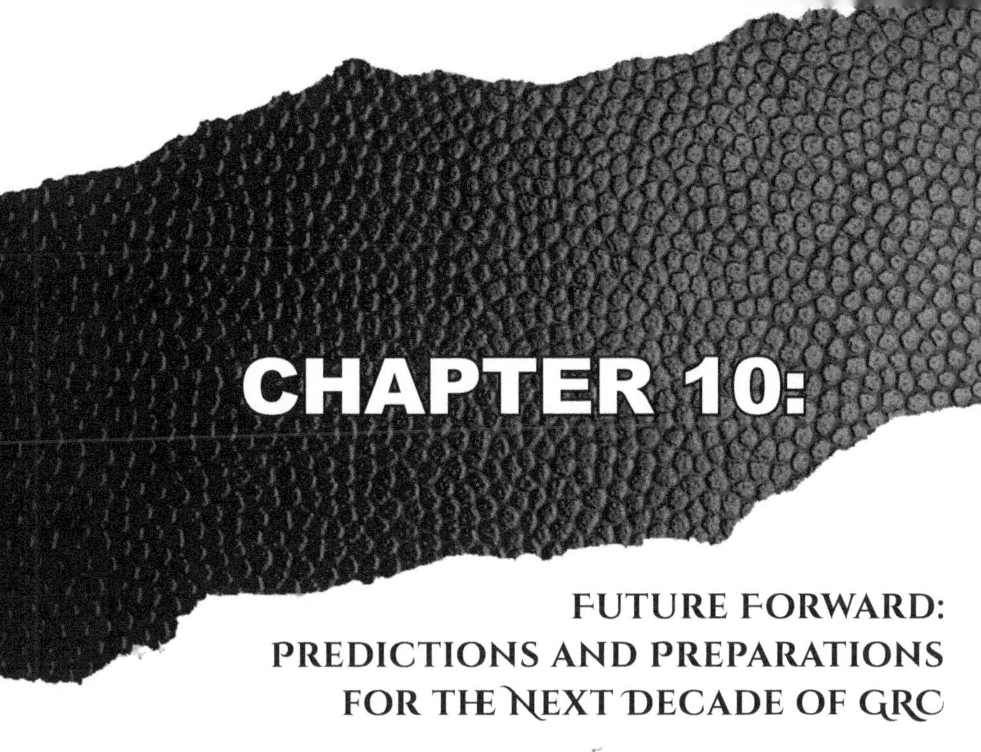

CHAPTER 10:

FUTURE FORWARD: PREDICTIONS AND PREPARATIONS FOR THE NEXT DECADE OF GRC

REFLECTING ON THE EVOLUTION OF GRC OVER THE PREVIOUS DECADE

Over the past decade, Governance, Risk, and Compliance (GRC) has undergone a transformative journey, shaped by technological advancements, evolving regulatory landscapes, and a heightened awareness of the interconnectedness of business processes. The shift towards digitalization has been a central theme, with organizations increasingly relying on data-driven insights, automation, and artificial intelligence to enhance their GRC practices. The integration of Environmental, Social, and Governance (ESG) considerations into GRC frameworks also marks a significant development, reflecting a broader recognition of the impact that businesses have on the world.

During this period, GRC professionals have navigated complex challenges, including the rise of cyber threats, dynamic regulatory changes, and the imperative to embed ethical considerations into every facet of organizational decision-making. The role of GRC has expanded beyond mere compliance to become a strategic driver, influencing business operations, fostering transparency, and contributing to long-term sustainability.

ANTICIPATING THE DYNAMICS THAT WILL SHAPE THE NEXT DECADE

Looking forward, the next decade promises to bring even more profound changes to the GRC landscape. Technological advancements, particularly in artificial intelligence and data analytics, will revolutionize risk management and compliance processes. The digital transformation will continue to reshape the way organizations operate, introducing new risks and opportunities that GRC professionals must navigate adeptly.

The regulatory environment is expected to become more complex and globally interconnected. As societies grapple with challenges like climate change and social inequality, regulatory frameworks will likely place a greater emphasis on ESG factors, requiring organizations to integrate sustainability into their core GRC strategies. Cybersecurity threats will persist and evolve, demanding innovative approaches to safeguarding digital assets and ensuring data privacy.

Decentralization, accelerated by remote work trends, will bring about new governance challenges. GRC professionals will need to adapt strategies to manage risks in a more distributed and interconnected business environment. The increasing interconnectedness of global markets and supply chains will necessitate a more collaborative approach to GRC, with organizations working together to address common challenges.

Purpose of the Chapter: Guiding GRC Professionals Toward Future Success

The purpose of this chapter is to serve as a compass for GRC professionals navigating the complexities of the next decade. By reflecting on the evolution of GRC over the previous years, we can distill key learnings and insights that provide a foundation for future success. Anticipating the dynamics that will shape the next decade allows us to proactively prepare for the challenges and opportunities that lie ahead.

THIS CHAPTER AIMS TO:

1. Provide Strategic Insights: Offer a strategic perspective on the evolving role of GRC in the broader business context, emphasizing the strategic importance of GRC in driving organizational success.

2. Explore Emerging Trends: Delve into emerging trends in technology, regulation, and global business landscapes, helping GRC professionals stay ahead of the curve and adapt their strategies accordingly.

3. Offer Practical Guidance: Provide practical guidance and actionable strategies for GRC professionals to enhance their skill sets, embrace innovation, and navigate the future with confidence.

4. Encourage a Forward-Thinking Mindset: Foster a forward-thinking mindset among GRC professionals, encouraging them to view challenges as opportunities for growth and adaptation.

   By reflecting on the past and anticipating the future, this chapter aims to empower GRC professionals to not only adapt to change but to proactively shape the future of governance, risk management, and compliance in a dynamic and interconnected world.

EMERGING TECHNOLOGIES (BLOCKCHAIN, IoT) AND THEIR GRC IMPLICATIONS

The integration of emerging technologies like blockchain and the Internet of Things (IoT) significantly influences Governance, Risk, and Compliance (GRC) practices. Technological advancements are driving regulatory change at a breakneck pace. From blockchain to artificial intelligence, new technologies are creating new risks and opportunities that regulators must address. GRC professionals must be prepared to navigate this new terrain. (Iris Carbon 2023).

Blockchain, with its transparent and decentralized ledger, enhances the reliability of GRC processes. It fosters transparency and traceability in transactions, automates compliance through smart contracts, and ensures data integrity and security. In supply chain management, blockchain facilitates end-to-end traceability, mitigating risks related to product recalls or compliance breaches. Additionally, blockchain enables decentralized identity management, reducing the risk of identity theft.

The proliferation of IoT devices presents challenges and opportunities for GRC professionals. The vast data generated by these devices raises concerns about data privacy and security. GRC frameworks need to adapt to handle the challenges of securing interconnected devices and managing the associated cybersecurity risks. Compliance with data protection regulations, especially concerning personal data collected by IoT devices, becomes a priority. Industries reliant on IoT, such as healthcare and smart cities, require GRC frameworks to navigate evolving regulatory landscapes and effectively manage associated risks.

THE IMPACT OF QUANTUM COMPUTING ON GRC PROCESSES

Quantum computing introduces both promise and challenge to GRC processes. Its potential to break widely used encryption algorithms poses a threat to the confidentiality of GRC data. GRC professionals need to anticipate the need for quantum-resistant encryption methods to safeguard sensitive information. On a positive note, quantum computing's ability to process vast datasets at unprecedented speeds can enhance risk analysis and modeling within GRC processes.

In the context of blockchain, quantum-resistant cryptographic techniques can reinforce the security of distributed ledgers, ensuring the continued integrity of GRC-related transactions. Quantum-resistant authentication methods can also enhance access controls within GRC systems, protecting against quantum-enabled attacks on traditional authentication mechanisms.

However, the emergence of quantum computing introduces novel risks that GRC professionals must understand. These include potential algorithmic bias in quantum algorithms and geopolitical implications tied to advancements in quantum technology. Long-term strategic planning becomes essential for GRC professionals to navigate the evolving landscape of quantum computing, ensuring the resilience and security of GRC processes in the face of advancing computational capabilities.

REGULATORY RESPONSES TO TECHNOLOGICAL ADVANCEMENT

Regulatory responses to technological advancements reflect a dynamic effort by governing bodies to address the challenges and harness the benefits brought about by rapid innovation. As technologies continue to evolve, regulatory frameworks must adapt to ensure responsible use, protect consumers, and maintain the integrity of various industries. Here's an exploration of how regulators respond to technological advancements:

1. **Understanding and Monitoring Technological Changes:**

    Regulatory bodies engage in continuous monitoring and analysis of technological trends to comprehend the implications for different sectors. This involves collaborating with industry experts, staying abreast of emerging technologies, and assessing their potential impact on existing regulatory frameworks.

2. **Issuing Guidance and Standards:**

Regulators often issue guidance documents and industry standards to provide clarity on the responsible deployment of new technologies. These documents serve as reference points for organizations, outlining best practices, compliance requirements, and ethical considerations associated with technological advancements.

3. **Incorporating Technology in Regulations:**

Regulatory frameworks are updated to incorporate technological considerations. This may involve amending existing regulations or introducing new ones that specifically address the challenges and opportunities presented by advanced technologies. For example, data protection regulations are continually evolving to address the complexities of digital data handling.

4. **Risk-Based Approaches:**

Regulators adopt risk-based approaches, acknowledging that not all technological advancements pose the same level of risk. This allows for a nuanced regulatory response, with more stringent measures applied to technologies that have a higher potential for adverse impacts on consumers, businesses, or societal well-being.

5. **Collaborative Initiatives:**

Collaboration between regulatory bodies, industry stakeholders, and technology experts is increasingly common. Such collaborative initiatives aim to foster open dialogue, share insights, and develop cohesive regulatory strategies that balance innovation with risk management. Global partnerships and information-sharing forums contribute to a more unified regulatory approach.

6. **Flexibility in Regulatory Frameworks:**

Regulators recognize the need for flexibility in regulatory frameworks to accommodate the fast-paced nature of technological advancements. This adaptability allows regulations to evolve alongside technological developments, ensuring that they remain effective in addressing emerging challenges and opportunities.

7. **Regulatory Sandboxes:**

Some regulatory bodies establish regulatory sandboxes—controlled environments that enable businesses to test innovative technologies in a live but supervised setting. This approach allows regulators to observe the real-world impact of new technologies, understand potential risks, and make informed adjustments to regulations.

8. **Consumer Protection Measures:**

A crucial aspect of regulatory responses is the emphasis on protecting consumers. Regulations often include provisions to ensure fair business practices, data privacy, and the security of consumer information in the context of evolving technologies. This includes measures to address issues such as online fraud, cybersecurity threats, and misleading advertising.

9. **Continuous Dialogue with Stakeholders:**

Regulators actively engage in a continuous dialogue with industry stakeholders, advocacy groups, and the general public. This inclusive approach ensures that regulatory responses take into account diverse perspectives, promote transparency, and foster a shared understanding of the challenges posed by technological advancements.

10. Enforcement and Penalties:

Regulatory bodies enforce compliance with established standards through audits, investigations, and penalties for non-compliance. This proactive enforcement serves as a deterrent to unethical or irresponsible use of technology and reinforces the importance of adhering to regulatory guidelines.

CYBERSECURITY CHALLENGES AND SOLUTIONS

The Escalating Threat Landscape: Cybersecurity Predictions

The contemporary digital landscape is marked by an escalating and ever-evolving threat landscape in cybersecurity. Predicting the future of these threats is essential for organizations to proactively fortify their defenses. Anticipated trends include:

1. Sophistication of Cyber Attacks:

Cybercriminals are expected to employ increasingly sophisticated techniques, leveraging artificial intelligence and machine learning to create more complex and adaptive attacks.

2. Ransomware Evolution:

Ransomware attacks are likely to become more targeted and stealthier, with threat actors customizing their approaches to specific industries and organizations, demanding higher ransoms.

3. Supply Chain Vulnerabilities:

The interconnected nature of global supply chains creates new avenues for cyber threats. Predictions include increased attacks targeting supply chain vulnerabilities to disrupt operations and compromise critical data.

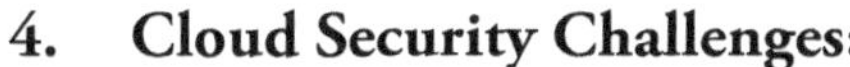

4. **Cloud Security Challenges:**

   As organizations continue to migrate to cloud environments, cybersecurity threats are expected to target cloud infrastructure. This emphasizes the need for robust cloud security measures and continuous monitoring.

5. **Zero-Day Exploits and APTs:**

   Zero-day exploits and Advanced Persistent Threats (APTs) are likely to proliferate, challenging organizations to enhance their threat detection and response capabilities to identify and mitigate these sophisticated attacks.

INNOVATIVE APPROACHES TO CYBER RISK MANAGEMENT

In the face of an evolving threat landscape, organizations are adopting innovative approaches to enhance cyber risk management:

1. **Threat Intelligence Integration:**

   Organizations are integrating threat intelligence into their cybersecurity strategies, leveraging real-time data to identify emerging threats, understand attack patterns, and fortify defenses.

2. **Behavioral Analytics:**

   Behavioral analytics and machine learning are being employed to detect anomalies in user behavior, network traffic, and system activities, allowing for early identification of potential security incidents.

3. **Deception Technology:**

   Deception technology involves deploying decoy systems and misinformation to mislead attackers. This proactive approach aims to divert and identify malicious actors before they can compromise critical systems.

4. **Zero Trust Architecture:**

    Zero Trust Architecture assumes that no entity, whether inside or outside the organization, should be trusted by default. This model verifies every user and device attempting to connect to the network, reducing the risk of unauthorized access.

5. **Cybersecurity Automation:**

    Automation is becoming integral to cybersecurity, streamlining routine tasks, enabling rapid response to threats, and allowing cybersecurity professionals to focus on more complex aspects of threat mitigation.

STRATEGIES FOR SECURING THE DIGITAL TRANSFORMATION IN GRC:

The ongoing digital transformation poses both opportunities and challenges for Governance, Risk, and Compliance (GRC). To secure this transformation effectively, organizations are adopting strategic approaches:

1. **Integrated Risk Management (IRM):**

    IRM frameworks are being embraced to integrate risk management into the core of digital transformation initiatives. This involves assessing risks holistically, considering the interconnectedness of processes and systems.

2. **Continuous Monitoring and Adaptive Controls:**

    Traditional periodic risk assessments are being complemented by continuous monitoring. Adaptive controls are implemented to dynamically adjust security measures based on real-time threat intelligence and risk assessments.

3. Cross-Functional Collaboration:

GRC professionals are collaborating across departments to ensure that cybersecurity considerations are embedded in every stage of the digital transformation journey. This includes involving cybersecurity experts in project planning and implementation.

4. User Education and Awareness:

Employees are often the first line of defense against cyber threats. Robust training programs and awareness initiatives are implemented to educate users about cybersecurity best practices, phishing prevention, and the importance of data security.

5. Third-Party Risk Management:

As organizations increasingly rely on third-party vendors and partners, effective third-party risk management is crucial. GRC frameworks are extended to encompass the cybersecurity practices of external entities, ensuring a comprehensive approach to risk mitigation.

6. Incident Response Planning:

GRC strategies include well-defined incident response plans that are regularly tested and updated. This ensures a swift and coordinated response to any cybersecurity incidents, minimizing potential damage and downtime.

GRC In The Era of Decentralization: Implications From Remote Work and Governance Considerations

1. **The Rise of Remote Work and Its GRC Implications:**

    The widespread adoption of remote work has reshaped the traditional workplace, introducing new challenges and opportunities for Governance, Risk, and Compliance (GRC). The implications span various aspects of organizational management:

2. **Governance Challenges:**

    Remote work necessitates a reevaluation of governance structures. The physical decentralization of the workforce may disrupt traditional hierarchies, requiring organizations to establish clear lines of authority, communication channels, and decision-making processes in virtual environments.

3. **Data Governance and Privacy:**

    With employees working from various locations, data governance becomes paramount. GRC professionals must ensure secure remote access to sensitive information, adhere to data protection regulations, and establish protocols for data privacy to prevent breaches and maintain compliance.

4. **Cybersecurity Risks:**

    The shift to remote work expands the attack surface for cyber threats. GRC frameworks need to evolve to address cybersecurity risks associated with remote work, including securing remote access, implementing encrypted communications, and continuously monitoring for potential security incidents.

5. **Compliance Challenges:**

Remote work introduces challenges in ensuring compliance with industry-specific regulations. GRC professionals need to adapt policies and procedures to meet compliance requirements while accommodating the flexible nature of remote work arrangements.

6. **Employee Training and Awareness:**

Robust training programs become essential to educate remote employees on compliance protocols, cybersecurity best practices, and the importance of adhering to organizational policies. GRC initiatives should focus on raising awareness and promoting a culture of compliance.

7. **Audit and Monitoring:**

Remote work necessitates a shift in audit and monitoring practices. GRC teams should leverage technology to conduct virtual audits, monitor compliance in real-time, and identify potential risks associated with remote work, ensuring that organizational standards are consistently upheld.

8. **Business Continuity Planning:**

GRC strategies should prioritize business continuity planning for remote work scenarios. This involves preparing for disruptions, ensuring remote access to critical systems, and implementing measures to maintain operational resilience in the face of unforeseen challenges.

DECENTRALIZED TECHNOLOGIES (E.G., DEFI) AND GOVERNANCE CONSIDERATIONS:

The rise of decentralized technologies, exemplified by Decentralized Finance (DeFi), introduces a paradigm shift in financial services. This shift brings distinct challenges and opportunities for Governance, Risk, and Compliance (GRC).

DeFi platforms heavily rely on smart contracts, introducing unique risks. GRC frameworks must address the inherent risks associated with smart contracts, including vulnerabilities, coding errors, and the potential for financial loss due to flaws in contract execution.

The decentralized nature of DeFi introduces regulatory challenges. GRC professionals must navigate the evolving regulatory landscape to ensure compliance with existing financial regulations and anticipate new regulations specific to decentralized technologies.

TOKEN GOVERNANCE:

Governance in DeFi involves decision-making related to protocol upgrades, changes to smart contracts, and the distribution of governance tokens. GRC frameworks must adapt to address the decentralized governance models unique to these technologies.

DeFi platforms often involve yield farming, where users provide liquidity in exchange for tokens. GRC strategies need to incorporate risk management measures to assess the risks associated with different yield farming strategies and ensure a balanced risk-reward profile.

SMART CONTRACT AUDITS:

Rigorous smart contract audits become a crucial aspect of GRC considerations. Engaging with cybersecurity experts to assess the security, functionality, and compliance of smart contracts before deployment helps mitigate potential risks.

GRC initiatives must focus on educating users about the risks involved in decentralized technologies. This includes understanding the mechanics of smart contracts, managing private keys securely, and being aware of potential scams and fraudulent activities in decentralized ecosystems.

As decentralized technologies expand, GRC frameworks should address the challenges of cross-chain interoperability. This involves ensuring that different blockchain networks can seamlessly interact while managing associated risks.

NAVIGATING GRC CHALLENGES IN A DISTRIBUTED ECOSYSTEM:

The advent of distributed ecosystems, characterized by decentralized technologies, remote work, and interconnected networks, brings forth a myriad of Governance, Risk, and Compliance (GRC) challenges. Navigating these challenges requires a proactive and adaptive approach to ensure organizational resilience and compliance with regulatory standards:

1. **Decentralized Governance Models:**

    Distributed ecosystems often rely on decentralized governance models, introducing challenges in decision-making, transparency, and accountability. Establishing clear governance frameworks that align with the decentralized nature of the ecosystem. This involves defining roles, responsibilities, and decision-making processes to ensure effective oversight and compliance.

2. **Remote Work Dynamics:**

    Remote work introduces complexities in managing data governance, ensuring cybersecurity, and maintaining compliance with industry regulations. Implementing robust data governance policies, cybersecurity measures, and compliance protocols tailored to remote work scenarios. Regular training and awareness programs can empower employees to adhere to organizational standards in dispersed work environments.

3. **Cybersecurity Risks in Distributed Networks:**

Distributed ecosystems amplify the attack surface for cybersecurity threats, requiring a comprehensive approach to risk management. Employing advanced cybersecurity measures, including encryption, multi-factor authentication, and continuous monitoring. Regular risk assessments and penetration testing help identify vulnerabilities and strengthen defenses.

4. **Regulatory Ambiguity in Decentralized Technologies:**

The evolving nature of decentralized technologies introduces regulatory uncertainties, requiring organizations to navigate complex legal landscapes. Staying informed about regulatory developments, actively engaging with regulatory bodies, and adapting GRC frameworks to align with emerging legal requirements. Collaboration with legal experts is crucial to ensuring compliance in decentralized ecosystems.

5. **Decentralized Finance (DeFi) Risks:**

DeFi platforms introduce unique risks, such as smart contract vulnerabilities, regulatory ambiguity, and user education challenges. Conducting thorough smart contract audits, staying abreast of regulatory changes in the DeFi space, and implementing user education programs to enhance awareness of risks and responsible usage.

6. **Supply Chain Risks in Decentralized Ecosystems:**

The interconnected nature of distributed ecosystems increases the risk of supply chain vulnerabilities and third-party risks. Implementing robust third-party risk management protocols, conducting due diligence on suppliers and partners, and ensuring the security of the entire supply chain. Continuous monitoring helps detect and address potential risks promptly.

7. **Cross-Platform and Cross-Border Compliance:**

Distributed ecosystems often operate across multiple platforms and borders, introducing challenges in maintaining uniform compliance standards. Developing GRC frameworks that are flexible enough to accommodate cross-platform and cross-border operations. This includes adapting to different regulatory requirements, ensuring consistent adherence to compliance standards, and actively participating in industry initiatives to promote best practices.

8. **Data Privacy and Sovereignty Concerns:**

Distributed ecosystems may encounter data privacy and sovereignty concerns, particularly when operating in regions with varying data protection regulations. Implementing data privacy measures that align with the strictest regulations applicable to the ecosystem. This involves understanding the legal requirements of different jurisdictions and implementing technologies that support compliance with diverse data protection standards.

9. **Dynamic Business Models and Continuous Adaptation:**

The dynamic nature of distributed ecosystems requires organizations to continuously adapt their business models and GRC strategies. Fostering a culture of adaptability and innovation within the organization. Implementing agile GRC strategies that can evolve alongside changes in the ecosystem's structure and technology landscape.

COLLABORATIVE GRC ECOSYSTEMS

Collaborative Governance, Risk, and Compliance (GRC) platforms are transformative tools that empower organizations to streamline their processes, enhance communication, and fortify their overall risk management strategies. The benefits of adopting collaborative GRC platforms include:

1. **Centralized Information Hub:**

   Collaborative GRC platforms serve as centralized information hubs, consolidating data from various departments and functions. This ensures that all stakeholders have access to real-time, accurate information, fostering a unified understanding of risk and compliance landscapes.

2. **Enhanced Communication and Collaboration:**

   These platforms facilitate seamless communication and collaboration among different teams and departments. Integrated communication tools enable timely exchange of information, breaking down silos and fostering a culture of collaboration crucial for effective GRC.

3. **Real-Time Risk Visibility:**

   Collaborative GRC platforms offer real-time visibility into risk profiles. This enables proactive risk management by allowing organizations to identify, assess, and respond to emerging risks promptly, minimizing potential negative impacts.

4. **Agile Compliance Management:**

   The collaborative nature of these platforms supports agile compliance management. Organizations can adapt quickly to changes in regulations, industry standards, or internal policies, ensuring continuous compliance and reducing the risk of penalties or fines.

5. **Efficient Audit Processes:**

   Collaborative GRC platforms streamline audit processes by providing auditors with access to a centralized repository of information. This accelerates audit cycles, enhances transparency, and allows for efficient collaboration between auditors and internal teams.

6. **Automated Workflow Integration:**

   Integration with workflow automation tools simplifies and accelerates GRC processes. Automated workflows ensure that tasks related to risk management, compliance, and governance are assigned, tracked, and completed efficiently, reducing manual effort and minimizing errors.

7. **Risk Appetite Alignment:**

   Collaborative GRC platforms facilitate the alignment of risk appetite across different business units. This ensures that risk-taking is consistent with organizational objectives, promoting a unified approach to risk management throughout the organization.

8. **Data Analytics for Informed Decision-Making:**

   These platforms often incorporate data analytics capabilities, providing organizations with actionable insights. Informed decision-making becomes a reality as organizations can analyze historical data, identify trends, and make data-driven choices to optimize their GRC strategies.

9. **Interconnectedness of GRC Processes Across Organizations:**

   Interconnecting GRC processes across organizations amplifies the collective strength of risk management efforts. This interconnectedness brings about several benefits:

10. Holistic Risk Management:

Interconnected GRC processes enable organizations to adopt a holistic approach to risk management. Rather than managing risks in isolated silos, organizations can view and address risks comprehensively, considering the interconnected nature of various processes.

11. Cross-Functional Collaboration:

The interconnectedness of GRC processes fosters cross-functional collaboration. Different departments and business units can collaborate seamlessly, sharing insights and working collectively to address risks and ensure compliance.

12. Consistent Risk Language:

Interconnected GRC processes promote the use of a consistent risk language across the organization. This common understanding of risk terminology facilitates effective communication and ensures that everyone is on the same page when assessing and managing risks.

13. Unified Risk Reporting:

Benefit: Organizations can generate unified risk reports that provide a comprehensive view of risk exposure across the entire enterprise. This enables leadership to make informed decisions and allocate resources strategically based on a consolidated understanding of risks.

14. Efficient Resource Allocation:

Interconnected GRC processes allow for more efficient resource allocation. Organizations can prioritize risks based on their impact on different functions, facilitating the allocation of resources to areas with the highest risk exposure.

Industry-Specific Collaborations and Their GRC Benefits:

Collaborations between organizations within the same industry amplify the collective strength of GRC efforts, leading to various benefits.

Industry-specific collaborations facilitate the sharing of threat intelligence. Organizations can collectively stay informed about emerging threats, vulnerabilities, and best practices, enhancing their ability to proactively address industry-specific risks.

Collaborations enable benchmarking against industry peers. Organizations can compare their GRC practices with others in the same sector, identify best practices, and strive for continuous improvement based on industry standards.

Furthermore, they also provide a platform for sharing regulatory insights and advocating for industry-specific regulatory changes. This collective approach ensures that organizations within the industry can influence and adapt to regulatory developments more effectively.

Collaborations in addition help to strengthen supply chain resilience. By collectively addressing GRC challenges in the supply chain, organizations can build a more resilient and interconnected network that is better equipped to handle disruptions and uncertainties.

TRAINING AND SKILL DEVELOPMENT:

Another benefit of Industry-specific collaborations is that they facilitate joint training programs and skill development initiatives. This ensures that professionals within the industry are equipped with the necessary skills and knowledge to navigate evolving GRC landscapes.

INCIDENT RESPONSE COORDINATION:

In the event of a security incident, industry collaborations enhance incident response coordination. Organizations can share information about incidents, collaborate on response strategies, and collectively strengthen the industry's ability to mitigate and recover from threats.

GRC Skills And Talent Development

Emerging Skills Required for Future GRC Professionals

As the landscape of Governance, Risk, and Compliance (GRC) continues to evolve, the demand for a nuanced skill set among professionals in this field becomes increasingly apparent.

Firstly, the proficiency in Data Analytics and Interpretation is paramount. With the exponential growth of data, GRC professionals need the ability to not just handle but derive meaningful insights from vast datasets. This skill is foundational for informed decision-making and recognizing patterns within complex data structures.

In tandem, Cybersecurity Expertise is now a prerequisite. The sophisticated nature of contemporary cyber threats necessitates a deep understanding of cybersecurity principles. This expertise empowers GRC professionals to effectively manage digital risks and safeguard organizational integrity.

Moreover, the integration of technology in compliance processes has given rise to the need for Regulatory Technology (RegTech) Knowledge. GRC professionals must now be well-versed in leveraging technological solutions to streamline and fortify regulatory compliance.

Digital transformations demand a solid grasp of technology, highlighting the necessity for Digital Literacy. GRC professionals must not only understand emerging technologies but also discern their implications for risk and compliance management.

Ethical considerations extend to the realm of GRC through Ethical Hacking and Penetration Testing. Understanding vulnerabilities in systems is not merely a security measure but a proactive strategy to identify weaknesses and fortify against potential threats.

Beyond technical competencies, soft skills such as Communication and Collaboration have become imperative. Effective communication and collaboration across departments are essential for conveying complex GRC concepts and fostering a holistic approach to risk management.

Crisis Management and Incident Response have become skills that go beyond theoretical understanding. GRC professionals need practical expertise to navigate unforeseen events, minimize damage, and expedite recovery in times of crisis.

Finally, a comprehensive understanding of Legal and Regulatory Acumen is indispensable. GRC professionals need to interpret and implement compliance requirements accurately, reducing legal risks and ensuring adherence to regulatory standards.

Importance of Continuous Learning in GRC:

The GRC landscape is dynamic, and adaptability is key. Continuous learning allows professionals to adapt to new risks, stay abreast of regulatory updates, integrate evolving technologies effectively, refine existing skills, and anticipate industry trends.

STRATEGIES FOR ATTRACTING AND RETAINING GRC TALENT:

In the competitive arena of talent acquisition and retention, organizations are adopting diverse strategies. Competitive compensation packages, professional development opportunities, work-life balance initiatives, recognition and appreciation programs, collaborative work environments, mentorship programs, clear career pathways, employee well-being initiatives, an inclusive and diverse culture, and engaging in challenging and meaningful work are among the multifaceted approaches organizations are leveraging.

The narrative of GRC professionals is evolving. Beyond the technical acumen, the narrative now includes a blend of adaptability, ethical considerations, and a holistic understanding of the organization's strategic goals. Continuous learning is not merely a phase but a perpetual journey, and attracting and retaining top GRC talent is not just a strategic objective but a narrative of organizational culture and commitment to excellence.

GRC And Corporate Culture: Towards A Better GRC Practice

Organizational culture, often regarded as the collective mindset and behavior shared among its members, influences how GRC principles are embraced and executed.

Organizational culture serves as the bedrock upon which GRC practices are built. A culture that values transparency, accountability, and ethical conduct inherently aligns with effective GRC. Conversely, a culture marked by resistance to change, opacity, or a lax approach to compliance may pose challenges to the implementation of robust GRC strategies.

The effectiveness of GRC practices, in turn, molds and reflects the organizational culture. Consistent adherence to compliance standards, proactive risk management, and transparent governance contribute to a culture of trust and reliability. Conversely, reactive responses to risks or non-compliance can erode trust and compromise the organizational culture.

Fostering a GRC Mindset Across All Levels of the Organization

Fostering a GRC mindset requires a concerted effort to instill a sense of responsibility and awareness at every level of the organization. It begins with leadership setting the tone and demonstrating a commitment to GRC principles. Leaders need to articulate the importance of compliance and risk management, emphasizing their relevance to the organization's overall success.

Communication plays a pivotal role in fostering a GRC mindset. Regular training sessions, workshops, and communication channels that educate employees about the significance of GRC practices create a shared understanding. This understanding, when embedded into the organizational culture, empowers employees to make decisions aligned with compliance requirements and risk mitigation strategies.

Inclusive decision-making processes contribute to a GRC mindset, ensuring that diverse perspectives are considered when assessing risks and formulating compliance strategies. Moreover, recognizing and rewarding individuals who embody a GRC mindset further reinforces its importance across all levels.

The Cultural Shift Toward Proactive GRC Strategies

The shift from reactive to proactive GRC strategies reflects a maturation of organizational culture. Traditionally, GRC practices were often viewed as a set of rules to be followed in response to external pressures. However, the contemporary landscape demands a more forward-thinking approach.

A cultural shift toward proactive GRC strategies involves anticipating risks, identifying opportunities, and integrating GRC considerations into strategic planning. This proactive stance necessitates a continuous evaluation of the risk landscape, staying ahead of regulatory changes, and adapting to the evolving business environment.

Leadership plays a pivotal role in driving this cultural shift. By encouraging a forward-thinking mindset, leaders set the stage for departments and individuals to embrace proactive GRC practices. Technologies such as data analytics and artificial intelligence further enable organizations to predict and assess risks, facilitating a proactive rather than reactive response.

FUTURISTIC GRC SCENARIOS AND PREDICTIONS

As we gaze into the future, Governance, Risk, and Compliance (GRC) are poised to undergo significant transformations, driven by technological advancements, evolving regulatory landscapes, and changing business paradigms.

1. **Advanced Technology Integration:**

   Artificial Intelligence (AI) and machine learning will play a pivotal role in automating routine GRC tasks, enabling real-time risk assessments and predictive analytics.

   Prediction: GRC platforms will harness the power of AI for more accurate risk predictions, streamlined compliance processes, and enhanced decision-making.

2. **Blockchain for Immutable Compliance Records:**

   Blockchain technology will be widely adopted for maintaining immutable compliance records, ensuring transparency and traceability.

   Prediction: Blockchain will revolutionize audit processes, providing a decentralized and secure ledger for compliance documentation.

3. **Global Regulatory Convergence:**

   Regulatory frameworks across nations will converge, creating a more standardized global compliance environment.

   Prediction: GRC professionals will navigate a unified set of compliance standards, reducing complexity and enhancing cross-border business operations.

4. **Integrated Risk and Sustainability Reporting:**

   Organizations will seamlessly integrate risk and sustainability reporting to provide stakeholders with a comprehensive view of corporate responsibility.

   Prediction: GRC frameworks will evolve to incorporate Environmental, Social, and Governance (ESG) factors into risk assessments and compliance evaluations.

5. **Cybersecurity as a Core GRC Component:**

   Cybersecurity will become an intrinsic component of GRC strategies, with a heightened focus on protecting digital assets.

   Prediction: GRC frameworks will prioritize cybersecurity risk assessments, acknowledging the interconnected nature of digital threats.

GRC's Potential Role in Shaping Global Business Landscapes

The evolving role of GRC in shaping global business landscapes transcends traditional risk management and compliance functions. GRC is positioned to become a strategic driver for sustainable and resilient organizations.

1. **Strategic Decision Support:**

   GRC frameworks will evolve to provide strategic decision support, offering insights into potential risks and opportunities that align with broader business objectives.

2. **Holistic Stakeholder Engagement:**

   GRC practices will extend beyond regulatory compliance to encompass a holistic approach to stakeholder engagement. Organizations will proactively address stakeholder concerns related to ethical practices, environmental impact, and social responsibility.

3. **Agile and Adaptable Governance Models:**

   GRC will foster agile governance models that can swiftly adapt to changes in the business environment. This adaptability will be crucial for navigating uncertainties and seizing emerging opportunities.

4. **Data-Driven Predictive Modeling:**

   GRC's integration with data-driven predictive modeling will empower organizations to foresee potential risks and adjust strategies accordingly, enhancing overall business resilience.

PREPARING FOR UNFORESEEN CHALLENGES AND OPPORTUNITIES

As organizations brace for unforeseen challenges and opportunities, GRC professionals will play a pivotal role in ensuring preparedness and adaptability.

1. **Scenario Planning and Sensitivity Analysis:**

    GRC frameworks will include advanced scenario planning and sensitivity analysis, enabling organizations to anticipate a spectrum of potential future scenarios and assess their resilience.

2. **Continuous Monitoring and Adaptive Strategies:**

    GRC practices will shift towards continuous monitoring, enabling organizations to adapt their strategies dynamically in response to evolving risks and opportunities.

    3. Crisis Management and Resilience Building:

    GRC will focus on building organizational resilience through effective crisis management strategies. This involves not only responding to crises but proactively fortifying against potential disruptions.

3. **Collaborative Risk Intelligence Networks:**

    GRC professionals will engage in collaborative risk intelligence networks, sharing insights and best practices across industries to collectively prepare for unforeseen challenges.

4. **Ethical AI and Responsible Innovation:**

    GRC frameworks will emphasize ethical considerations in the deployment of AI and other emerging technologies. Responsible innovation will be a cornerstone of risk management and compliance in the face of evolving technological landscapes.

The future of GRC holds transformative potential, shaping not only how organizations manage risks and comply with regulations but also influencing strategic decision-making and global business landscapes. The adaptability of GRC frameworks will be instrumental in preparing organizations for the uncertainties and opportunities that lie ahead in our ever-changing world.

BIBLIOGRAPHY

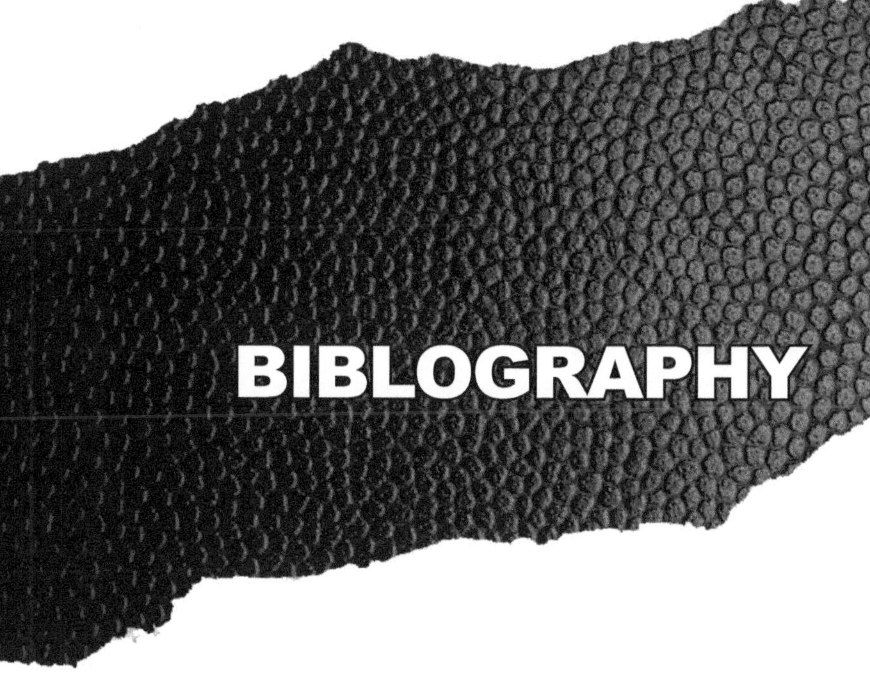

3 Risks and Consequences of Regulatory Non-Compliance with Examples. (n.d.). Retrieved from Nimonik Inc. website: https://nimonik.com/resources/non-compliance-risks/

Anthony Peter Spanakos. (2022). International Law in a Transcivilizational World? Tensions Between International Law and Civilization. *WORLD SCIENTIFIC EBooks*, 3–27. https://doi.org/10.1142/9789811256158_0001

CARBON, T. I. (2023, June 21). The Future of GRC: Anticipating Evolving Challenges and Adapting to New Regulatory Landscapes. Retrieved November 18, 2023, from IRIS CARBON® website: https://iriscarbon.com/the-future-of-grc-anticipating-evolving-challenges-and-adapting-to-new-regulatory-landscapes/

Damodaran, A. (n.d.). *DANGER AND OPPORTUNITY: THE ESSENCE OF RISK MANAGEMENT!* Retrieved from https://pages.stern.nyu.edu/~adamodar/pdfiles/country/RiskforPATH.pdf

Deloitte. (n.d.). 4 Ways to Engage Executives in Cyber Risk. Retrieved November 18, 2023, from WSJ website: https://deloitte.wsj.com/cio/4-ways-to-engage-executives-in-cyber-risk-1437364906

Enterprise Risk Management A Guide for EBMOs to promote efficiency and business resilience. (n.d.). Retrieved from https://www.ilo.org/wcmsp5/groups/public/---ed_dialogue/---act_emp/documents/publication/wcms_865180.pdf

Globalizing Your Compliance Program | Insights | Ropes & Gray LLP. (n.d.). Retrieved November 18, 2023, from www.ropesgray.com website: https://www.ropesgray.com/en/insights/alerts/2018/01/globalizing-your-compliance-program

Isaca. (2019). COBIT | Control Objectives for Information Technologies | ISACA. Retrieved from Isaca.org website: https://www.isaca.org/resources/cobit

isorobot. (n.d.). Retrieved November 18, 2023, from isorobot.io website: https://isorobot.io/blog/grc-in-the-age-of-globalization-trends-and-forecasts

Laufer, W. S. (2017). A Very Special Regulatory Milestone. *SSRN Electronic Journal.* https://doi.org/10.2139/ssrn.3034699

Mergers & Acquisitions. (n.d.). Retrieved from LII / Legal Information Institute website: https://www.law.cornell.edu/wex/mergers_acquisitions

National Institute of Standards and Technology. (2016, June 30). Cybersecurity. Retrieved from NIST website: https://www.nist.gov/cybersecurity

Navigating the Risks and Challenges of Widespread Technology Adoption. (n.d.). Retrieved from www.linkedin.com website: https://www.linkedin.com/pulse/navigating-risks-challenges-widespread-technology-adoption-ahmed

NCCoE. (2019). Retrieved from Nist.gov website: https://www.nccoe.nist.gov/

paul.hernandez@nist.gov. (2021, April 9). Executive Order 14028, Improving the Nation's Cybersecurity. Retrieved from NIST website: https://www.nist.gov/itl/executive-order-14028-improving-nations-cybersecurity

Sherehiy, B, Karwowski, W, & Layer J.K. (2007). *A review of enterprise agility: Concepts, frameworks, and attributes. International Journal of Industrial Ergonomics* (pp. 445–460). Hershey, PA: Information Science Reference.

The GRC Framework: A Practical Guide to GRC. (2022, February 25). Retrieved from CIO Insight website: https://www.cioinsight.com/it-management/grc-framework/

Wikipedia. (2019, March 4). Industrial Revolution. Retrieved from Wikipedia website: https://en.wikipedia.org/wiki/Industrial_Revolution

ABOUT THE AUTHOR

The Author, Tolulope Michael, is a proud Computer Science graduate from the esteemed and prestigious Lagos State University. His love for technology, combined with a strong interest in cybersecurity, has driven him to dedicate close to two decades of his life to this field.

Over the years, he has gained valuable experience in various domains of cybersecurity, including Penetration Testing, Application Security Engineering, Cloud Security Engineering, and Governance, Risk and Compliance (GRC). He is proud to say that he has contributed to the growth of the industry, leaving a lasting impact with his expertise and knowledge.

In his quest to help others succeed in cybersecurity, he created ExcelMindCyber, a platform designed to provide comprehensive education in this field. His flagship program, "The Ultimate Cybersecurity Program" has already made a significant impact, helping many individuals realize their potential and earn multiple six figures.

He is grateful for the opportunity to share his passion and knowledge with others, and it brings him immense joy to see his students find success and fulfillment in this field. His journey in cybersecurity has been a rewarding one, and he is proud to be a part of this industry.He hopes to continue making a difference in the lives of those who share his love for cybersecurity, and is committed to helping them achieve their goals. This is his story, and he is proud to tell it.

With a clear and accessible writing style, he provides a roadmap for individuals looking to break into the field of cybersecurity, offering practical advice and actionable tips that will help you succeed in your journey. Whether you're a student, a professional looking for a change, or simply someone with an interest in cybersecurity, the author's insights and guidance will help you build the foundation you need for an exciting and rewarding career.